PORTUGAL

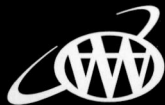

SPIRAL GUIDES

Travel With Someone You Trust®

Contents

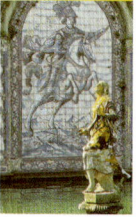
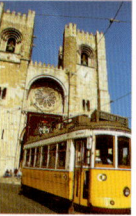
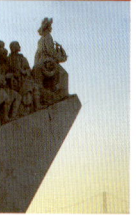
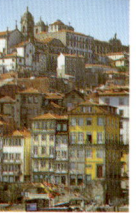

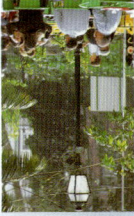

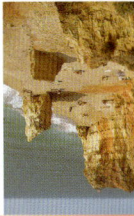

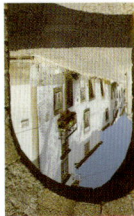

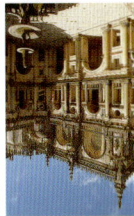

Written by Tony Kelly
Produced by Duncan Baird Publishers, London, England
Listings sections by Andrew Benson
Researchers: Chris and Melanie Rice
Updated by Emma Rowley Ruas
American editor Tracy Larson

Edited, designed and produced by AA Publishing
© Automobile Association Developments Limited 2006, 2008
Maps © Automobile Association Developments Limited 2006, 2008

Published in the United States by AAA Publishing,
1000 AAA Drive, Heathrow, Florida 32746
Published in the United Kingdom by AA Publishing

ISBN-13: 978-1-59508-277-0

Cover design and binding style by AA Publishing

Color separation by Keenes, Andover

Printed and bound in China by Leo Paper Products

10 9 8 7 6 5 4 3 2 1

A03439
Maps in this title produced from mapping © MAIRDUMONT /
Falk Verlag 2008
(except p.185)
Transport map © Communicarta Ltd, UK

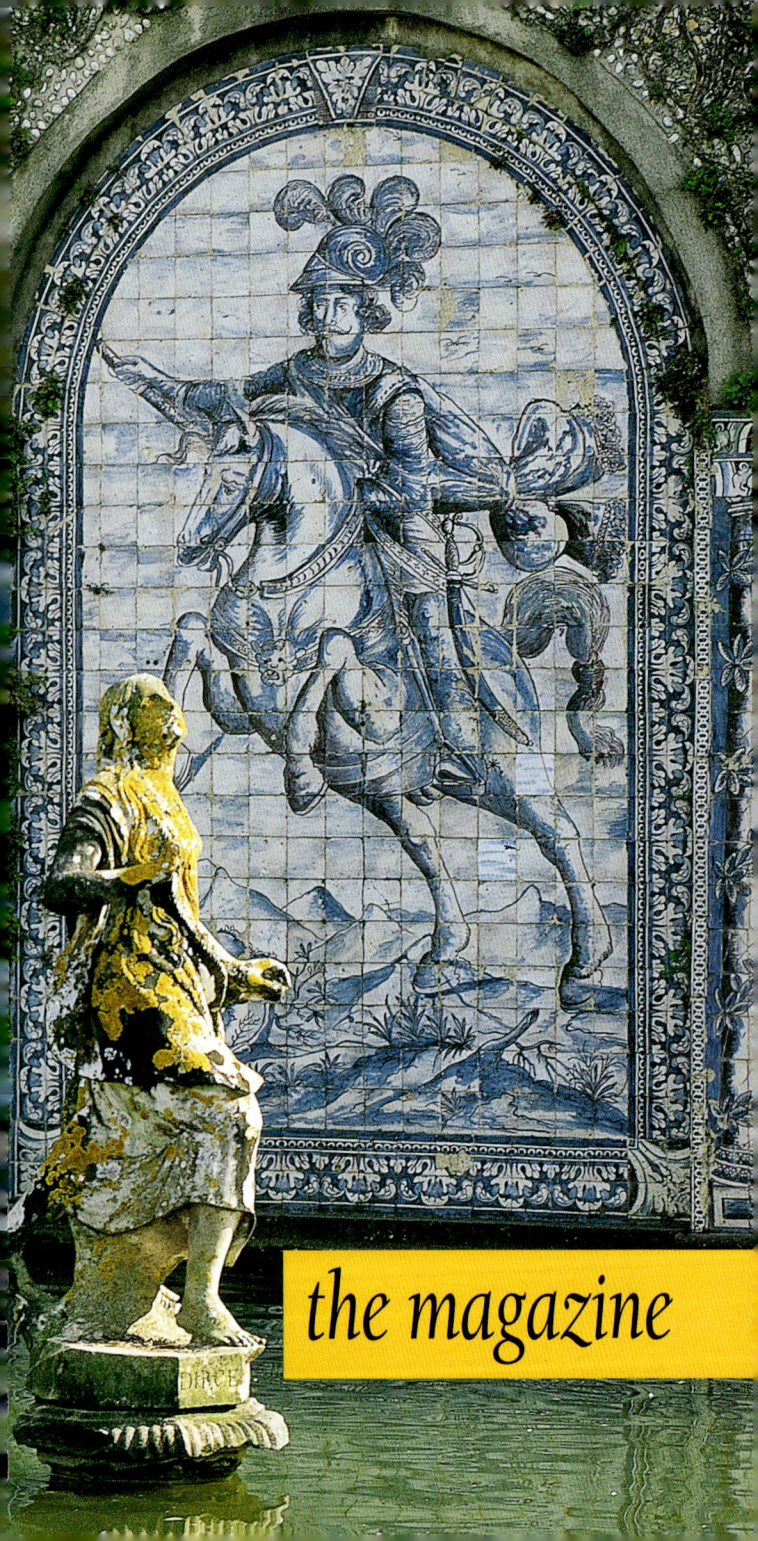

the magazine

The Sea

When Lisbon hosted Expo'98, the last World Exposition of the second millennium (➤ 58), it chose the world's oceans as its theme. Stuck out on the edge of Europe facing the Atlantic, and at odds for much of its history with its only land neighbour, Spain, Portugal has always enjoyed a close relationship with the sea. It defines Portugal's national identity, and its influence can be seen in everything from architecture to cuisine.

The Age of Discovery

The Portuguese like to look back to the golden age when their explorers sailed uncharted waters in search of new lands. The greatest of all Portuguese heroes is Henry the Navigator (1394–1460), Grand Master of the Order of Christ and architect of the *descobrimentos* (discoveries), which paved the way for Portugal to become the greatest maritime nation. The third son of João I and Philippa of Lancaster, Henry took part in the capture of Ceuta on the Moroccan coast in 1415, but he never sailed again, instead retiring to Sagres (➤ 156) where he established a school of navigation to train the nation's best minds. Here, new forms of astrolabe and sextant (navigational instruments) were developed and a design for a new type of ship, the caravel, a cross between a traditional Douro cargo boat (Henry had been brought up with them in Porto) and an Arab *dhow*, was drawn up.

Left: A statue of the great explorer Henry the Navigator at Lagos

Background: The striking Monument to the Discoveries at Belém, Lisbon

1419
Madeira

1427
The Azores

1460
Cape Verde

1482
Diego Cão reaches the mouth of the Congo, leading to the Portuguese conquest of Angola

1488
Dias rounds the Cape of Good Hope, South Africa

1498
Vasco da Gama discovers a sea route to India

1500
Pedro Álvares Cabral discovers Brazil

1519
The Portuguese sailor Fernão de Magalhães (Ferdinand Magellan) leads the first circumnavigation of the world, though he is killed in the Philippines en route (the journey was completed under the leadership of Juan Sebastian del Cano, a Spanish voyager). Magellan is considered the first circumnavigator of the world because he had previously sailed from the Philippines to Europe, thus completing a global journey.

Manueline Art

King Dom Manuel I is known as Manuel the Fortunate as it was during his reign (1495–1521) that the sea route to India was discovered, bringing riches to Portugal in the form of spices, ivory and gold. The king has lent his name to a uniquely Portuguese version of late Gothic architecture, inspired both by the florid forms of Indian art and by the *descobrimentos* (discoveries) themselves. The most typical symbols of Manueline art are the armillary sphere (a navigational device consisting of a celestial globe with the earth at the centre, which became the emblem of Manuel I), the cross of the Order of Christ, seafaring imagery such as anchors and knotted ropes, and exotic fauna and flora from the newly discovered lands.

The finest examples of Manueline art are the monastery and tower at Belém (➤ 46), the cloisters and unfinished chapels of the abbey at Batalha (➤ 112–113) and the windows of the Convento do Cristo at Tomar (➤ 116).

Top: The tower at Belém, a gem of Manueline art

Centre: Knotted rope imagery at the Convento do Cristo, Tomar

"There is no peril so great that the hope of reward will not be greater."

To learn more about Portugal's relationship with the sea, visit the Museu de Marinha in Belém (➤ 48–49) which is devoted to Portugal's maritime history.

The caravel revolutionised sea travel. Its triangular sails allowed sailors to take advantage of side winds and travel much faster. They were used by Columbus (1451–1506) in voyages to the New World.

During Henry's lifetime, Madeira and the Azores were discovered and the explorer Gil Eanes rounded the fearsome Cape Bojador in west Africa, at that time the end of the known world beyond which were thought to lurk sea monsters and unknown hidden perils. The holy grail was the discovery of a sea route to India which allowed Portugal to control the trade in oriental spices, silks and carpets that crossed Asia.

It was Vasco da Gama who achieved this in 1498, returning to Lisbon triumphant.

The Portuguese went on to establish colonies in Angola and Mozambique as well as trading posts in Goa, Timor and Macau.

In the meantime, Pedro Álvares Cabral had discovered Brazil, awarded to Portugal under the 1494 Treaty of Tordesillas, which divided the thus far known world into Spanish and Portuguese spheres of influence. The fact that Portugal chose a dividing line that just happened to give them Brazil has led many to suspect that they knew it was there all along.

The Sea Today

The Portuguese fishing fleet may have declined due to overfishing, but fishing is an important industry and brightly coloured fishing boats are a familiar sight in ports like Peniche and Nazaré on the west coast, and Lagos and Olhão in the Algarve.

These days, the sea is yielding a more significant harvest, as tourists are attracted to the beaches of the Algarve, Costa de Lisboa, Costa de Prata and Costa Verde.

Background: A giant map of the world at Belém shows Portuguese discoveries

Top left: Algar Seco, a typical Algarve beach

Centre left: Fishermen still bring in the catch at Burgau, in the Algarve

Bacalhau

The Portuguese passion for *bacalhau* (dried salted cod) has its origins in the fishing fleets that sailed the waters off Newfoundland in the early 16th century. At that time there was an abundance of cod, but it had to be preserved for the journey back to Portugal. Despite the presence of numerous fresh fish off the coast, *bacalhau* remains a Portuguese favourite and there are said to be 365 different ways of cooking it.

Salt cod on sale near the market in Porto

Vintage Port

In exceptional years, a vintage may be declared and the very best wine will be transferred into bottles after just two years in the cask. It will continue to mature in the bottle for at least 10 years, developing a dark colour, a heady aroma and a crusty sediment. Vintage port should be stored on its side until 24 hours before drinking, and decanted at least two hours before being served. Unlike other ports, it needs to be consumed within a day of being opened. All vintage port is special, but the 1994 vintage is shaping up to be one of the best ever and should be laid down for drinking from around 2010.

the story of port

IN PORTUGAL, PORT IS A DRINK TO BE ENJOYED BY ANYONE AT ANY TIME, WHETHER IT IS A WHITE PORT AND TONIC ON THE ROCKS AT THE START OF THE EVENING, OR AN AGED TAWNY WITH CHOCOLATE CAKE TO ROUND OFF A MEAL.

Port is produced solely along a 100km (62-mile) stretch of the River Douro, in the oldest demarcated wine region in the world. The climate here is extreme, with bitingly cold winters and searingly hot summers, but the schist stone in the soil has the perfect properties, absorbing humidity in winter and releasing it in summer, preserving heat in the day to release it at night.

Wine has been made in the Douro region since the Romans were here, but the origins of port lie in the 17th century, when British traders, cut off from their supplies of claret by wars with France, developed a taste for strong Portuguese wines. The Methuen Treaty of 1703 lowered the duty on Portuguese wine coming into Britain in return for concessions for British textile merchants in Portugal. But the wines did not travel well, so the port shippers began adding brandy to fortify them during their long sea voyage. Port was born, and with it the household names (Croft, Dow, Taylor, Warre) that still control much of the port trade.

The traditional grape varieties include Tinta Roriz (known as Tempranillo in Spain) and Touriga Nacional. The grapes are harvested by hand in autumn, and either crushed by foot in stone vats or fermented in steel tanks. After two days, the fermentation process is stopped by the addition of grape spirit and the wine is transferred into pipes – wooden casks with a capacity of around 500 litres. The following spring they are transported down river to mature in the port lodges at Vila Nova de Gaia (▶ 84).

Above: Barrels of port mature in the lodges of Vila Nova de Gaia

Left: Port comes in both red and white styles

Styles of Port
White: Churchill's – dry or sweet, served chilled as an apéritif
Ruby: Sandeman's Rich Ruby – dark, full-bodied and fruity
Tawny: Dow's Ten-Year-Old Tawny – amber-coloured, aged in wood for ten years or more
Colheita: Barros – complex, spicy, single-harvest tawny aged for at least seven years
LBV (Late Bottled Vintage): Taylor's – single-harvest wine aged in wood for four to six years
Vintage: Graham's 1986 (▶ opposite)

For a wide range of ports by the glass, visit the **Solar do Vinho do Porto** in Lisbon (►71) or **Porto** (►81).

Top: Grapes are grown on the slopes of the Douro Valley

Centre: Taylor's is one of the oldest names in port

Not Just Mateus Rosé

The sweet Mateus Rosé, exported worldwide in distinctive, bulb-shaped bottles, has perhaps given Portuguese wine a bad name (although it is currently being given an image makeover) – but there are some excellent wines if you know where to look. As well as port, the Douro Valley produces strong, serious reds, while from the Beiras come the full-bodied reds of the Dão region and the intense, fruity reds of Bairrada, made with the Baga grape. Some of the best new red wines come from Alentejo, particularly around Redondo and Reguengos. And don't forget *vinho verde*, the young, slightly sparkling "green" wine of the Minho, which comes as both red and white.

Bulls...

Just as in Spain, the **bullfight** is considered an art form rather than a sport, and few people are bothered about the cruelty involved. The big difference is that in Portugal bulls are not killed in the ring, though they are invariably mortally wounded and dispatched out of sight after the fight.

The *tourada* begins with a *cavaleiro*, a rider in 18th-century costume, with silk jacket, knee-length boots and plumed tricorne hat. The *cavaleiro* performs elaborate dressage manoeuvres before piercing the bull with darts, preparing the way for the *pega*, when *forcados*, dressed in scarlet cummerbunds, leap onto the bull and wrestle it to the ground –

but usually not before at least one of them has been tossed into the air.

Bullfights take place between Easter and October in towns across southern Portugal, particularly in Lisbon and Santarém. They are also staged in the Algarve, primarily for tourists attracted by the misleading slogan: "The bull is not killed".

Another popular tradition is **bull-running** in the streets at Vila Franca de Xira, north of Lisbon, during the Festa do Colete Encarnado (Festival of the Red Waistcoat) in early July and the Feira de Outubro in early October. As in Pamplona in Spain, this event involves members of the public running through the streets with bulls.

To experience the drama of Portuguese popular culture head for a bullfight, a football match or a traditional religious *festa*

BULLS, BALLS AND BELLS

Balls...

If bullfighting is a passion, **football** is an obsession. Lisbon is equally divided between supporters of the red Benfica and the green Sporting, while in Porto Boavista challenge the national and former European champions FC Porto who monopolise the game.

The big names are Eusébio, born in Mozambique and star of the Benfica team that won the European Cup in 1962, Luís Figo, who played for FC Barcelona and Real Madrid before moving to Inter Milan, and the current "golden boy" of football, Cristiano Ronaldo, currently at Manchester United. Portugal hosted the European football championships in 2004 for which new stadia were built all over the country.

...and Bells

Nothing quite matches the colour and spectacle of a Portuguese **festa**. Every town and village has its own saint's day, marked by religious processions, music, dancing and parades. Many of these festivals combine Christian and pagan elements, and all provide an excuse for partying, drinking, flirting and fireworks.

RICARDO...VIVE PRA SEMP
NO NOSSO CORAÇÃO!

Festa!

Carnival (Feb/Mar): Masked dances, fancy-dress costumes and processions of floats mark the end of winter and the arrival of Lent. Some of the most colourful parades are in Loulé and Elvas.

Holy Week (Mar/Apr): Torchlit processions of hooded and barefoot penitents take place on the Thursday and Friday before Easter in Braga.

Festa das Cruzes (first weekend in May): A country fair in Barcelos, with processions of crosses along flower-strewn streets.

Festas dos Santos Populares (12–29 Jun): Three weeks of merrymaking takes place in Lisbon to mark the feasts of the "popular saints", Santo António, São João and São Pedro. On 12 June, the *bairros* of Lisbon are decorated with streamers and paper lanterns and people pour into Alfama to eat grilled sardines at tables set up on the street.

Festa de São João (23–24 Jun): Bonfires and fireworks mark the summer solstice in Porto. There's a regatta on the River Douro and the strange custom of people hitting each other over the head with giant leeks, bunches of garlic and plastic hammers.

Romaria de Nossa Senhora da Agonía (weekend nearest 20 Aug): A huge, traditional *romaria* (religious festival) in Viana do Castelo with bullfights, fireworks over the River Lima, folk dancing and the blessing of fishing boats.

Romaria de Nossa Senhora da Nazaré (8 Sep): Religious processions, folk dancing and bullfights take place in the fishing village of Nazaré.

Feiras Novas (third weekend in Sep): There's a large market and fairground with fireworks, brass bands and parades in Ponte de Lima, a centre of traditional Minho culture.

Festa dos Rapazes (25 Dec–6 Jan): Christmas in Portugal is a family affair, a time for eating *bacalhau* (salt cod) and *bolo rei* (fruit cake) – except in the villages around Bragança, where young men put on masks, cowbells and suits of ribbons and run through their villages in an ancient rite of passage which dates back to pre-Christian times.

Children in traditional dress enjoy a festival in the Minho

ON THE TILES

You see them at railway stations and churches, grocery shops and fountains, royal palaces and backstreet bars. You find them on sale in Algarve fishing villages and see them covering up entire buildings in Lisbon. If visitors to Portugal take away one single image that defines Portuguese architecture, it is usually the "azulejo" tile.

Azulejos are not unique to Portugal, but it is perhaps here that they have achieved their finest expression. Similar glazed and painted tiles are found across the Arab world and in the Spanish region of Andalucía, from where *azulejos* originally came.

The name probably derives from an Arabic phrase meaning "azure polished stone" and they were first introduced to Portugal in the late 15th century when Manuel I imported Hispano-Arabic tiles from Seville for his royal palace at Sintra (► 60).

These early tiles were called *alicatados* and were made of monochrome pieces of glazed earthenware that were cut into shapes or separated by strips to form mosaic-like geometric patterns.

The majolica technique was introduced from Italy during the 16th century. This involved coating the clay in a layer of white enamel on to which the artist could paint directly. In the 17th century, the fashion was for *tapetes* (carpet tiles), painted blue and yellow and resembling Moorish tapestries and rugs.

The 18th century saw both the arrival of mass production – the first factory was set up after the 1755 earthquake in

The entrance hall of São Bento railway station in Porto is beautifully decorated with *azulejos*

Lisbon – and also the development of the familiar blue and white tiles, heavily influenced by Chinese porcelain.

The custom of covering entire house- and shopfronts with *azulejos* began in Lisbon during the mid-19th century and came from Brazil, where Portuguese settlers used it as a way of keeping out the tropical rain.

Azulejos continue to be a popular decoration, brightening up private *patios* and courtyards, public parks and gardens, and several of the Metro stations in Lisbon.

Below: Modern designs at Porches, the pottery capital of the Algarve

Bottom: *Azulejos* decorate the gardens of an aristocratic palace in Lisbon

Where to See *Azulejos*

- Museu Nacional do Azulejo, Lisbon (► 65)
- Palácio Nacional, Sintra (► 60)
- Sé Velha, Coimbra (► 108)
- Igreja dos Lóios, Évora (► 133)
- Nossa Senhora da Consolação, Elvas (► 141)
- Museu Regional, Beja (► 142)
- Igreja de São Lourenço, Almansil (► 151)

How to Make an *Azulejo*

- Most *azulejos* conform to a standard size of 14cm by 14cm (5.5 by 5.5 inches).
- The clay is cut to size and then fired in a kiln.
- It is glazed with a layer of white enamel, made by mixing water with powdered glass.
- The design is drawn in charcoal, with a rabbit's brush (tail) used to erase mistakes.
- The tile is then painted in colour and fired at a temperature of 980°C.

Amália

Amália Rodrigues (1920–99) was Portugal's greatest diva and the best-known voice of *fado* for 50 years. Her own life could have been the subject for a *fado* song – the girl from a Lisbon slum who ended up on Broadway but whose life was marred by faithless lovers and suicide attempts. When she died, there were three days of national mourning and she became the first woman to be honoured in the national pantheon (➤ 56).

Lisbon's *Fado* Clubs

- **Parreirinha de Alfama**, Beco de Espírito Santo 1, tel: 218 868 209
- **Clube de Fado**, Rua São João da Praça 92, tel: 218 882 694
- **A Baiúca**, Rua de São Miguel 20, tel: 218 867 284
- **Adega do Ribatejo**, Rua do Diário do Notícias 23, tel: 213 468 343
- **Adega Machado**, Rua do Norte 91, tel: 213 224 640
- **Arcadas do Faia**, Rua da Barroca 54, tel: 213 426 742
- **Senhor Vinho**, Rua do Meio à Lapa 18, tel: 213 972 681
- **Casa de Linhares Restaurante Bacalhau de Molho**, Beco dos Armazens do Linho 2, tel: 218 865 088

FADO – LISBON'S URBAN BLUES

The lights are dimmed and the drinkers put down their glasses. All eyes are on the musicians, one with a *guitarra* (a Portuguese guitar like a mandolin), the other with a *viola* (acoustic Spanish guitar). There is absolute silence as a woman dressed in black rises to sing, head thrown back, eyes half-closed. She sings of love and death, of triumph and tragedy, of destiny and *fado* (fate). Above all she sings of *saudade*, that uniquely Portuguese notion best translated as a longing for that which has been lost, from a broken love affair to the days when Portugal was great.

Fado has its origins in the working-class *bairros* of Lisbon in the early 19th century. At first, it was played in taverns and brothels and then, in the 1920s, the first *casas de fado* opened, with professional singers making recordings and putting on shows for tourists. It is only now that *fado* is making a comeback among young Portuguese as a genuine art form. It is melancholic, dramatic and heart-wrenching – think of the blues born in the poor neighbourhoods of America.

All female *fadistas* wear a black shawl in memory of Maria Severa (1810–36), the first great *fado* singer, whose scandalous affair with a bull-fighter and tragically early death have been the subject of many songs.

The best places to hear *fado* are in the clubs of Alfama and Bairro Alto. At Parreirinha de Alfama (► opposite), *fado* legend Argentina Santos continues to sing in her backstreet cellar club, with black-and-white photos of *fadistas* on the walls. A few streets away, guitarist Mário Pacheco plays every night in his intimate Clube de Fado, one of the newest of Lisbon's *fado* clubs (► opposite). These places have a minimum charge and you are expected to order a meal, but beyond that there is little commercialism and most of the customers are Portuguese.

For the full, raw, spontaneous experience, head for the bars and clubs where *fado amador* is played. These usually have house musicians but anyone can turn up and sing.

Former bank clerk Henrique Gascon opened A Baiúca in Alfama (► opposite) so that he would have somewhere to listen to *fado* with his friends. Now it is packed most nights.

In Bairro Alto, Adega do Ribatejo (► opposite) is a popular meeting place, where waitresses Sara Cristina and Maria Raquel can be seen swapping aprons for black shawls and turning into *fadistas* for the night.

CHANGING

PORTUGAL IS CHANGING, AND CHANGING FAST. THE CARNATION REVOLUTION OF 1974, WHEN THE PEOPLE OF LISBON STUFFED CARNATIONS DOWN THE BARRELS OF SOLDIERS' GUNS, BROUGHT TO AN END MORE THAN 40 YEARS OF DICTATORSHIP UNDER ANTÓNIO SALAZAR AND TOOK PORTUGAL INTO THE EUROPEAN MAINSTREAM.

Portugal in Figures

- Population: 10.5 million
- Births: 120,000 per year
- Deaths: 105,000 per year
- Marriages: 63,000 per year
- Divorces: 19,000 per year
- Literacy: Male 95%, female 90%

In 1986, Portugal entered the European Union; in 2002, it adopted the euro as its currency. Meanwhile, the end of the colonial wars and the granting of independence to the former African colonies brought thousands of Angolans, Cape Verdeans and Mozambicans to Lisbon, creating a vibrant, racially diverse, tolerant city.

The most obvious change has been in the visible signs of wealth. In 1985, Portugal had just one motorway that ran between Porto and Lisbon; now there are dozens of new roads, financed by European Union grants, opening up the interior and linking previously inaccessible regions with Lisbon and Spain.

The staging of Expo'98 in Lisbon on the 500th anniversary of Vasco da Gama's epic journey to India unleashed a building

The futuristic buildings of the Parque das Nações, Lisbon

PORTUGAL

boom in the capital, bringing about new bridges, Metro lines, skyscrapers and shopping malls. Buoyed by the success of Expo'98, Portugal then bid for the Euro 2004 football championships, which it won, and vast sums of money were spent on building new stadia and upgrading hotels.

Portugal has one of the fastest growth rates in the European Union, yet large areas of poverty remain everywhere. Salaries are low. Infant mortality rates are among the highest in Europe. There are shanty towns on the fringes of Lisbon and Porto, and there are people in Trás-os-Montes without access to running water.

At the same time, the influence of the Catholic church is in decline. The religious festivals are as popular as ever, but Sunday attendance is at a record low and Catholic priests are no longer seen as the guardians of public morality.

Although abortion is only legal up to 12 weeks (or if the mother's life is at risk), contraception is widely available, birth rates are falling and divorce is on the increase. Sex outside marriage is no longer taboo, and homosexuality is more widely accepted. The tourist office in Lisbon has a guide to gay discos and bars.

Meanwhile, in Alfama, a widow who will wear black until she dies gathers flowers for her husband's grave.

Despite the popularity of Fátima, church attendance is in decline

Background: A modern suspension bridge at Portimão in the Algarve

Below: Many widows still dress in black

BEYOND THE MOUNTAINS

An ancient granite sculpture of a pig, nearly 3m (3.3yards) long, stands in the main square of Murça, a small town on the old road from Bragança to Vila Real. The locals have grown rather fond of this pig and have named their wine Porca de Murça in its honour. But like so much about Trás-os-Montes, its origins are shrouded in mystery. More than 200 of these *berrões* have been found across the region, many of them within circular stone walls that suggest a pagan shrine. They were probably placed there by Celto-Iberian tribes more than 2,000 years ago and were used in fertility cults.

Background: Much of northern Portugal is still mountain wilderness

Wild Portugal
You can also experience the wild side of Portugal at:
• Parque Nacional da Peneda-Gerês (➤ 91)
• Serra da Estrela (➤ 119)
• Serra de Monchique (➤ 154–155)

Museums
To find out more about Trás-os-Montes folk traditions, visit the local museums in Bragança (➤ 94–95) and Miranda do Douro (➤ 95).

It would not be surprising if the ancient people of Trás-os-Montes worshipped pigs. Cut off from the rest of Portugal by high mountain ranges, this is a land of rugged moorland where life has always been hard. The Terra Fria (cold lands) in the north of the province has a climate which is often described as "nine months of winter and three months of hell". In such a climate, pigs are a lifeline – they can be slaughtered in winter and turned into hams and sausages to keep you going through the barren months ahead.

The very name Trás-os-Montes (Beyond the Mountains) conjures up visions of a world apart. This is a place where the winter solstice is still marked by masked dancers in multicoloured suits running through the village with cowbells round their waists in a ritual that dates back to pagan times. Until recently, when people were ill, they used folk remedies or consulted the local witch.

This sense of otherworldliness has always attracted outsiders, including Jews who fled here from the Spanish Inquisition during the 15th century. Their legacy can be seen in the *alheiras* (chicken sausages), which are still a speciality of Mirandela, but which were first made as a way of fooling the Inquisitors that they had renounced their Jewish ways and started to eat pork.

Some of the wildest parts of Trás-os-Montes are in the Parque Natural de Montesinho, between Bragança and the Spanish border. The heather-clad uplands rise to 1,480m (4,855 feet) while the lower slopes support chestnut and holm oak. Golden eagles hover above the hills, wolves hide in the forests, and at weekends

A medieval pillory rises out of a granite pig in the regional capital of Bragança

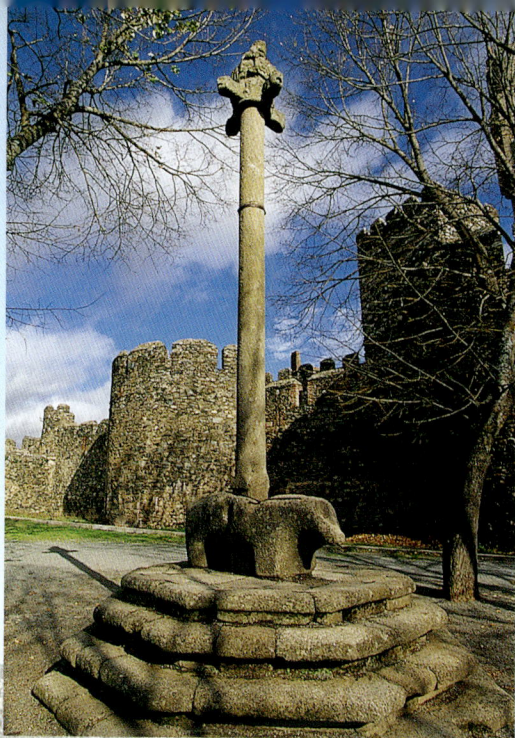

Golden eagles can be seen in the Montesinho natural park

the local farmers go hunting for partridge, deer and wild boar. At least 90 villages are scattered about the park, with horseshoe-shaped dovecotes and slate-roofed houses where the oxen sleep downstairs and a granite staircase leads to the living quarters above.

The village of Rio de Onor, right on the border, is half-Spanish, half-Portuguese. The only sign that you are crossing from one country to another is a stone block marked with the letters "E" (España) and "P" (Portugal) and the change to a tarmac road on the Spanish side.

A study by the Spanish anthropologist António Jorge Dias in 1953 found that the people of Rio de Onor lived a communal existence, sharing land and cattle with their Spanish neighbours quite independently of the State and speaking a dialect common to them both, Rionorês.

Although the village has become depopulated in recent years, some of these traditions still survive.

But Trás-os-Montes is changing. A new highway from Porto to Bragança has opened up the province as it is on the route to northern Spain. Even in the villages, cars and tractors are replacing horse-carts and bullock-ploughs. The emigrants who abandoned Trás-os-Montes for lack of work opportunities are returning to build chic new houses (casas de emigrante) with the money they have made in France, Germany, Luxembourg and the United States, bringing with them cosmopolitan values and a taste for fast food.

POUSADAS AND SOLARES

ON 19 APRIL, 1942, THE FIRST POUSADA OPENED IN THE BORDER TOWN OF ELVAS TO CATER FOR TRAVELLERS FROM SPAIN. THE PRICE OF A DOUBLE ROOM WAS 80 ESCUDOS (€0.40). THE POUSADAS WERE STATE-RUN INNS ALONG THE LINES OF THE SPANISH PARADORES, OFFERING SIMPLE HOSPITALITY AND REGIONAL CUISINE, AND WERE THE BRAINCHILD OF THE MINISTER FOR POPULAR CULTURE AND TOURISM, ANTÓNIO FERRO. "AT THE CURRENT TIME, NEARLY ALL CONSTRUCTION IN EUROPE IS INTENDED FOR WAR," HE SAID AT THE OPENING CEREMONY. "OUR POUSADAS WILL BE FORTRESSES OF PEACE, REFUGES OF GRACE AND QUIET."

in the centre of the walled village.

António Ferro wanted the *pousadas* to be "small hotels where people could feel at home". For him, rustic furniture and local crafts were part of the experience, which was summed up as "comfort without ostentation".

Ironically, as levels of service rise ever higher, the *pousadas* are in danger of moving away from their roots. "If a guest walks into one of our *pousadas* and feels as if he has returned to his own house, then we will have achieved what we were striving for," Ferro said.

Sixty years later, there are now 40 *pousadas*, but they are no longer state-owned. *All* of them are housed in historic buildings or situated in places of natural beauty, or both.

You can stay at a restored castle in Óbidos (▶ 124) or Estremoz (▶ 144), a convent in Évora (▶ 133) or Beja (▶ 142), or a village house in Monsanto (▶ 124) or Marvão (▶ 138–139).

Perhaps the finest of all the *pousadas* is **Pousada de Santa Marinha**, in a 12th-century convent overlooking the historic city of Guimarães (▶ 93). The rooms are in former monks' cells around the cloisters, with tile-lined stairways and corridors filled with antiques.

By contrast, the simple *pousada* at **Ourém**, just outside Fátima (▶ 114), is a tasteful modern conversion of a group of medieval houses

Solares de Portugal

If you really want to feel at home, you could stay in a manor house with a Portuguese family.

The Count of Calheiros, president of the Solares de Portugal (▶ 35), has been welcoming guests to his ancestral home (Paço de Calheiros, tel: 258 947 164) since 1985. The house, built in the 17th century, stands at the end of an avenue of magnolia trees with a stone fountain in the yard. Chestnut ceilings are weighed down with chandeliers, and family portraits hang on the walls. The chapel has a carved 17th-century altarpiece and a vault where the last count is buried. The old stables have been turned into apartments and there is a swimming pool and tennis court in the grounds. From the terrace there are views over the vineyards to

Ponte de Lima, the headquarters of Solares de Portugal and the town with the largest concentration of manor houses in the scheme.

A few hours east in Trás-os-Montes, Brazilian artist, Maria Francisca Pessanha introduces visitors to **Solar das Arcas** (tel: 278 400 010), a 17th-century mansion built for the descendants of a Genoese navigator who arrived in Portugal in the 14th century at the invitation of Dom Dinis. The library has shelves of antique books. The apartments have wooden furniture, granite fireplaces and Maria Francisca's modern art on the walls. From your room, the only sounds you can hear are church bells and the horses' hooves on the village street. The Pessanhas will offer you their own wine and home-cured sausages, and give you advice on walking, cycling and horse-riding in the area.

Solares de Portugal offers around 100 properties, from manor houses and country estates to rustic farmhouses and cottages. Most are in the Minho, but others are scattered across Portugal, right down to the Alentejo and the Algarve. Most are in quiet rural locations and many have swimming pools. However, what makes this experience really special is that you are staying in family houses rather than hotels, with a real insight into Portuguese life.

Useful Addresses
• **Pousadas de Portugal**, Rua Soares de Passos 3, Alto de Santo Amaro, 1300-314 Lisbon, tel: 218 442 001 (► 35)
• **Solares de Portugal**, Praça da República 4990, Ponte de Lima, Lisbon, tel: 258 741 672 (► 35)

Ten Memorable Experiences

• A blustery morning at **Belém** (▶ 46–49), feeling the ocean breeze and the taste of adventure as you recall the voyages of Portugal's 15th-century explorers.

• A ride on the **No 28 tram** in Lisbon (▶ 66).

• An evening at one of **Lisbon's fado clubs** (▶ 18).

• Touring the port lodges of **Vila Nova de Gaia** (▶ 84).

• Exploring the **Douro Valley** by road, river or rail, or taking the **scenic train line** from Tua to Mirandela (▶ 178).

• Joining the crowds at the Thursday **market in Barcelos** (▶ 94).

• The **view** from the summit of Serra da Estrela (▶ 119).

• A **boat trip** from Lagos or Carvoeiro in summer to explore the cliffs, caves and cove beaches of the Algarve (▶ 159–161).

• Standing on the cliffs at **Cabo de São Vicente** (▶ 157–158) to watch the sun setting over the Atlantic Ocean.

• Spending the night in a **private manor house** (▶ 26–27).

Best Museums...

• **Museu Calouste Gulbenkian** (▶ 50) for its fabulous world-class collection.

• **Museu Nacional de Arte Antiga** (▶ 63), with a collection of ancient Portuguese art.

• **Museu Nacional do Azulejo** (▶ 65) for an insight into Portuguese tile art.

A ride on the No 28 tram is an essential Lisbon experience

Azulejo tiles at their best at the Museu Nacional do Azulejo

• Lovers of the eccentric will enjoy the **Toy Museum** at Sintra (➤ 61) and the **matchbox museum** at Tomar (➤ 117), as well as the quirky museums at **Miranda do Douro** (➤ 95) and **Lagos** (➤ 165).

The Saturday market at Estremoz

If You Only Visit One Market...
...make it the Thursday market at **Barcelos** (➤ 94), which has all the colour and atmosphere of a medieval fair. There are other good markets at **Estremoz** (➤ 146) and **Loulé** (➤ 164).

Best Castles in the Air
Portugal has a wealth of romantic ruined castles, many in hilltop towns along the Spanish border. Among the best are **Castelo de São Jorge**, Lisbon (➤ 52) and the castles at **Sintra** (➤ 61), **Guimarães** (➤ 93), **Bragança** (➤ 94), **Silves** (➤ 165) and the walled villages of **Óbidos** (➤ 121) and **Marvão** (➤ 138–139).

The impressive castle walls at Óbidos

Best Places for People-Watching
The terrace of **Café Nicola** (➤ 175) or **Pastelaria Suiça** (➤ 175) on the Rossio in Lisbon.

Best Churches
The **Mosteiro dos Jerónimos** at Belém (➤ 48) and the abbeys at **Alcobaça** (➤ 110) and **Batalha** (➤ 112).

Évora's grisly but fascinating bone chapel

Best Bone Chapels
Fans of the macabre will enjoy the bone chapels at **Évora** (➤ 134) and **Faro** (➤ 163).

Best for Kids
• **Algarve beaches**, boat trips and **waterparks** (➤ 159–161, 170).
• **Oceanário**, Lisbon (➤ 58), Europe's largest aquarium.
• **Portugal dos Pequenitos**, Coimbra (➤ 106).

The golden sands of Albufeira in the Algarve

...that Portuguese is spoken by more than 200 million people worldwide and is the official language of Brazil and five African nations, making it the world's seventh language and more common than French?

...that according to figures produced by the United Nations, the Portuguese have the second highest calorie consumption per capita in the world, behind Argentina?

...that Portugal is one of the oldest nation states in Europe, having declared its independence under Afonso Henriques in 1139 and existed within its present borders since the reconquest of Moorish Algarve in 1249?

...that Portugal has the longest working hours in the European Union (apart from Great Britain), the lowest salaries and the highest participation of women in the workforce?

...that although the last king, Manuel II, went into exile in 1910, his successor, Dom Duarte, Duke of Bragança, still claims the title of head of the royal house of Portugal?

...that although the population of Portugal is around ten million, a further three million Portuguese citizens live abroad?

...that Portugal is Britain's oldest ally? The alliance was formed by the 1386 Treaty of Windsor, and sealed by the marriage of Philippa of Lancaster to João I the same year.

...that Portuguese novelist José Saramago won the Nobel Prize for Literature in 1998? His travelogue *Journey to Portugal* (1990) describes a six-month journey around his own country.

DID...?

DID...?

DID YOU KNOW...?

DID YOU KNOW...?

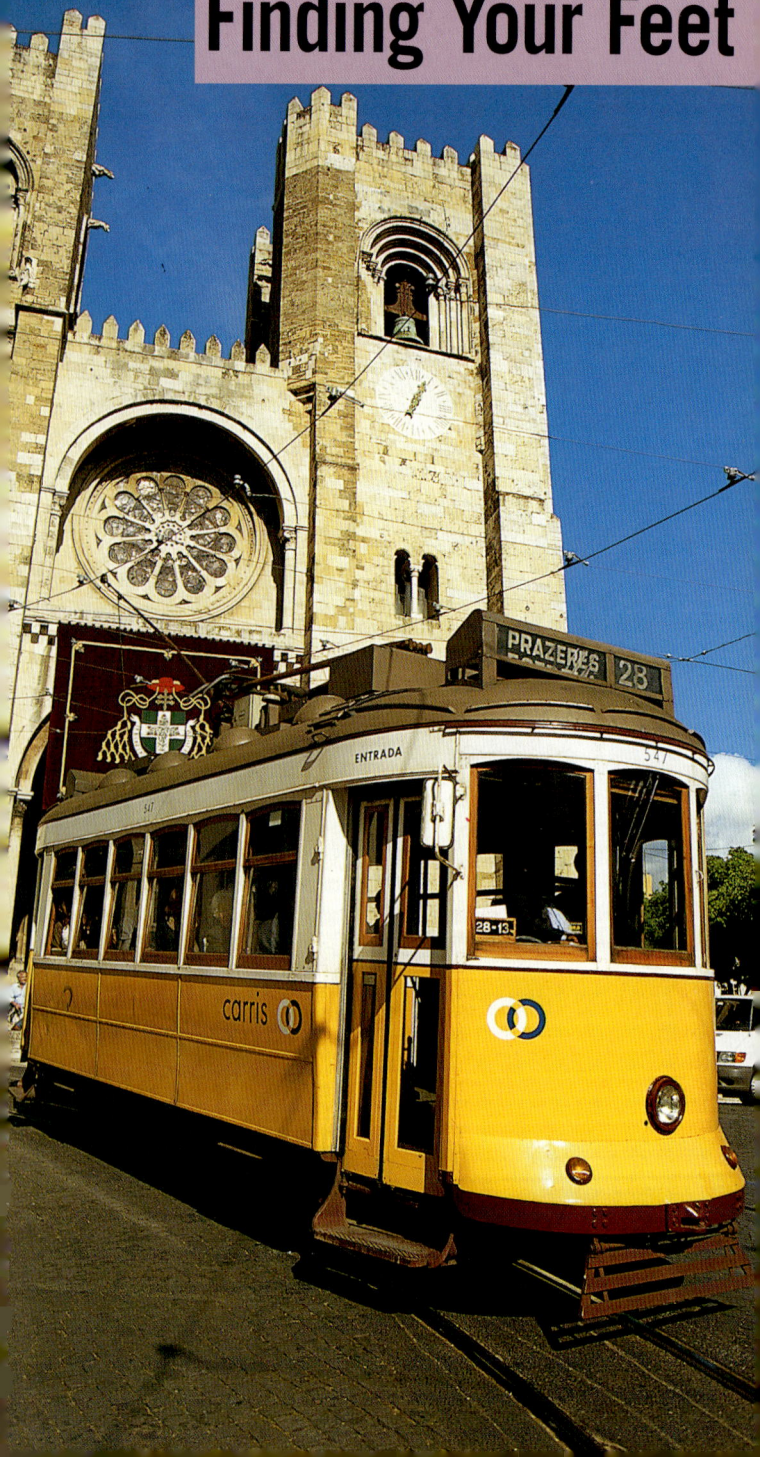

First Two Hours

Arriving by Air

There are international airports at Lisbon, Porto and Faro. All three have tourist offices, post offices, currency exchange facilities and car hire outlets.

Lisbon

■ **Portela Airport** (www.ana.pt) is 7km (4.3 miles) north of the city centre. Tel: 218 413 500 (enquiries), tel: 218 413 700 (arrivals/ departures).

■ The **Aerobus** (inexpensive; free for passengers flying with TAP, the Portuguese national airline) departs for central Lisbon from outside the arrivals hall every 20 minutes 7:40am–8:45pm daily. The route takes in Avenida da Liberdade, Rossio, Praça do Comércio and Cais do Sodré (for trains to Estoril and Cascais). Tickets are also valid for one day on Lisbon's buses, trams and funiculars.

■ A **taxi** to central Lisbon should cost around €15–€20, with supplements for extra luggage or night travel. Fares are metered, so make sure that the meter is switched on. An alternative is to buy a pre-paid taxi voucher from the tourist office in the arrivals hall.

Porto

■ **Francisco Sá Carneiro Airport** is 11km (6.8 miles) north of the city centre. Tel: 229 432 400; www.ana.pt.

■ **Buses** 87 and 601 (www.stcp.pt) run daily from 5:13am–9pm every 30 minutes and the fare is €1.30.

■ On the **Metro** (www.metrodoporto.pt) take the Violeta Line (E), running from 6am–1am every 20 minutes (€1.25) taking 20–35 minutes to the centre.

■ A **taxi** to central Porto should cost around €15–18, with supplements for extra luggage or night travel.

Faro

■ **Faro Airport** is 6km (3.7 miles) west of the city centre. Tel: 289 800 800; www.ana.pt

■ From the airport take buses No 16 and No 14 into Faro.

■ **Taxi** fares to Faro and the various resorts are listed in the arrivals hall, but it is worth checking the price with the driver before you set off.

Tourist Information Offices

Most tourist office staff speak excellent English, and have maps and information in English. There are tourist offices in all main towns and cities.

■ **Lisbon**: The main office (daily 9–7) is the **Lisboa Welcome Center**, Rua do Arsenal 15, tel: 210 312 700; www.visitlisboa.com. This also has a bookshop, art gallery, café and shops selling local crafts and design. There are tourist offices on Praça dos Restauradores (daily 9–8) and information kiosks at Belém, Rua Augusta and Castelo de São Jorge.

■ **Porto**: The main tourist office is at Rua Clube dos Fenianos 25, near the top of Avenida dos Aliados (tel: 223 393 470).

■ **Faro**: The tourist office is at Rua da Misericórdia 8 (near the entrance to the old town), tel: 289 803 604. There is also an office at the airport.

■ **The Algarve**: There are also tourist offices at Albufeira, Alcoutim, Carvoeiro, Lagos, Loulé, Monchique, Monte Gordo, Portimão, Praia da Rocha, Sagres, Silves and Tavira.

Getting Around

Portugal's compact size makes it easy to get around. There are good bus and train connections between the major cities, but to get to the more out-of-the-way places you will need a car.

Driving

- Drivers **bringing their own cars** into Portugal need a driving licence, registration document, insurance certificate and nationality sticker.
- **Car rental** is available at all airports and in major towns and resorts. To rent a car you must be over 21 and have a passport, driving licence and credit card. You can book in advance through the major international car rental agencies (► below). Local firms offer competitive rates, but you should check carefully the level of insurance cover and excess. Keep the car-rental documents and your driving licence with you at all times.
- Theft from rental cars is common. Never leave items on display in the car, and take all valuables with you or lock them out of sight.

Avis: tel: 218 435 550 (Lisbon Airport); www.avis.com
Europcar: tel: 218 401 176 or 800 201 002 for reservations
(Lisbon Airport); www.europcar.com
Hertz: tel: 218 438 660 (Lisbon Airport); www.hertz.com

Driving Essentials

- Drive on the **right**.
- **Seat belts** are compulsory for the driver and all passengers.
- The legal **alcohol** limit is 0.05 per cent.
- **Speed limits** are 120kph (74mph) on motorways, 90kph (56mph) on main roads, 50kph (31mph) in urban areas, unless otherwise indicated.
- **Driving standards** are generally poor and Portugal has one of the highest accident rates in Europe. The N125 across the Algarve is notorious for its high number of accidents. If you are involved in an accident, use the orange SOS phone on a motorway to call the police.
- A network of **motorways** and **main roads** connects Lisbon, Porto and the major cities. Motorways are prefaced with A and incur tolls. Other main roads are prefaced with IP or IC, or N (for *nacional*).
- **Check regulations before you travel** – www.theAA.com has comprehensive European driving information.

Buses and Trains

- Bus and train services connect the main towns and cities. On both, children under 4 travel free, under-12s travel half fare, and over-65s receive a discount.
- **Bus** services are operated by **private companies**.
- **Train** services are operated by **Caminhos de Ferros Portugueses** (**CP**, tel: 808 208 208; www.cp.pt). Tickets can be purchased in advance from stations. **CP** also sells a rail pass valid for 7, 14 or 21 days.
- The Alfa Pendular from Lisbon to Porto via Coimbra is a **fast train service**.
- There are five main **railway stations** in **Lisbon**. Trains depart from Sete Rios for Sintra, from Cais do Sodré for Estoril and Cascais, Obidos and the west coast from Santa Apolónia or Oriente for Porto and Madrid and from Entrecampos for Faro and Evora.

City Transport

- **Lisbon** has an excellent network of buses, trams, Metro trains and *elevadores* (funiculars).
- **Single tickets** can be bought on buses or at Metro stations and validated at the machines behind the driver or at the station barriers. Less expensive options include a two-journey ticket or a one-day or three-day pass, valid on buses and trams, from the Carris ticket booth on Praça da Figueira. You can also buy a four-day or seven-day *passe turístico*, valid on Metro, buses and trams, on production of your passport. Metro stations sell 10-ticket *cadernetas*, which are good value for multiple journeys. Tourist offices sell the **Lisbon Card**, valid for up to three days, which gives unlimited travel on public transport and free or discounted admission to more than 20 museums and places of interest.
- **Porto** has a good network of local **buses**. Single-journey tickets and one-day passes can be bought on the bus. Tourist offices sell one- or two-day passes called the **Porto Card**, which include discounts at museums and on river cruises, and free travel on buses, trams and the Metro. A new Metro system with seven different lines named from A through G now covers much of the city and is an efficient way to get around (www.metro-porto.pt).

Admission Charges

The cost of admission for museums and places of interest featured in this guide is indicated by the following price categories.

Inexpensive = under €3
Moderate = €3–6
Expensive = over €6

Accommodation

Especially outside Lisbon and the Algarve, accommodation in Portugal is very good value. Independent travellers can choose from a wide range of places and the luxury end of the market is refreshingly informal.

Booking

- Advance booking is vital in the **high season** (July and August) or if your stay coincides with events such as local festivals or pilgrimages. In quiet periods rates can drop to 40 per cent of the high-season price, but beware that in coastal resorts places may shut completely in the winter.
- **Tourist offices** have comprehensive lists of official accommodation or the addresses of *dormidas* or *quartos* (rooms for rent).
- Many hotels and tourist complexes in the Algarve are **block booked** throughout the summer; either reserve months ahead or choose a guesthouse, *pousada* or *estalagem* instead.

Hotels

- Hotels are invariably **clean and safe**, but you might find alternative types of accommodation (► oppposite) more attractive and welcoming than budget hotels, especially in cities.
- An **official price list** must be displayed inside the door of every room.
- **IVA** (VAT) or sales tax must be included in the advertised room rate; breakfast tends to be included and varies from continental style to a copious buffet.

- You may be **charged extra** for using a garage or gym.
- **Extra beds** are often supplied for a small fee.
- **Children** (usually under four years) can stay free or at a discount in their parents' room.

Pousadas and Accommodation with Character

- *Pousadas* (which means "a place to rest") are privately owned hotels located throughout the country (many in the Alentejo), aimed at tourists looking for somewhere special to stay, usually near centres of interest.
- They are set in **fabulous surroundings** and have elements of traditional architecture and furnishing, as well as good to excellent restaurants – open to non-residents – where you can sample Portuguese specialities and wine, often in highly atmospheric dining rooms.
- **Standards of comfort** are reliably high.
- Numbering 44 in all, there are four categories: historical *pousadas*, converted castles and monasteries; historic design *pousadas*, as above but with modern boutique-style elements; nature *pousadas,* in spectacular natural settings; charm *pousadas,* often in converted village houses. All *pousadas* are good value for money and even the most expensive, such as those at Estremoz (➤ 144) and Guimarães (➤ 97), cost less than the equivalent luxury establishments in most other countries.
- *Pousadas* are popular with honeymooners, who receive special treatment, and they also offer discounts to families, the under-30s and those aged 60 or over.
- The *pousadas* described in this guide are not necessarily the best, but form part of a balanced selection of accommodation for each region. For a complete listing and detailed information, including promotions and booking facilities, contact **Pousadas de Portugal**, Rua Soares de Passos 3, Alto de Santo Amaro, 1300-314 Lisbon; tel: 218 442 001, fax: 218 442 085/7; www.pousadas.pt
- On a more intimate scale, the **Solares de Portugal**, and other similar schemes, offer a huge choice of alternative accommodation across the whole country in the mid-budget range. Government-approved but privately owned, these tend to be farmhouses and country houses with around 12 rooms, sometimes with facilities such as swimming pools but seldom offering meals other than breakfast.
  A complete list is available from the following:
  • **Solares de Portugal**, Praça da República 4990, Ponte de Lima; tel: 258 741 672, fax: 258 741 444; www.solaresdeportugal.pt
  • **Privetur**, Largo das Pereiras, 4990 Ponte de Lima; tel: 258 743 923; www.privetur.co.uk
  • **CENTER** (Centro de Tourismo no Espaço Rural), Praça da República 4990, Ponte de Lima; tel: 258 931 750; www.center.pt
- Also look out for the official green tree symbol awarded to government-approved country guesthouses often advertised as a *turismo rural*. These also offer charming accommodation in manors and farms, usually on a bed-and-breakfast basis, plus facilities such as horse-riding.
- Traditional Alentejo farmhouses, known as *montes*, have grouped together to form **Turismo Montes Alentejanos,** Avenida da Liberdade 115, 7400-217 Ponte de Sôr; tel: 242 291 226; www.montesalentejanos.com

Pensões and *Residencials*

- In addition to rooms for rent, at the lower end of the budget range is the *residencial*. These are nearly always clean and comfortable, if basic, but do not provide any meals, except possibly breakfast. The *pensão* is another alternative, sometimes offering no meals at all, or sometimes breakfast

and an evening meal. Alternatively, there is the *hospedaria*, the lowliest of all. Some rooms have their own bathroom, sometimes at a far higher rate than if you share facilities. In value terms, these are often better value than a low- to mid-budget hotel, and some of these places have wonderful character.

Youth Hostels

- *Pousadas de Juventude* (youth hostels) are good on the whole and some are excellent – clean, safe and friendly.
- In **high season** you should book ahead, either through your local youth hostel association or the **Portuguese Youth Hostel Association** (Movijovem), Rua Lúcio de Azevedo 27, 1600-146 Lisbon, tel: 707 203 030 (reservations); www.pousadasjuventude.pt; reservas@movijovem.pt
- Of all the 30 or so hostels, the one in **Leiria** has the best reputation, while the most expensive are in the big cities and the Algarve (where the favourite is at Alcoutim). The hostels in Lagos, Portimão, Coimbra and Penhas da Saúde are all acclaimed. Expect to pay around €9–€43 a night, depending on location, room type and time of year.

Camping

- *Parques de Campismo* (campsites) are usually well run, with facilities ranging from basic to quite luxurious, again at relatively low prices.
- The best ones in **prime seaside locations**, especially in the Algarve where there are several, are crowded in high season – and be warned that theft can be a problem.
- Only a few require an **international camping carnet**, available from national organisations. Charges hover around the €5 per person mark.
- Sites belonging to **ORBITUR** are more expensive but slightly better: ORBITUR, Rua Diogo Couto 1/8°, 1149-042 Lisbon; tel: 218 117 070, fax: 218 117 034; www.orbitur.pt
- For more details contact the **Portuguese Camping Federation**, Avenida Coronel Eduardo Galhardo 24 D, 1199-007 Lisbon, tel: 218 126 890, www.fcmportugal.com, or **Roteiro Campista**, Rua do Giestal, 5-1° Fte, 1300-274 Lisbon, tel: 213 642 370, fax: 213 619 284 for the invaluable booklet of the same name (www.roteiro-campista.pt).

Self-Catering

- Self-catering apartments and villas are found mostly along the **south coast**, though they can be found throughout Portugal.
- **Facilities** range from a basic refrigerator and cooker to fully equipped kitchens, swimming pools, large gardens and a regular maid service.
- It's worth **booking privately** rather than through a tour operator to get better value for money.
- Local and national **tourist offices** should be able to supply contact names and addresses.
- Also try www.ownersdirect.co.uk or www.holidaylettings.co.uk

---

Prices
The symbols refer to the average cost of a double room with bathroom in high season. Singles often cost more than half the double rate.
€ = under €60
€€ = €60–€120
€€€ = €121–€180
€€€€ = over €180

Food and Drink

There are said to be 365 ways of preparing the national favourite, *bacalhau* (salt cod, the traditinal staple, ➤ 9) so you are sure to find it on the menu. Be adventurous and seek out other specialities and, given the subtle regional variations, the advent of several imaginative chefs, plus some remarkably low prices, you can enjoy some memorable meals without breaking the bank.

Eating Out – A Practical Guide

- Strict **dress codes** are almost non-existent, though Sunday best is still customary in the provinces. Jacket and tie is *de rigueur* in only a handful of restaurants in Lisbon and Porto.
- A notch up the scale and mostly found in cities, *cervejarias* (beer houses) also serve food. *Marisquerias* specialise in *marisco* (seafood), where *gambas* (prawns), lobster and luxury fish, served by weight, can send your bill through the roof.
- **Restaurant terraces** (as opposed to café *esplanadas*) are a rarity, so the coolness of deep cellars where some dining rooms are located may prove welcome in the height of summer.

Portuguese Cuisine

- **Seafood**, usually top rate and priced accordingly, is served all along Portugal's long coasts, while inland, lamb, pork and game (in season) are the features.
- Portugal's answer to "**surf and turf**" is *carne de porco à alentejana* (pork simmered with clams and fresh coriander).
- *Bacalhau* (salt cod, soaked to remove most of the salt) is a favourite (➤ 9). There are several different recipes, such as à Gomes de Sá (with hard-boiled egg, boiled potatoes and black olives), *à brás* (stir-fried with eggs, onions and potatoes), *à minhota* (with fried potatoes) and *com natas* (baked in a rich cream sauce).
- *Churrasco* (barbecued meat), sometimes served Brazilian-style (*rodízio*), is the house speciality of many roadside grills and can be great value.
- *Leitão* (suckling pig) is the speciality of the region between Lisbon and Coimbra, but is considered a delicacy nationwide.
- **Vegetarians** have a fairly hard time in Portugal – ask for salads or side orders such as spinach. Although rice and potatoes are frequently on the menu, the only true concession to vegetarians will be omelettes.

Practicalities

- All but the most modest places now accept **credit cards**, but check first in case you don't have enough cash on you.
- **Lunch** is over by 2pm, maybe 3pm in the south. **Dinner** is served around 8pm and you may find it hard to find a kitchen open after 10 or 11pm, especially in rural areas.
- In Lisbon, fashionable places serve until very late into the night, while *cervejarias* (beer houses) may stay open all afternoon too. Some establishments may close Sunday evening, many more are closed all day Monday.
- Standard servings are **enormous**, except in chic restaurants: you can often ask for *meia dose* (half portion) for one person.
- **Service** is rarely included and never compulsory, but a 10 per cent tip will always be welcome even in cafés and tea-rooms.
- The *ementa turística* (daily set menu) can be very good value (as little as €5–€6), but is normally only available at lunchtime.

Snacks and Sweets

■ The Portuguese are great on **snacks** (*petiscos* are the local answer to *tapas*), while *lanche* (afternoon tea) is faithfully observed.

■ With a good breakfast (coffee or tea, bread and jam or cheese, cold meats and eggs) you can probably survive until the evening by eating in cafés, *confeitarias* and *pastelerias* (cake shops), and *casas de chá* (tea-rooms).

■ **Coffee** is good and popular and a few sumptuous cafés have survived modernisation in towns and cities. *Bica* (*um café* in Porto and Lisbon) is a strong espresso, while *galão* is a milky coffee served in a glass, perfect with a *torrada* (thick slices of toasted bread dripping with butter).

■ In addition to *sandes* (sandwiches), *pregos* (bread rolls with hot slices of beef) and *bifanas* (like *pregos* but with pork), try *rissóis* (deep-fried meat or prawn patties) and *pastéis de bacalhau* (mini cod fishcakes).

■ Portuguese **cakes** (*pastéis* or *bolos*) are very sweet. The main ingredient is sugar, followed by almonds, honey and egg yolks, and sometimes all four. The regional and local variations on these themes are countless. The best are the cheese-based *queijadas* from Sintra and custard-filled *pastéis de nata* (especially the fabulous ones at Belém – ➤ 69).

■ **Dessert** fans will appreciate *arroz doce* (rice pudding with cinnamon), *pudim flan* (crème caramel) and a whole range of nut and chocolate concoctions. Baked apple (*maçã*) and quince (*marmelo*) are delicious.

Cover Charges and Starters

■ In nearly every restaurant there's a **cover charge** – ostensibly for the bread – and in more expensive places this can be quite high.

■ *Acepipes* – an array of olives, ham, cheese (traditionally served before rather than after meals) and pickles – can keep you going until the main course arrives but, even if unsolicited, they will be itemised on your bill if you so much as touch them. Politely but pointedly refuse them if you don't want to be charged.

■ *Entradas* (starters) come in the form of vegetable soups (such as *caldo verde*, containing strips of kale cabbage) or seafood, or maybe a salad.

Drinks

■ **Mineral water** is excellent and inexpensive – ask for *agua sem gas* (still) or *agua com gas* (sparkling) served *fresca* (chilled) or *natural* (room temperature).

■ Apart from **vinho do Porto** (port, ➤ 10) and **Mateus Rosé**, there are excellent **wines** to sample, the best coming from the Dão and Douro valleys, plus full-bodied reds from Bairrada and the Alentejo. Or there's *vinho verde* – slightly sparkling young wine from the Minho (mostly whites).

■ **Beer** is popular in big cities and on tap should be ordered by the *imperial* (in the south) or *fino* (in the north).

■ There are some good **brandies** (*conhaque*) as well as *aguardente*, *bagaço* and *medronho*, made in the Algarve from arbutus berries. Cherry-based *ginginha* is a popular tipple, especially in Lisbon.

Prices
The following symbols indicate the average price per person for a three-course à la carte meal, excluding drinks and tips.
€ = under €12
€€ = €12–€24
€€€ = €25–€36
€€€€ = over €36

Shopping

Traditional markets across Portugal can be colourful spectacles as well as great places to shop. Ceramics are often on sale along with foods, but the finest items are only sold during local fairs (*feiras*). With its juxtaposition of extravagant boutiques and dusty groceries alongside state-of-the-art shopping malls and beguiling bookstores, Lisbon is Portugal's undisputed shopping capital, though Porto does its best. Every town and city has a busy commercial street or two where you can pick up bargains. Perhaps the best gifts are food or wine related, though sometimes you can come across interesting arts and crafts. Footwear and other leather goods are also good value.

Opening Hours

- Shops usually open daily 9–7, except Sunday, with a two-hour lunch break – *sestas* (siestas) are rare outside the rural interior.
- Modern shopping centres open 10am–midnight, seven days a week.

Clothes and Footwear

- Items such as belts, bags, wallets, shoes, jackets and purses are less expensive than in the rest of western Europe. Leather gloves are also a bargain, still sold in old-fashioned booth-like shops.
- **Home-grown designers** are worth investigating, though few have branches outside Lisbon.

Food and Wine

- In addition to wine and port, brandy, *aguardente* (firewater) and, in the Algarve, *medronho* (► 169) make good gifts. Decanters and other wine-connoisseur paraphernalia can be interesting – some are designed by fashionable artists.
- The easiest foodstuffs to transport include olive oil (try and get "luxury" oil – 0.1 or 0.2 per cent acidity, packaged in smart, corked bottles), cheese (some of it at astronomical prices, so beware), *bacalhau*, and non-perishable cakes and biscuits.
- Pine nuts, almonds and dried and candied fruit are very good value compared with prices in most other countries.

Art and Crafts

- Ceramics, basket- and wicker-ware, and copper pans tend to be the traditional items appealing to all tastes. Pottery and porcelain can be more of an acquired taste.
- The yellow-dotted brown earthenware dishes from Barcelos are universally popular – as is the "Galo" (rooster) commemorating a folk legend originating in the eponymous northern town, and now a national symbol (► 94).

Souvenirs

- *Azulejos* (traditional glazed tiles) range from mass-produced souvenirs to whole sets of antique tiles. Measure up before you come to Portugal and you can have a set tailor-made, to your own design.
- "*Scissor chairs*" are distinctive seats from Monchique in the Algarve.
- *Cataplanas* are metal cooking pans used to make seafood dishes.
- *Arraiolos carpets* are exquisite (and expensive) rugs made in the picturesque town of the same name, to ancient designs.
- *Fado* (► 18) – a CD or cassette of Portuguese "blues" by Amália (► 18) or one of her disciples.

Entertainment

Information

- In the Algarve there are three monthly **English-language publications**: *Essential Algarve*, *Welcome to the Algarve* and *Algarve Guide*, all available from tourist offices and hotels. In Lisbon you can find *Follow Me* for the Greater Lisbon area, and for Sintra and Cascais *What's In Sintra* and *What's in Cascais*. Elsewhere you'll have to rely on weekly English-language newspapers *The Portugal News* and *The Resident*, Portuguese-language publications, such as the daily press, tourist office information and posters and flyers. Or check out the various websites (➤ 188).

Music and Other Cultural Entertainments

- Having both served as European Capital of Culture, Lisbon and Porto are better equipped with dance, music and other performing arts than ever before (➤ 44, 80). Provincial centres such as Faro, Évora, Braga and Coimbra are no cultural deserts either; elsewhere classical concerts are held in churches and monasteries – look out for posters.
- ***Fado*** (➤ 18) is the most famous musical form – the better-known Lisbon version is performed in special *casas* in the capital, most of them aimed at tourists, but internationally famed stars sing in venues across the country. The folksier, academic variant unique to Coimbra is harder to track down, though a couple of places in the city stage regular sessions.
- **Ballet, opera and jazz** are mostly confined to big cities, though some music clubs in the Algarve resorts cater to highbrow tastes.

Festivals

- For local colour and a taste of traditions, there's nothing better than a local **festival** – the calendar is packed with them (➤ 15).
- The most important festivals are covered in the regional listings, but look out for others – it's important to know if only because accommodation can be scarce. Check at local tourist offices.

Spectator Sports

- Luís Figo and Cristiano Ronaldo are the most prominent Portuguese **footballers** since Eusébio. Porto and Lisbon's rival teams, Benfica, Boavista, FC Porto and Sporting, have the national championship stitched up between them and fans might like to see them play at home (➤ 74).
- **Roller-hockey** is the only sport at which Portugal regularly excels internationally (➤ 74), while **bullfighting** (*touradas*) – less cruel than in Spain but still not a sight for animal-lovers (➤ 13) – is making a comeback in some areas after years as an admittedly impressive tourist attraction.

Sport and Outdoor Pursuits

- The Algarve is a sports paradise, and some of Europe's best **golfing** fairways, **tennis courts** and **diving clubs** are to be found along Portugal's warm southern coast (➤ 170).
- The western seaboard – where wind and rollers are perennially reliable – is better for **surfing**, **windsurfing** or just a refreshing dip.
- Inland unspoiled mountain scenery lends itself to **hiking**, **mountain-biking**, **hang-gliding** and **horse-riding** – ask at local tourist offices for outfits.
- **Boating**, **fishing** and other **watersports** can be practised at sea or on inland waterways; many places hire equipment (➤ individual chapters).

Lisbon and Around

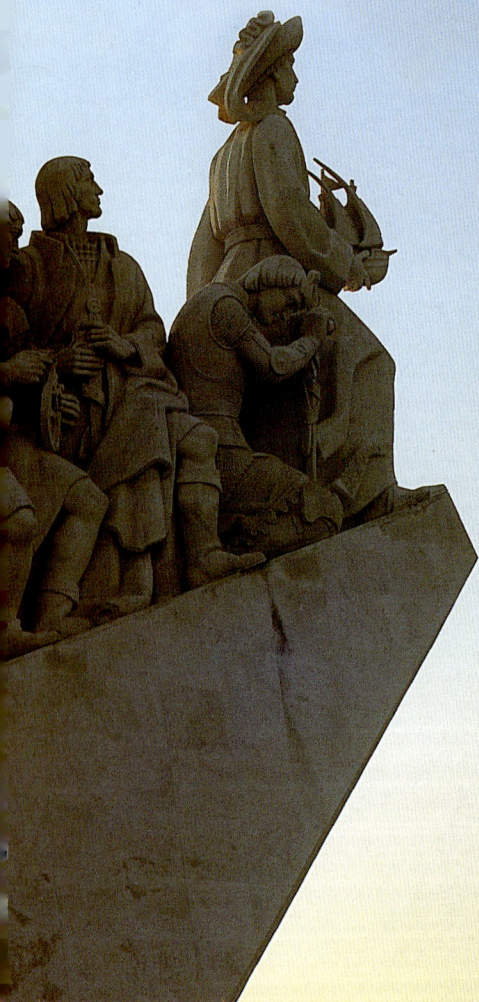

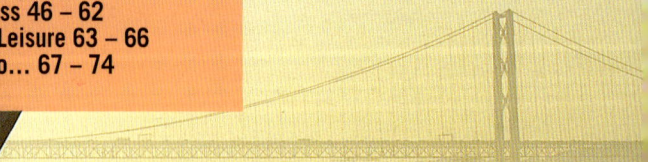

Getting Your Bearings

The capital of Portugal since around 1255, Lisbon (Lisboa) is one of Europe's smallest and most atmospheric capitals. Built in a rambling heap on seven hills on the north bank of the Tagus (Tejo) estuary, it has a vibrant, multicultural appeal that stems from the large number of immigrants from its former African and Asian colonies. One in ten of Portugal's population live here, creating a lively, Latin atmosphere.

The best way to arrive in Lisbon, and to get a sense of the city's layout, is on one of the ferries across the River Tagus. In front of you is Praça do Comércio, the former parade ground and symbolic entrance to the city. Ahead, beyond a triumphal arch, Rua Augusta leads through the Baixa (lower town), the downtown business and shopping district. To one side stands the Bairro Alto (upper town); to the other, Alfama, crowned by a splendid Moorish castle. Across the water, beyond Ponte 25 de Abril, a giant statue of Christ gazes down from the south bank.

The present-day shape of Lisbon is largely the result of the most traumatic incident in the city's history, the earthquake of 1755. It struck on All Saints' Day, when most of the population were at church, causing a tidal wave and hundreds of fires as buildings full of lighted candles collapsed in ruins. At least 40,000 people were killed. The subsequent rebuilding of the Baixa on a grid plan was largely the work of one man, the chief minister, Marquês de Pombal.

Two buildings that mostly survived the destruction were the Manueline tower and monastery at Belém, inspired by the discoveries (▶ 7) and built on the riches that made Lisbon great – spices from India and gold from Brazil.

In the last few years, Lisbon has seen another transformation, with new dockside leisure facilities, one of Europe's longest bridges and European Union funding for new façades. Perhaps, at last, Lisbon is once again looking to the future rather than harking back to a golden age.

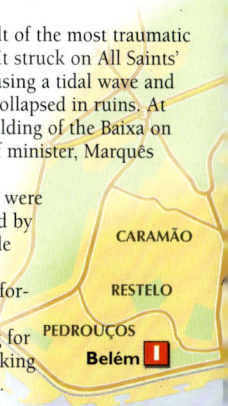

CARAMÃO

RESTELO

PEDROUÇOS

Belém 🔳

Torres Vedras

Alenquer

Ericeira

Mafra 🔳

Malveira

Montelavar

Sintra 🔳

Loures

Cabo da Roca

Amadora
A5

Parque das Nações 🔳

🔳 **LISBOA**

Almada

Moita

Estoril & Cascais 🔳

Barreiro

0 —— 20 km
0 —— 10 mile

Top: A Manueline carving at the Torre de Belém

Above: The Ponte 25 de Abril stretches across the River Tagus

AVENIDA DAS FORÇAS ARMADAS

OLAIAS

Museu Calouste Gulbenkian 2

REGO

ARCO CEGO

ALTO DO PINA

PICHELEIRA

Parque Eduardo VII 10

ESTEFÂNIA

CAMPOLIDE

SÃO SEBASTIÃO

BAIRRO LOPES

Museu Nacional do Azulejo 11

CAMPO DE OURIQUE

RATO

AVENIDA DA LIBERDADE

AVENIDA ALMIRANTE REIS

GRAÇA

Castelo de São Jorge 3

AVENIDA INFANTE DOM HENRIQUE

PADA AJUDA

AVENIDA DA PONTE

8 **Estrêla**

Bairro Alto 9

BAIXA

4 **Alfama**

Museu Nacional de Arte Antiga

7

ALCÂNTARA

ANTO MARÓ

AVENIDA VINTE E QUATRO DE JULHO

T e j o

PONTE 25 DE ABRIL

IP7

Page 41: The Monument to the Discoveries at Belém

Museums and monasteries, beaches and bars: Lisbon and its surrounding area is full of variety. Start with Portugal's maritime history and end with a charming fishing village.

Lisbon and Around in Four Days

Day One

Morning

From Praça do Comércio, take tram No 15 to 🚊 **Belém** (➤ 44–49) to savour the glories of Portugal's maritime past. Walk along the waterfront to the Torre de Belém, then visit the Museu de Marinha and Mosteiro dos Jerónimos (below and bottom), built to celebrate the achievements of Portuguese explorers. Unwind with a sandwich and a pastry at the Antiga Confeitaria de Belém (➤ 69).

Afternoon and Evening

Return by tram as far as the Alcântara docks and climb the steps to the 🔴 **Museu Nacional de Arte Antiga** (➤ 63) to explore this fine collection of Portuguese art. If clubbing is your thing, head back down to the revitalised docks area and take your pick from the clubs on and around Avenida 24 de Julho (➤ 74). Otherwise return to Belém to take in a concert at the Centro Cultural de Belém (➤ 74) – as well as three auditoria, there are free concerts on weekday evenings at the terrace bar.

Day Two

Morning

Take the Metro to São Sebastião to visit **2 Museu Calouste Gulbenkian** (left; ► 50), then stroll through the sculpture park for lunch at the Centro de Arte Moderna (► 51).

Afternoon and Evening

Walk downhill to central Lisbon through **10 Parque Eduardo VII** (► 64) and along the tree-lined Avenida da Liberdade. Continue walking through the heart of the Baixa, then head into **4 Alfama** (► 54) to explore its steep streets and cobbled lanes. Climb to **3 Castelo de São Jorge** (► 52) to watch the sun set over the River Tagus, then wander back down to Alfama and spend the evening in one of its traditional *fado* clubs (► 18).

Day Three

Morning

Take the Metro to Oriente to spend a few hours in the **5 Parque das Nações** (► 58). Visit the oceanarium and ride the cable-car along the waterfront before having lunch at one of the riverside restaurants.

Afternoon and Evening

Shop for souvenirs in the Centro Comercial Vasco da Gama, then take the Metro to Rossio for a drink at a pavement café. Take the Elevador da Glória up to the Bairro Alto to sample its legendary nightlife – perhaps an apéritif at the Solar do Vinho do Porto (► 71), followed by an African meal at Água do Bengo (► 69) and then some *fado*.

Day Four

Morning and Afternoon

Take the train from Cais do Sodré to **12 Estoril** (► 65) and stroll along the seafront to **12 Cascais** (► 65). After exploring this fishing port, get on a bus to **6 Sintra** (► 60) and have lunch at Tulhas (► 72) in the centre of town. Hop on the bus for the climb to Castelo dos Mouros and Palácio da Pena (right). Walk back through the pinewoods to Sintra or take the bus to the station to return to Lisbon by train.

❶ Belém

More than anywhere else in Portugal, it is at Belém that you feel the pull of the Atlantic and the excitement of the great Age of Discovery. For more than a century, Portuguese ships left from Belém in search of new worlds, bringing back untold riches from unknown lands. Add to that its status as Lisbon's museum district, along with the crowning glories of Manueline architecture, and there are plenty of attractions here.

The best way to reach Belém is on the No 15 tram that clatters along the waterfront from central Lisbon.

On arrival, head for the **Padrão dos Descobrimentos** (Monument to the Discoveries), built in 1960 to mark the 500th anniversary of Prince Henry the Navigator's death. A *padrão* was a stone cairn surmounted by a cross, built by Portuguese explorers to mark their presence on new territory; this modern version neatly combines the form of a caravel, a cross and a sword. The prow of a ship faces out to sea with an image of Prince Henry at the helm. Behind him are other heroes of the discoveries, including Gil Eanes, Vasco da Gama, Pedro Álvares Cabral and poet Luís de Camões, who celebrated the Age of Discovery in his epic work *Os Lusíadas* (*The Lusiads*).

Above: Walk across the world of the Portuguese explorers

Take the lift to the top of the tower, which is 52m (171 feet) high, for views over the harbour, then wander around the marble map of the world at its base, with dates showing Portuguese conquests in Africa, Asia and America.

Manueline Masterpiece

Just along the waterfront is the **Torre de Belém**, built by Dom Manuel I between 1515 and 1520 to guard the entrance to Lisbon harbour. This elegant fortress is a good example of what has come to be called the Manueline style, a Portuguese version of late Gothic architecture inspired by the discoveries and particularly associated with Dom Manuel.

The hallmark of this style is the extravagant use of seafaring imagery, with windows and doorways decorated with stone carvings of knotted ropes, anchors, globes, exotic fauna and flora and other maritime motifs. Two symbols which are ever present in Manueline architecture are the armillary sphere (emblem of Dom Manuel, ➤ 7) and the Cross of the Order of Christ.

You can go right inside the tower and up onto the terrace for closer views.

Above: The Torre de Belém is Lisbon's most emblematic building

The Place to Go

The other main sights of Belém are across the railway line, around the Praça do Império gardens.

On one side is the **Centro Cultural de Belém**, conceived as a showpiece for Portugal's presidency of the European Union in 1992. Built out of the same limestone as the Mosteiro dos Jerónimos, it was initially controversial as it was a modern building right beside the monastery, but it has now been widely accepted and blends in surprisingly well with its surroundings.

Below: Portuguese heroes are carved in stone

Already it has become one of Lisbon's most vibrant cultural centres, with art galleries, a design museum, concerts, bookshops and trendy cafés.

A Long History

However, the sight that really takes your breath away as you look across the gardens is the **Mosteiro dos Jerónimos**, begun in 1502 on the site of a former hermitage founded by Prince Henry the Navigator. It was here in 1497 that Vasco da Gama spent his final night before setting off to discover a sea route to India, and Dom Manuel vowed that he would build a great church to the Virgin if the voyage was successful. The monastery, begun by French architect Diogo de Boytac and continued by Spaniard João de Castilho, is full of Manueline flourishes, especially the south portal, with its stonework saints and figure of Prince Henry on a pedestal. Immediately inside the church are the tombs of Vasco da Gama and Luís de Camões. Go through a separate entrance to reach the two-storey cloister, a masterpiece of Manueline art embellished by rich maritime tracery. It was in these cloisters that the treaty of accession for Portugal's entry to the European Union was signed in 1986.

Maritime History

A 19th-century wing of the monastery houses the **Museu de Marinha**, devoted to Portugal's maritime history. Among the large collection of model boats, maps, navigational instruments and Oriental art, there is graffiti, carved onto the African rocks by Portuguese explorer Diogo Cão in 1483: "To this place came the ships of the enlightened King John the Second of Portugal." Other highlights are the model of Vasco da Gama's flagship; the maps of the known world divided into Spanish and Portuguese spheres of influence, with crude drawings of palm trees and African slaves kneeling at the Cross; and the reconstruction of the state rooms from the royal yacht *Amélia*, right down to the king's private piano and roulette table.

Top: The Manueline cloisters of the Mosteiro dos Jerónimos

Inset: Looking down over the nave

A separate building contains the royal barges, including the sumptuous gilded barge built for the wedding of João VI in 1780, rowed by 78 oarsmen and last used to transport Britain's Queen Elizabeth II on the River Tagus in 1957.

Travelling by Coach

Another popular museum is the **Museu Nacional dos Coches**, featuring coaches from the 17th to the 19th century. Don't miss the set of three coaches sent by Dom João V to Pope Clement VI, an extravagant display of royal wealth aimed at winning concessions for the Portuguese church. The coaches are rich in allegory from the time of the discoveries, with dragons trampling slaves underfoot and angels lifting Lisbon to glory.

TAKING A BREAK

Treat yourself to a coffee and a custard tart at the **Antiga Confeitaria de Belém** (➤ 69).

✚ 196 off A1 🚋 Tram 15 🚉 Belém (Lisbon to Cascais line)

Padrão dos Descobrimentos
✉ Avenida de Brasília ☎ 213 031 950; www.padraodescobrimentos
.egeac.pt 🕐 May–Sep daily 10–6:30; Oct–Apr 10–5:30 💰 Inexpensive

Torre de Belém
✉ Avenida de Brasília ☎ 213 620 034; www.mosteirojeronimos.pt
🕐 Oct–Apr Tue–Sun 10–5; May–Sep Tue–Sun 10–6:30. Last entry 30 mins before closing 💰 Moderate (free Sun 10–2)

Mosteiro dos Jerónimos
✉ Praça do Império ☎ 213 620 034; www.mosteirojeronimos.pt
🕐 Oct–Apr Tue–Sun 10–5; May–Sep Tue–Sun 10–6 💰 Church free, cloisters moderate (free Sun 10–2)

The gilded age was a bonus for Portugal's state coaches

Museu de Marinha
✉ Praça do Império ☎ 213 620 010;
www.museu.marinha.pt 🕐 Oct–Apr Tue–Sun 10–5;
May–Sep Tue–Sun 10–6 💰 Moderate

Museu Nacional dos Coches
✉ Praça Afonso de Albuquerque ☎ 213 610 850;
www.museudoscoches-ipmuseus.pt 🕐 Tue–Sun 10–5:30
💰 Moderate (free Sun 10–2)

BELÉM: INSIDE INFO

Top tip Visit Belém on a Sunday morning when many of the museums and sights have free entrance. Avoid Mondays when almost everything is closed.

In more depth The **Museu da Electricidade** (www.fundacao.edp.pt; Sun–Sat 10–6), housed inside the thermo-electric power station at the eastern end of Belém contains original generators and energy-themed exhibitions.

2 Museu Calouste Gulbenkian

The most significant museum in Portugal is the result of one man's passionate collecting, encompassing the entire history of both Eastern and Western art. What makes it all the more enjoyable is that although each piece is worth seeing, the small size of the collection means that it can be thoroughly explored in a visit of a couple of hours.

Calouste Gulbenkian (1869–1955) was an Armenian oil magnate who earned his nickname "Mr Five Per Cent" when he negotiated a five per cent stake in the newly discovered oilfields of Iraq.

He spent much of his wealth acquiring works of art, from Roman coins to old masters bought from the Hermitage Museum in St Petersburg. During World War II he came to live in Portugal, bequeathing his fortune and his art collection to the Portuguese. The foundation, which was established after his death, is now one of the largest cultural institutions in the world, supporting museums, orchestras and charitable projects in all aspects of Portuguese life.

The **Museu Calouste Gulbenkian** was opened in 1969 and contains the most precious objects from Gulbenkian's collection. It begins with a small room devoted to ancient Egyptian art, including funerary statues, bronze sculptures and an alabaster bowl dating from 2700BC. The next room contains classical art from Greece and Rome, together with a life-size relief of an Assyrian warrior from the 9th century BC.

Some of the greatest treasures are found in the **Gallery of Islamic and Oriental Art**, which features Persian rugs, Ottoman ceramics, enamelled glassware and a beautiful late 13th-century glazed ceramic *mihrab* (a prayer niche indicating the direction of Mecca) from a Persian mosque. Also in this room is a small case of illuminated gospel manuscripts from Gulbenkian's native Armenia.

Above: The entrance to the museum

Left: A portrait of Alexander the Great by Rembrandt

Far left: A 14th-century mosque lamp

Above: Relaxing in the sculpture garden

This leads into the **Far East Gallery**, which has Chinese and Japanese porcelain, jade, lacquered boxes and screens.

The largest part of the museum is devoted to **European art** from the 13th to the 20th centuries. It begins with early illuminated gospels and a 14th-century French triptych depicting scenes from the life of the Virgin.

Among the paintings to look out for are *Portrait of an Old Man* by Rembrandt, *Flight Into Egypt* by Rubens (which features a terrified Mary clutching Jesus to her breast as the beasts of the forest surround her) and Rubens' sensual portrait of his second wife, Helena Fourment. From the Impressionist period there is *Self-Portrait* by Degas and *Boy Blowing Bubbles* by Manet. Other prominent European artists represented in the museum include Gainsborough, Turner, Renoir and Monet, along with some superb marble sculptures by Rodin.

The Gulbenkian Foundation is also responsible for the **Centro de Arte Moderna** (same hours as the museum), devoted to 20th-century Portuguese art. Walk through the attractive sculpture gardens and past an amphitheatre where open-air concerts are held in summer.

TAKING A BREAK

Take a **picnic** to the sculpture gardens or visit the café of the **Centro de Arte Moderna**, which has a good lunchtime cold buffet.

✚ 196 off A5 ✉ Avenida de Berna 45 ☎ 217 823 000; www.museu.gulbenkian.pt 🕐 Tue–Sun 10–5:45 🚇 São Sebastião or Praça de Espanha 🚌 16, 56, 718, 726, 742, 746 💶 Moderate (free on Sun)

MUSEU CALOUSTE GULBENKIAN: INSIDE INFO

Top tips The Gulbenkian Foundation has its own **orchestra and choir** and also hosts concerts by visiting musicians. Ask for a programme at the museum reception desk or contact the box office (tel: 217 823 000).

• As well as paintings and sculpture, the European art galleries contain fine examples of **decorative arts**, including 18th-century Louis XV furniture from France and a set of Italian tapestries depicting children playing in the woods.

Hidden gem Don't miss the **René Lalique Gallery** at the end of the European Art section, with stunning art nouveau jewellery by the French decorative artist, René Lalique, who was a friend of Calouste Gulbenkian.

3 Castelo de São Jorge

Dominating the skyline above the Alfama district, the Castelo de São Jorge (St George's Castle) has a long and chequered history. Yet despite its bloody past this is now one of the most peaceful spots in Lisbon. The gardens make a pleasant place to escape for an hour or two, and there are fine views over the city and the river from its walkways and terraces.

The castle occupies the site where Phoenician traders set up their first camp when they occupied Lisbon during the 8th century BC. It was fortified by the Romans and again by the Visigoths, and the Moorish rulers built their palace here.

The castle was taken for the Christians in 1147 by Afonso Henriques, Portugal's first king, who captured it after a 17-week siege, with the help of British and French crusaders. The victorious battle saw the death of the Portuguese knight Martim Moniz, who is honoured in the name of a Metro station and a nearby square.

After the Christian conquest, the Portuguese kings used the Moorish palace as their royal palace until Dom Manuel I moved it to Terreiro do Paço, on the site of Praça do Comércio.

You enter the outer walls through the Arco de São Jorge, where a niche houses an image of the saint. This leads you into the *bairro* of **Santa Cruz**, a village-like quarter of medieval houses around the 18th-century church of Santa Cruz do Castelo. A separate gateway leads into the castle proper, and a parade ground dominated by a statue of Afonso Henriques.

Top right: The castle stands on a hill above Alfama

Far right: The view from the castle walls

Below: Climb on to the towers for the best views

From the terrace there are wonderful **views** over the River Tagus, named the *mar de palha* (sea of straw) by locals because of the way it shimmers in the sun.

Walkways lead around the walls, and you can climb up onto the battlements and the roofs of the 10 towers for more superb views. In summer, peacocks strut around the gardens and artists set up their stalls beneath the ramparts.

Part of the old royal palace now contains **Olisipónia**, a multimedia exhibition. The video sequence takes you on a tour of Lisbon's history, including a simulation of the 1755 earthquake, with commentary and sound effects.

The other attraction here is the **Câmara Escura**, housed in one of the inner towers, a device that provides live 360° images of the city and the people below going about their business.

TAKING A BREAK

There is a café and a restaurant within the castle, or for something different try a Goan curry at **Arco da Castelo** (► 70).

✚ 197 E4

Castelo
☎ 218 800 620; www.castelosaojorge.egeac.pt
🕐 Mar–Oct daily 9–8:30; Nov–Feb daily 9–5:30
🚌 37; tram 12, 28 💰 Moderate

Olisipónia
🕐 As castle, above 💰 Included in castle entry

Câmara Escura
🕐 Mar–Oct daily 10–5; Nov–Feb daily 11–2:30
💰 Included in castle entry

CASTELO DE SÃO JORGE: INSIDE INFO

Top tips The castle can be reached by a short, steep climb from the **Miradouro de Santa Luzia**, but if you want to avoid the walk, **bus 37** goes all the way to the outer walls.

• The castle terrace is a great place from where to watch the **sun set**.

④ Alfama

The oldest quarter of Lisbon is also its most charming. Alfama sprawls across a hill between the Castelo de São Jorge and the River Tagus, a maze of cobbled lanes, alleyways, staircases and secret gardens whose Moorish streetplan has largely survived the damage caused by the 1755 earthquake.

This is a district for aimless strolling through lanes where you will be rewarded with endless surprises as you discover a pretty courtyard, a public washing place or a statue of the Virgin in a niche high on a wall. Although Alfama is undergoing some changes, it is still primarily a working-class *bairro*, with a densely populated community of fishermen – who spend their spare time in local *tascas* (bars) – and their wives, who set up stalls on the street. The scent of charcoal and grilled sardines is ever present as the life of the community goes on in dilapidated houses with wrought-iron balconies and *azulejo* panels on the walls.

Below left: A 14th-century Gothic tomb in the cathedral

Cathedral and Teatro Romano

The name Alfama probably derives from the Arabic *al hama* (fountain) and there is evidence of Roman and Moorish settlements here. The Christians built their **sé** (cathedral) on the site of the main mosque, soon after Afonso Henriques captured the city in 1147. Built in Romanesque style and closely resembling a fortress, it has twin towers either side of a rose window on the main façade. The Gothic cloisters contain the excavated remains of the Roman city.

Just above the cathedral, the **Teatro Romano** is a partly excavated Roman theatre, built during the reign of Emperor Augustus and rebuilt under

Right: An aristocratic drawing room in the Museu de Artes Decorativas

Below: The cathedral was extensively rebuilt after the 1755 earthquake

Nero in the 1st century AD. The theatre itself is found in a shed on Rua de São Mamede, and there is a small museum across the street displaying archaeological finds.

Miradouro de Santa Luzia

Walk (or take tram 28) uphill from the cathedral to reach **Miradouro de Santa Luzia**, a pretty garden with fine views over Alfama and the River Tagus. Notice the tiled panels on the south wall of the nearby church, one depicting Lisbon before the earthquake, the other showing Christian soldiers with helmets, swords and shields attacking the Castelo de São Jorge (▶ 52), which is defended by turbanned Moors.

Museu de Artes Decorativas

Around the corner is the **Museu de Artes Decorativas**, containing the applied arts collection of the Portuguese banker, Ricardo do Espírito Santo Silva. The collection is particularly rich in Portuguese furniture, as well as ceramics, clocks, fans and guns, all displayed in an authentic re-creation of a 17th-century aristocratic home. Don't miss the *Giraffe Parade*, a colourful 16th-century Flemish tapestry in the main hall that depicts knights, turbanned Moors and people riding elephants and giraffes.

There are more views over the Alfama rooftops from the terrace at **Largo das Portas do Sol**, opposite the museum. Notice here the statue of São Vicente, Lisbon's patron saint, bearing the city's symbol, a boat with two ravens (the relics of the saint were said to have been brought to Lisbon by Afonso Henriques in a boat piloted by ravens).

Two Churches

Looking east from the terrace, the skyline is dominated by two white marble churches, the vast bulk of **São Vicente de Fora** and the domed church of **Santa Engrácia**. You can hop back on the tram to visit them.

São Vicente de Fora means "St Vincent Beyond the Wall" as the church was originally outside the city walls. The first church was built on this site soon after the Christian conquest, though the current one dates from 1629. Go through a side entrance to visit the monastery and cloisters. There is a fine 18th-century sacristy with walls of inlaid polychrome marble

Above: Enjoying the views from Largo das Portas do Sol

and a set of *azulejo* tiles depicting the fables of the 17th-century French satirist La Fontaine.

The former monks' refectory is now the pantheon of the House of Bragança, containing the tombs of monarchs from Catherine of Bragança (Queen of England) to the assassinated Dom Carlos I and his son, Dom Manuel II, who died in exile in England in 1932.

The baroque church of **Santa Engrácia**, by contrast, has become the national pantheon, with monuments to Portuguese heroes such as explorers Vasco da Gama and Luís de Camões, as well as the *fadista* Amália Rodrigues (►18). You can take the lift up to the rooftop for fabulous views over the River Tagus and the city.

The open ground between the two churches, **Campo de Santa Clara**, is the setting for Lisbon's liveliest flea market, the Feira da Ladra (Thieves' Market) which takes place on Tuesday and Saturday mornings.

Fado

Alfama is the true home of the traditional music of *fado* (►18), and there are several clubs in the back streets where you can hear it performed each night.

To find out more about this uniquely Portuguese music, visit the **Museu do Fado**, on the southern edge of Alfama, close to the river. This excellent new museum describes the history and traditions of *fado* and of the Portuguese guitar, a mandolin-type instrument that was introduced by

Left: The church of "St Vincent Beyond the Wall"

British traders in the 18th century. There is plenty of *fado* music to listen to, and the shop sells *fado* books and CDs.

TAKING A BREAK

The largest concentration of restaurants is at the foot of Rua de São Pedro, on and around Largo do Chafariz de Dentro. Try **Os Corvos** (Beco do Alfurja 4, tel: 218 884 508, €€) for traditional Portuguese cuisine fresh from the market, or **Lautasco** (Beco de Azinhal 7A, tel: 218 860 173, €€) for seafood *cataplana* (steamed with strips of ham).

⊞ 197 F3 🚋 Tram 12, 28, bus 37

Sé
⊞ 197 E2 ✉ Largo da Sé ☎ 218 876 628 🕐 Museum daily 10–5; cloisters 10–6; cathedral daily 9–7 🎫 Church free, cloisters inexpensive

Museu de Teatro Romano
⊞ 197 E2 ✉ Pátío de Aljube 5, Rua Augusto Rosa ☎ 217 513 200 🕐 Tue–Sun 10–1, 2–6 🎫 Free

Museu de Artes Decorativas
⊞ 197 E3 ✉ Largo das Portas do Sol 2 ☎ 218 881 991; www.fress.pt 🕐 Tue–Sun 10–5 🎫 Moderate

São Vicente de Fora
⊞ 197 off F4 ✉ Largo de São Vicente ☎ 218 824 400 🕐 Church Tue–Sat 9–4, Sun 9–12:30; cloisters Tue–Sat 10–5, Sun 19–11:30 🚌 Bus 37 🎫 Free

Santa Engrácia (Panteão Nacional)
⊞ 197 F4 ✉ Campo de Santa Clara ☎ 218 854 820 🕐 Tue–Sun 10–5 🚌 Bus 34 🎫 Inexpensive (free Sun 10–2)

Museu do Fado
⊞ 197 F2 ✉ Largo do Chafariz de Dentro 1 ☎ 218 823 470; www.museudofado.egeac.pt 🕐 Tue–Sun 10–5:30 🎫 Inexpensive

Above: Outdoor dining in a courtyard on Beco do Azinhal

ALFAMA: INSIDE INFO

Top tips Come here on **weekday mornings** when the street life is at its most lively and a fish market is set up along Rua de São Pedro.
• A decent pair of **walking shoes** is a good idea as there are lots of hills and cobbled streets.
• Alfama is a poor area with a reputation for **petty crime**, so avoid flaunting anything valuable and take care when wandering at night.

Hidden gem There are hidden gems all over Alfama, but one particularly charming spot is the **courtyard** at the top of **Escadinha de Santo Estêvão**, between Rua dos Remédios and Santo Estêvão church.

5 Parque das Nações

The former Expo'98 site has become an open-air playground where Lisboetas flock at weekends to enjoy its restaurants, bars, sculpture gardens and riverside walks. With stunning modern architecture and a range of high-tech attractions, a day out at "the invented city" offers a completely different experience of Lisbon.

Top: The wide, open plazas are a showcase for modern sculpture

Inset: Get up close and personal to the marine life at the Oceanário

The hosting of the World Exposition in 1998 gave Lisbon the opportunity for a major project in urban renewal. A derelict area of warehouses and oil refineries, 5km (3 miles) east of the city, was transformed into a riverside park for the exhibition. When Expo'98 closed, the site was renamed Parque das Nações and a long-term plan was conceived to turn it into a business and residential zone – in effect a new city with superb cultural and sporting facilities. The project is now complete and already more people are visiting this area than when Expo'98 was in full swing.

Most visitors arrive at the **Estação do Oriente**, an airy, light, steel-and-glass Metro station. This leads straight into the Vasco da Gama **shopping mall**, another popular excursion. Walk through the mall and you emerge on the waterfront.

The biggest draw here is the **Oceanário**, one of the largest aquarium in Europe. It is based around an enormous central tank, the size of four Olympic swimming pools, with

windows at two levels that allow you to watch the sharks swimming near the surface and flat-fish on the seabed.

Ranged around this are four separate tanks devoted to the ecosystems of the North Atlantic, South Atlantic, Pacific and Indian oceans. More than 15,000 marine animals and birds are on show, including puffins, penguins, sea otters and spider crabs, together with some superb examples of coral reefs.

From here you can walk or take the cable-car along the banks of the River Tagus, passing the Garcia de Orta gardens. The ride ends close to **Torre Vasco da Gama**, Lisbon's tallest building, which rises 145m (476 feet) above the river.

The River Tagus is spanned by the extraordinary 18km (11-mile) bridge, **Ponte Vasco da Gama**, which passes directly over water for 10km (6 miles) of its length and almost seems to be floating.

TAKING A BREAK

There are more than 40 restaurants in the area, offering a choice of fast food, Brazilian, Cuban, Chinese, Italian, Spanish and Portuguese cuisine. You'll find everything from ice-cream parlours, pizza houses and *tapas* bars to traditional restaurants serving Portugese dishes.

✚ 200 B2 ☎ 218 919 333; www.parquedasnacoes.pt

Oceanário
☎ 218 917 002; www.oceanario.pt 🕐 Nov–Mar daily 10–6 (last entry); Apr–Oct 10–7 (last entry) 💰 Expensive

Teleférico (cable-car)
☎ 218 956 143; www.parquedasnacoes 🕐 Jun–Sep Mon–Fri 11–8, Sat–Sun 10–9; Oct–May Mon–Fri 11–7, Sat–Sun 10–8 💰 Moderate

Above: The site's landmark tower looks like the sail of a ship

Left: Fountains and walkways decorate the ornamental gardens

PARQUE DAS NAÇÕES: INSIDE INFO

Top tips If you have small children with you, you can get around the various attractions on a **miniature road train** that makes regular circuits of the park.
• The **Cartão do Parque**, valid for two days, gives free entry to the Oceanário and cable-car, as well as discounts at other attractions, and is good value if you intend doing them all.

In more depth Try the bowling alley **BIL (Bowling Internacional de Lisboa)** if the weather is against you (Mon–Thu noon–2am, Fri noon–4am, Sat 11am–4am, Sun 11am–2am, moderate) and also the **Pavilhão do Conhecimento** (Tue–Fri 10–6, Sat–Sun 11–7, moderate), an interactive science museum.

6 Sintra

If you only have time for one excursion from Lisbon, you should definitely make it Sintra. Once the summer residence of the kings of Portugal, this is still where wealthy Lisboetas come to escape the city, in whitewashed *quintas* set on green hillsides among fairy-tale palaces, pinewoods and granite crags.

Palácio Nacional

The centre of the town is dominated by the Palácio Nacional, with its two enormous conical chimneys. This royal palace was begun by João I in the late 14th century and completed by Manuel I in the Manueline style.

Look out for the **Sala dos Cisnes** (Swan Room) and **Sala das Pegas** (Magpie Room), named after the birds in the ceiling frescoes. The **Sala dos Brasões** (Arms Room) has *azulejo* walls depicting hunting scenes and a coffered gilded ceiling with the coats of arms of 72 noble families.

Also in the palace is the **bedchamber of Afonso VI**, the deranged king held prisoner here by his brother Pedro II, who added insult to injury by marrying his queen.

Left: A detail from the Manueline Palácio da Pena

Below: The Palácio Nacional's conical chimneys are hard to miss

Above: The
battlements
of the Castelo
dos Mouros
are worth
the climb

The Castle

The other main sights of Sintra are found on the hills above the
town. The **Castelo dos Mouros** (Moors' Castle) was built in
the 9th century and captured by Afonso Henriques in 1147.

You can walk around the ramparts, with views stretching
beyond Lisbon and out to sea, to reach the royal tower, where
there is a fine view of the Palácio da Pena, on a granite peak.

Palácio da Pena

The climb to the Palácio da Pena takes you through the wood-
lands of Parque da Pena, dotted with lakes and follies. With
its minarets, towers and golden domes, the palace is one of
the best-known images of Portugal. This intricate fantasy was
built in the 1840s by Prince Ferdinand of Saxe-Coburg-Gotha,
husband of Dona Maria II and honorary king of Portugal, on
the site of a monastery established by Manuel I to give thanks
for the sighting of Vasco da Gama's fleet returning from India.

This was the last royal palace to be built
in Portugal and the German architect, Baron
Eschwege, ran riot with his imagination.
Gargoyles gaze down from the doorways and
chandeliers are held up by life-size statues.
The queen's antechamber is decorated entirely
in Meissen porcelain, and the Arabic Room
features playful *trompe-l'œil* walls. Everything
is preserved as it was when Dom Manuel II
went into exile in 1910. From the belvedere you
can look out to Cruz Alta, the highest point of
the Serra de Sintra, marked by a stone cross and
a statue of Baron Eschwege.

Two Museums

There are two museums worth visiting in the
centre of town. The **Museu do Brinquedo** (Toy
Museum), in the old fire station, contains the
fascinating collection of João Arbués Moreira,
gathered over 50 years.

Among the toys on display are Egyptian
marbles, Roman bronze figures, hand-crafted
African vehicles and a large number of toy
soldiers and model cars.

The **Museu de Arte Moderna**, in the old
casino, features rotating exhibits from the
Berardo Collection of 20th-century art, including works by Dalí, Miró, Picasso and Warhol.

TAKING A BREAK

Queijadas are sweet cheese and cinnamon pastries that have been made in Sintra since Moorish times. You can try them at the **Fábrica das Queijadas da Sapa** (near the Palácio Nacional at Volta da Duche 12, Tue–Sun 9–7, €).

Below: The climb to Palácio da Pena

✚ 200 A2

Tourist Information Centre
✉ Praça da República 23 ☎ 219 231 157;
www.cm-sintra.pt

Palácio Nacional
✉ Largo Rainha D Amélia ☎ 219 106 840;
www.ippar.pt/english/monumentos/palacio_sintra
🕐 Thu–Tue 10–5 💶 Moderate (free Sun 10–2)

Castelo dos Mouros
☎ 219 237 300; www.parquesdesintra.pt
🕐 Nov–Apr daily 9:30–5; May–Oct 9–6 or 7
🚌 434 💶 Moderate

Palácio da Pena
✉ Estrada da Pena ☎ 219 105 340;
www.ippar.pt/english/monumentos/palacio_pena
🕐 Tue–Sun 10–5 or 6:30 🚌 434 💶 Moderate

Museu do Brinquedo
✉ Rua Visconde de Monserrate ☎ 219 242 171;
www.museu-do-brinquedo.pt 🕐 Tue–Sun 10–6
💶 Moderate

Museu de Arte Moderna
✉ Avenida Heliodoro Salgado ☎ 219 248 170;
www.cm-sintra.pt or www.berardocllection.com
🕐 Tue–Sun 10–5:30 💶 Moderate

SINTRA: INSIDE INFO

Top tips The main sights are connected by a **circular bus route** (No 434) that links the station, old town, Castelo dos Mouros and Palácio da Pena. A single ticket is valid for any number of journeys in a day. If you are coming from Estoril or Cascais, buy a Day Rover ticket (*bilhete turístico diário*), which includes travel within Sintra.

• The **Sintra Music Festival**, which takes place in June and July, is one of Portugal's top classical music festivals, with concerts by international artists at the Palácio da Pena, Palácio Nacional and Palácio de Queluz. Details from Sintra tourist information office.

In more depth Another of Portugal's royal palaces, **Palácio de Queluz** (tel: 214 343 860, Wed–Mon 10–4:30, moderate), lies close to the Sintra train line and can be visited on the way back to Lisbon. Built in the mid-18th century by the future Dom Pedro III, its formal gardens and rococo architecture were inspired by the Palais de Versailles outside Paris.

At Your Leisure

7 Museu Nacional de Arte Antiga

It may not have the treasures of the Museu Calouste Gulbenkian (► 50), but the National Museum of Ancient Art does have the most complete collection of Portuguese art, together with the cultures that influenced it. Among the items to look for are Indo-Portuguese furniture, Sino-Portuguese ceramics, a carved ivory salt cellar from Africa, and 16th-century lacquer screens showing the arrival of Portuguese explorers in Japan. Many of the religious paintings, such as Nuno Gonçalves' 15th-century *St Vincent Altarpiece*, were confiscated from churches following the dissolution of the monasteries in 1834. The museum also contains a complete baroque chapel from the Carmelite convent that once stood on this site, with gilded woodwork and outstanding *azulejo* tiles.

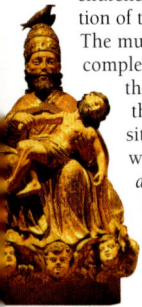

🔢 196 off A1 ✉ Rua das Janelas Verdes, Lapa ☎ 213 912 800; www.mnarteantiga-ipmuseus.pt 🕐 Wed–Sun 10–6, Tue 2–6 🚌 60, 713, 714, 732; tram 15, 18, 25 🎫 Moderate (free Sun 10–2)

8 Estrêla

The No 28 tram ride ends in Estrêla, a well-to-do neighbourhood some 2km (1.2 miles) west of Bairro Alto.

The area is dominated by the **Basílica da Estrêla**, a late 18th-century baroque church whose white dome is visible from across the city. Across the street, **Jardim da Estrêla** is one of Lisbon's prettiest public gardens, with a bandstand, play area and a small pond. Walk through the gardens to reach St George's Anglican church (service: Sun 11:30) and the **Cemitério Inglês**,

Lisbon for Kids
• **Parque das Nações** (► 58–59): the former Expo'98 site, now offering the Oceanário and Pavilhão do Conhecimento Virtual, with hands-on exhibits, and there's even a mini road train to take you round.
• **Planetário Calouste Gulbenkian**: the planetarium next to the Museu de Marinha (► 48–49) has special children's shows at weekends.
• **Museu da Carris**: take tram No 15 to visit the tram museum (Mon–Sat 10–4:30; www.carris.pt).
• **Jardim Zoológico**: take the Metro to Jardim Zoológico to visit Lisbon's zoo (Oct–Mar daily 10–6 (last entry 5); Apr–Sep 10–8, tel: 217 232 900).

where the 18th-century novelist Henry Fielding is buried.
🔢 196 off A3 🚊 Tram 25, 28
Basílica da Estrêla
✉ Largo da Estrêla ☎ 213 960 915 🕐 Mon–Sat 8:30–12, 1–7, Sun 10–11:45, 3–6:45 🎫 Free

Cemitério Inglês
✉ Rua de São Jorge à Estrêla ☎ 213 963 275 🕐 Mon–Sat 9–5, Sun 9–1 🎫 Free

9 Bairro Alto

The grid of 16th-century lanes which makes up the Bairro Alto (upper town) is best known as

Four Best Viewpoints
- **Castelo de São Jorge** (▶ 52): standing at the top of Alfama, there are fine views from the castle ramparts.
- **Miradouro de Santa Luzia**, Alfama (▶ 55): views over the River Tagus and Alfama.
- **Miradouro de São Pedro de Alcântara**, Bairro Alto (▶ 63, 174): views from the top of the Elevador da Glória over the Baixa and River Tagus.
- **Ponte 25 de Abril** (▶ 43): Stretching across the River Tagus, the views from the bridge are breathtaking.

Lisbon's nightlife quarter, where the plaintive strains of *fado* compete with African and Latin vibes.

Traditionally a working-class area, Bairro Alto has seen gentrification in recent years, with art galleries, cocktail bars and alternative fashion shops giving the area a bohemian appeal. If you like port, don't miss the **Solar do Vinho do Porto** (▶ 71).

Near here is the Jesuit **Igreja de São Roque**, whose plain façade belies the richness of its interior, especially its lavish side chapels. The Capela de São João Baptista, fourth on the left,

Inside the Estufa Fria greenhouse at Parque Eduardo VII

is a riot of marble, alabaster, lapis lazuli, amethyst, mosaic, silver and gold, built in Rome and taken to Lisbon on the orders of Dom João V.

Just down the hill, on the edge of the Chiado district, the **Museu Arqueológico do Carmo** occupies the old Carmelite convent, destroyed in the earthquake of 1755 and now a romantic Gothic shell. Among the items on display are Egyptian and Peruvian mummies, Roman mosaics and a stone bust of Afonso Henriques dating from the 12th century.

➕ 196 A3 🚋 Tram 28 or Elevador da Glória

Igreja de São Roque
➕ 196 A4 ✉ Largo Trindade Coelho ☎ 213 235 380 🕐 Church daily 8:30–5; museum Tue–Sun 10–5 💷 Church free; museum inexpensive

Museu Arqueológico do Carmo
➕ 196 B3 ✉ Largo do Carmo ☎ 213 478 629 🕐 May–Sep Mon–Sat 10–6; Oct–Apr Mon–Sat 10–5 💷 Inexpensive (free Sun 10–2)

⑩ Parque Eduardo VII

This large, formal park was laid out at the end of the 19th century and subsequently named after an English king, Edward VII. The best reason for coming here is the **view** from the terrace at the top of the park, where a stone monument commemorates

The mock castle on the beach at Estoril

the 1974 revolution. From here you look down over sweeping lawns and along the broad Avenida da Liberdade all the way to the River Tagus. Near here is a garden dedicated to the *fado* singer Amália Rodrigues (► 18). On one side of the park is a sports pavilion, named after the 1984 Olympic marathon champion Carlos Lopes; on the other side is the Estufa Fria greenhouse, with lakeside walks and hothouses full of tropical plants.

➕ 196 off A5 🚇 Marquês de Pombal, Parque, São Sebastião

Ⅲ Museu Nacional do Azulejo

It's worth making the short trek out of the centre of Lisbon to visit the National Tile Museum, housed in the former convent of Madre de Deus. The museum traces the development of *azulejo* tiles (► 16) from the 15th century onwards, in the setting of a lovely baroque church with Manueline cloisters and tiled walls. The highlight is an 18th-century panel of more than 1,300 tiles, which gives a panoramic view of pre-earthquake Lisbon. The 20th-century

galleries show how *azulejos* have moved out of monasteries and into shopping malls, Metro stations and the realms of abstract art.

➕ 197 off F2 ✉ Rua Madre de Deus 4 ☎ 218 100 340; www.mnazulejo-ipmuseus.pt 🕐 Wed–Sun 10–6, Tue 2–6 🚌 718, 742, 794 💳 Moderate (free Sun 10–2)

Ⅻ Estoril and Cascais

These twin resorts, linked by an attractive seafront promenade, lie at the heart of the Lisbon coast. **Estoril** is more cosmopolitan and chic, with a casino, golf course and racetrack and a mock castle on the beach. During World War II, when Portugal remained neutral, Estoril was a refuge for diplomats, spies and exiled royalty – King Juan Carlos of Spain spent his childhood here.

Although a growing resort, **Cascais** retains elements of its fishing village past, and there are still fish auctions every day beside the main beach, Praia da Ribeira.

Beyond Cascais, a coastal corniche leads past **Boca do Inferno** (Hell's Mouth), where waves crash against the cliffs, to the windswept dunes at Praia do Guincho, a

popular windsurfing beach, and Cabo da Roca, mainland Europe's westernmost point.

This area makes a good base for a short stay near Lisbon, combining a beach holiday with a city break. Trains to Lisbon follow a scenic line along the coast, via the resorts of São Pedro do Estoril and Carcavelos.

✚ 200 A2

🔟 Mafra

The pink marble **Palácio-Convento de Mafra**, 40km (25 miles) northwest of Lisbon, was built by Dom João V in 1717 to give thanks to God for the birth of a royal heir. Like El Escorial in Madrid, with which it is often compared, it served both as a royal palace and a monastery.

Financed by profits from Brazilian gold, the palace employed 50,000 workers in its construction; originally intended to hold 13 monks, it ended up accommodating 300 monks

and the entire royal family. You can visit the basilica and the palace on guided tours, including the monks' cells, the pharmacy, the trophy room and the magnificent baroque library. There are also tours of the royal hunting ground, now a wildlife park.

✚ 200 A3 ☎ 261 817 550; www.ippar.pt/english/monumentos/ palacio_mafra ⏰ Wed–Mon 10–4:30 💶 Moderate

Lisbon Rides

It is fun (and cheaper) to join the locals on public transport.

• **Ferries**: Commuter ferries cross the Tagus to Barreiro and Cacilhas. The boats for Barreiro depart from Terreiro do Paço, with superb views of the city.

• **Trams**: A ride on one of Lisbon's antique wooden trams is an experience in itself. The most enjoyable route is No 28, which rattles up and down the steep streets of Alfama on its way from Graça to Estrela.

• *Elevadors*: These ancient lifts and funiculars are part of Lisbon's public transport system. Take Elevador da Glória from Praça dos Restauradores to Bairro Alto, or Elevador de Santa Justa for views over Baixa.

A corridor in the spectacular Palacio-Convento de Mafra

Where to... Stay

Prices

Expect to pay for a double room with bathroom in high season

€ = under €60 €€ = €60–€120 €€€ = €121–€180 €€€€ = over €180

Albergaria Senhora do Monte €€–€€€

The pink and white décor and marble bathrooms in this modern hotel complement the romantic location, high up in the quiet *bairro* of Graça. With its picture windows overlooking the city as far as the river, the panoramic restaurant-bar (open to non-guests for drinks) is a wonderful place to linger over breakfast. More expensive rooms with south-facing terraces also have air-conditioning – ask for one when booking; they are worth the extra cost. It's a short tram ride into downtown Lisbon.

🔛 197 E5 ⊠ Calçada do Monte 39 ☎ 218 866 002, fax: 218 877 783; www.maisturismo.pt/sramonte 🚊 Tram 12, 28 🔘 All year

As Janelas Verdes Inn €€€–€€€€

The Lapa is one of central Lisbon's most desirable *bairros* and along this street is this top hotel and also the nearby Museu Nacional de Arte Antiga (▶ 63). At the Janelas Verdes you can choose from 29 charming rooms, some non-smoking and each decorated in a different but equally elegant style. Weather permitting, a copious buffet breakfast is served among bougainvilleas and giant rubber trees in the walled terrace garden. Cosy libraries (there are superb views across the Tagus from the rooftop library) and handsomely decorated salons, even a piano, evoke a home-from-home feel, helped along by the extra friendly staff.

🔛 196 off A1 ⊠ Rua das Janelas Verdes 47 ☎ 213 968 143; janelas.verdes@heritage.pt 🚊 Tram 25, Train Santos 🔘 All year

Pensão Londres €€

This simple, reliable *pensão* is wonderfully located in the Príncipe Real district, and many of the rooms command fabulous views across the rooftops to the Ponte 25 de Abril or Castelo São Jorge (▶ 52). Solid conversions have given almost all the rooms their own bathrooms. The largest doubles have attractive period furniture and some rooms have lovely stucco mouldings in the ceilings. A full breakfast is served in a charming dining room, which also has a fine view. And it's gay-friendly.

🔛 196 off A4 ⊠ Rua Pedro V 53/1-4 ☎ 213 462 203, fax: 213 465 682; pensaolondres@pensaolondres.com.pt; www.pensaolondres.com.pt 🚊 Elevador da Glória, Bus 58 🔘 All year

Regency Chiado €€€–€€€€

This bright, modern hotel was built by leading architect Álvaro Siza Vieira. The main attraction is the unbeatable view from the airy dining room, salon and bar – open to non-guests and a trendy meeting place. Try and get one of the rooms that also face the Castelo São Jorge (▶ 52), with stunning views across the Baixa to the cathedral and beyond. All the rooms and bathrooms are tastefully decorated, with oriental touches. The buffet breakfast is lavish.

🔛 196 C2 ⊠ Rua Nova do Almada 114 ☎ 213 256 100, fax: 213 256 161; www.regency-hotels-resorts.com; regencychiado@madeiraregency.pt 🚊 Metro Baixa-Chiado 🔘 All year

Residencial Duas Nações €–€€

Of all the basic *pensões* and *residenciais* in the central Baixa, this one offers the best value. Although the surrounding streets are pedestrianised, rooms facing on to the ever-busy Rua Augusta are best avoided. The building itself is a smart 19th-century townhouse, with a quaint lift, and there's a popular bar. Rooms are all simply decorated, some of them *en suite*. For breakfast you can either go to the pleasant dining room or, unusually for such a modest place, order it in your room.

✚ 196 C3 ☒ Rua da Vitória 41 ☎ 213 460 710, fax: 213 470 206; www.duasnacoes.com ⓜ Metro Baixa-Chiado ◎ All year

Residencial Santa Catarina €–€€

Santa Catarina is located along a quiet, cobbled street, not far from the top of the ancient Bica funicular. The upper floor rooms of this simple but charming family guesthouse have superb views across to the River Tagus, and the Santa Catarina viewpoint (▶ 80) is a short walk away. Similarly the nightlife and restaurants of the Bairro Alto are near by.

✚ 196 off A2 ☒ Rua Dr Luís de Almeida e Albuquerque 6 ☎ 213 466 106, fax: 213 477 227 ⓛ Tram 28, Elevador da Bica ◎ All year

Sé Guesthouse €€

Just behind the *sé* (cathedral), on the edge of Alfama, Lisbon's old town, this extremely friendly nine-room *pensão* is on the first floor of a beautiful townhouse. It is tastefully furnished with lovely wooden floors, African artefacts and antique furniture. The rooms are large and comfortable but the bathrooms are communal. Breakfast is copious. The owners speak English.

✚ 197 E2 ☒ Rua de São João da Praça 97/1 ☎ 218 864 400 ⓛ Tram 12 and 28 ◎ All year

Tryp Oriente €€

The comfortable, if rather functional, rooms at the Tryp Oriente come with a kitchenette, so you can self-cater if you wish. You also have the Parque das Nações (▶ 58) on the door-step, and all rooms have staggering views of its futuristic buildings, the "Sea of Straw" (River Tagus) and the impressive Ponte Vasco da Gama (▶ 59).

✚ 200 B2 ☒ Avenida Dom João II, Parque das Nações, ☎ 218 930 000, fax: 218 930 099; www.solmelia.com ⓜ Metro Oriente ◎ All year

Veneza €€–€€€

This professionally run Venetian-style palace, built in 1886, is one of the few townhouses on the Avenue da Liberdade that has managed to escape the demolition trucks. The interior is lavishly decorated in a traditional way with wrought iron, polished wood and stained glass, while colourful murals of Lisbon by Portuguese artist Pedro Luis Gomes adorn the monumental staircase, guarded by kitsch, torch-bearing statues. The 38 *en suite* rooms are rather more liveable, with under-stated décor, bright fabrics and mini-bar.

✚ 196 A5 ☒ Avenida da Liberdade 189 ☎ 213 522 618, fax: 213 526 678; www.3khoteis.com ⓜ Metro Avenida ◎ All year

York House €€€–€€€€

A tranquil and elegant place, for many this is the best spot to stay in Lisbon, so it is essential to book well in advance. In a discreet Lapa location, accessed by a shady stairway, this 17th-century Carmelite convent was first turned into a guesthouse in the late 19th century by two ladies from York in England – from whom it gets its oddly un-Portuguese name. In fair weather you can breakfast under the huge palm in the flower-filled courtyard. Inside are welcoming sitting rooms and labyrinthine corridors decorated with religious art, and a fine dining room serving refined

Portuguese cuisine. The 32 rooms are decorated either in a traditional or minimalist chic style.

➕ 196 off A1 ✉ Rua das Janelas Verdes 32 ☎ 213 962 435, fax: 213 972 793; www.yorkhouselisboa.com 🚋 Tram 25, Train Santos ⏰ All year

SINTRA

Lawrence's Hotel €€€€

A beautiful house near to central Sintra, Lawrence's claims to be the oldest hotel in Iberia. Its exquisitely decorated 11 rooms and five suites have the latest facilities, including air-conditioning and satellite TV; some have Jacuzzis in the huge bathrooms, and open fireplaces. At the top-class restaurant you can sample some of the best cooking in Sintra – even if you're not a hotel guest. A refined cellar backs up the Portuguese-influenced cuisine. Golfing holiday packages are also offered, with discount rates at the best local links.

➕ 200 A2 ✉ Rua Consiglieri Pedroso 38–40 ☎ 219 105 500, fax: 219 105 505; lawrenceshotel@gmail.com; www.lawrenceshotel.com ⏰ All year

Palácio de Seteais €€€–€€€€

The legendary microclimate, rural tranquillity and centuries of refinement are all good arguments for staying in this fabulous hillside setting, less than 30km (19 miles) from central Lisbon. A short way from Sintra, this aristocratic palace (the name means "seven sighs") was built in the 18th century for the Dutch consul. Later the Marquis of Marialva joined the two neo-classical buildings with a triumphal archway. The dining room and salon are decorated with frescoes. All with luxurious bathrooms, the rooms look out on to the gardens and terraces, where there's a pool, tennis courts and riding stables.

➕ 200 A2 ✉ Rua Barbosa do Bocage 10 ☎ 219 233 200, fax: 219 234 277; www.tivolihotels.com ⏰ All year

Where to...
Eat and Drink

Prices
Expect to pay per person for a three-course à la carte meal, excluding drinks and tips
€ = under €12   €€ = €12–€24   €€€ = €25–€36   €€€€ = over €36

LISBON

Água do Bengo €€

At this Angolan restaurant, palm oil and plantains, okra and beans, manioc and cashews, yams and dried shrimp are the basic ingredients, with fish and meat thrown in to make *mozongué*, *calulu* and *moamba* (stew-like dishes). It's delicious and different. Vegetarians will also find the meatless dishes to their taste.

➕ 196 A4 ✉ Rua da Teixeira 1 ☎ 213 477 516 🚇 Metro Restauradores and Elevador da Glória ⏰ Mon–Sat dinner

Antiga Confeitaria de Belém €

Although you can have sandwiches and other cakes, most people come to this place for one thing, the freshly baked *pastéis de nata*. You can find these crisp tartlets filled with egg-custard in *pastelarias* across the country, but those made here, to a secret recipe, are unanimously regarded as superior – and they are noticeably less sweet.

➕ 196 off A1 ✉ Rua de Belém 84–88 ☎ 213 637 423; www.pasteisdebelem.pt 🚋 Tram 15, Train Belém ⏰ Nov–Apr Mon–Sat 8am–11pm, Sun 8am–10pm; May–Oct daily 8am–midnight

Arco do Castelo €€

Anyone looking for something a bit different might like to test this Goan restaurant in Alfama. Portugal's colonial influence is clear – both pork and beef feature on the menu, with coconut, ginger and cardamom dominating. Try *balchão de porco* (pork and shrimp curry) or *sarapatel* (pork with lots of ginger). If you're baffled by the word *chamuças* on the menu, just say it out loud: it's the Portuguese spelling of *samosas*.

✚ 197 E2 **⊠** Rua Chão da Feira 25 **☎** 218 876 598 **🚊** Tram 12 and 28 **🕐** Mon–Sat 12:30–3:30, 6–10:30

A Bica do Sapato €€€€

Leading light Manuel Reis – who owns Lux, the nearby nightclub (▶ 74) – has an eye for location and impeccable taste in décor. Right on the waterfront at up-and-coming Santa Apolónia, this three-in-one temple to good food is currently the place to eat and be seen, whether in the stylish café-bar, the sushi section

or the restaurant. In the latter you can sample clever concoctions dreamed up by Joaquim Figueredo, Lisbon's most famous chef of the moment, who uses seafood as nobody else in the country dares.

✚ 197 E2 **⊠** Avenida Infante Dom Henrique, Armazém B **🚌** 218 810 320 **🚌** Bus 9, 28, 35, 81, 82, 90 **🕐** Restaurant Mon 8pm–11:30pm, Tue–Sat noon–2:30, 8–11:30. Sushi Bar Mon–Sat 7:30pm–1am. Café Mon 5pm–1am, Tue–Sat 12–3:30, 7:30–1am. Closed Sun

A Brasileira €

Few old-style cafés have survived in Lisbon, but this one thankfully has – the timeless atmosphere is enhanced by a handless clock at the far end of the mirrored salon. It's not only a meeting place for students, intellectuals and other regulars drawn by the excellent coffee and *pastéis*, it is also a shrine to Fernando Pessoa who frequented it – witness the bronze statue on the small esplanada, next to which

many tourists have their picture taken, often without having heard of the great 20th-century poet.

✚ 196 B3 **⊠** Rua Garrett 120 **☎** 213 469 541 **🚇** Metro Baixa-Chiado **🕐** Daily 8–2

Casa da Comida €€€€

Tucked away in a side street above the Rato, not far from Amoreiras shopping centre, this restaurant is one of Portugal's best, with prices to match. Unimpressive from the outside, inside it's a noble mansion, with a beautiful *patio* and sophisticated décor. Chef Jorge Vale, who welcomes guests personally, is master of the cordon bleu sauce. Yet he manages to combine French flair with traditional Portuguese dishes, using local clams and crab, pheasant and partridge. Desserts are amazing and, of course, there's an excellent wine cellar.

✚ 196 off A4 **⊠** Travessa das Amoreiras **☎** 213 885 376 **🚇** Metro Rato **🕐** Tue–Fri noon–3, 8–11; Sat, Mon 8–11. Closed Sun

Casa do Alentejo €-€€

Behind a run-of-the-mill façade and up a gloomy staircase, there's a fantastic, if slightly decadent, patrician mansion, with Moorish *patios* and beautiful skylights, decorated with carved wood, gleaming *azulejos* and huge palms. The reliably good and well-priced food served in two dining rooms, one more subdued, the other lined with bright tiles, gives you a taste of the Alentejo, with classic dishes such as *carne de porco a alentejana* (pork with coriander and clams). Exhibitions and other events are held in this house dedicated to "a people, a region and a culture".

✚ 196 B5 **⊠** Rua das Portas de Santo Antão 58 **☎** 213 405 140 **🚇** Metro Restauradores **🕐** Daily noon–3, 7–11

Comida de Santo €€-€€€

Of the many Brazilian restaurants in Lisbon, this one has the most reliably good food, served with a smile in tropical surroundings,

including a stylised jungle fresco. It can get very busy, especially on Sundays when nearly everywhere else is closed, so book. The *caipirinhas* (lime and white rum cocktails) are expertly prepared, as is the delicious Bahia-dominated cuisine. The portions of thick *vatapás* (spicy shrimp purée) and succulent chicken *muquecas* (cooked in coconut milk) are easily enough for two, as is the *feijoada* (pork and black bean stew) with its trimmings of toasted manioc and orange slices. Fresh mango and papaya round off your meal.

✚ 196 off A4 ⓜ Calçada Engenheiro Miguel Pais 39 ☎ 213 963 339 🚇 Metro Rato 🕓 Daily 12:30–3:30, 7:30–1am

Mercado de Santa Clara €–€€

One of the few places open for Sunday lunch, this wonderful spot above the market hall gets packed out for its special *feijoada* (bean stew) buffets and the *cozido à portuguesa* (a regional dish of mixed meats and sausages with vegetables). The rest of the week you can taste refined cuisine using fresh produce from the market: a range of *bacalhau* dishes, steaks and another local favourite, *iscas com elas* (fried liver in white wine). There are also great views of the Panteão Nacional and the river.

✚ 197 F4 ⓜ Campo Santa Clara 7 ☎ 218 873 986 🚋 Tram 28 🕓 Tue–Sat 12:30–3, 8–10:30, Sun 12:30–3

Pap'Açorda €€€

This Bairro Alto haunt of the famous and glamorous never seems to go out of fashion. Humorous but professional waiters, a lavish décor of crystal chandeliers and plentiful plants and a lively atmosphere are part of the explanation. But people also come for the expertly prepared food. The emphasis is on mussels, clams and other seafood. The house speciality is the Lisbon delicacy, *açorda*, a concoction of bread, oil, egg and coriander that tastes far better than it sounds or looks. The *açorda real*, with lobster and prawns, is truly "regal". To round off a delicious meal, the chocolate mousse is notoriously the best in town.

✚ 196 A3 ⓜ Rua da Atalaia 57–59 ☎ 213 464 811 🚇 Metro Baixa-Chiado. Bus 58, 790 🕓 Tue–Sat noon–2, 8–11

Pavilhão Chinês €

A classy tearoom and cocktail bar combined on the edge of the Bairro Alto, the Chinese Pavilion must also be one of the most eccentric bars in the world, let alone Lisbon. The walls, cabinets and ceilings of its three red lacquer salons are crammed with fans and oriental porcelain, statues and dolls, lead soldiers and iron helmets, all collected by Lisbon celebrity Luís Pinto Coelho, also responsible for the aptly named Paródia (Rua do Patrocínio 26) in Campo de Ourique. Both are unusual places for an aperitif.

✚ 196 off A4 ⓜ Rua Dom Pedro V 89 ☎ 213 424 729 🚇 Metro Restauradores and Elevador da Glória 🕓 Mon–Sat 6pm–2am, Sun 9pm–2am

Primeiro de Maio €€

With friendly service and a loyal clientele of journalists, intellectuals and bohemian types, this favourite dishes up Lisbon specials – it's one of the best places to try starters such as *pastéis de bacalhau* (bite-sized cod cakes), *peixinhos da horta* (green bean fritters) or *favas com enchidos* (broad beans and sausage). As an *adega* (wine cellar), one of the few traditional ones left in the Bairro Alto, it also has decent house wine and a range of bottled vintages.

✚ 196 A3 ⓜ Rua da Atalaia 8 ☎ 213 426 840 🚇 Metro Baixa-Chiado 🕓 Mon–Fri noon–3, 7–10:30, Sat 7–10:30

Solar do Vinho do Porto €–€€

A cosy but modern place, with comfortable sofas and a dimly lit bar, this is the perfect place to taste your way through a bewildering list of

Where to... Shop

Feira da Ladra (Campo de Santa Clara, São Vicente, Tuesday morning and Saturday) is Lisbon's flea market. **Mercado da Ribeira** (Cais do Sodré, Avenida 24 de Julho, closed Sunday) is the most interesting traditional market – the highlight is the spectacular fish stalls.

Lisbon is proud of its modern malls, not least **Armazéns do Chiado** (Rua do Carmo), housing some out-of-the-ordinary shops among the international chains.

The love-them-hate-them landmark towers of **Amoreiras** (Avenida Engenheiro Duarte Pacheco), the titanic **Centro Comercial Colombo** (Avenida Lusíada, Benfica), too big for some, and cut-above-the-rest newcomer **Centro Comercial Vasco**

---

over 300 ports, with the help of the expert staff. It's the ideal way to find out which ones are to your taste – to buy elsewhere afterwards (▶84) – and which ones are within your budget range. Vintage ports, however, can only be sampled by the bottle, so come with other port fans. Incidentally, there's another solar in port's home city of Porto, housed in the Museu Romântico, Rua de Entre Quintas (▶81).

🕂 196 A4 ☒ Rua de São Pedro de Alcântara 45 ☎ 213 475 707; www.ivp.pt 🚇 Metro Baixa-Chaido 🕒 Mon–Sat 11am–midnight

Tágide €€€€

For reliable, classic Portuguese cuisine with a pronounced French influence, Tágide remains at the pinnacle of gastronomic Lisbon. If you're by a window – book well ahead and specify this requirement – you're also treated to incredible views of the city and river that would distract you from the food were it not so delicious. Not sur-

prisingly the wine cellar is one of the most refined in the city, and you can choose a suitable wine to accompany different regional dishes. The baked bacalhau is the omnipresent house special and the cheese board is truly the talk of the town.

🕂 196 B2 ☒ Largo da Academia Nacional de Belas Artes 18 ☎ 213 404 011, fax: 213 404 019 🚇 Metro Baixa-Chiado 🕒 Mon–Sat noon–2:30, 7:30–10:30

Trindade €–€€

A boisterous but cheery cervejaria (beer house), Trindade's main purpose is to serve people going to the nearby beaches of the same name. The noise is amplified by the sound of crab claws being bashed open by mallets. Once a convent – hard to imagine now – it has beautiful vaulted ceilings and a splendid display of azulejos. Draught Portuguese beer such as Sagres, served ice-cold by the imperial (a smallish lager glass), is the

perfect accompaniment to the simple fish and seafood dishes – watch out as the latter can be very pricey.

🕂 196 B3 ☒ Rua Nova da Trindade 20 ☎ 213 423 506 🚇 Metro Baixa-Chiado 🕒 Daily noon–1am

Tulhas €€

A charming restaurant right in the centre of Sintra (▶60–62), near the tourist office, Tulhas is in a beautiful rustic building that used to be a barn. The food is varied, with both fish and meat dishes on the menu, and you should certainly try the house special, lombos de vitela com vinho de Madeira (medallions of veal in Madeira sauce).

An ementa turística (set menu of the day) makes this an ideal place for a quiet, authentic lunch during a day's sightseeing in this beautiful hilltop town.

🕂 200 A2 ☒ Rua Gil Vicente 4–6 ☎ 219 232 378 🕒 Thu–Tue noon–3:30, 7–10

da Gama Avenida Dom João II) out at the Parque das Nações, are great places to window shop.

As for supermarkets, perfect for spirits and picnic fare, look out for the many branches of **Pingo Doce** or its rival, **Pão de Açúcar**.

CLOTHES AND FOOTWEAR

In the hip Bairro Alto, **Eldorado** (Rua do Norte 23), **Fátima Lopes** (Rua da Atalaia 36) and **Manuel Alves & José Manuel Gonçalves** (Rua das Flores 105/1D) are three fashion boutiques, the first specialising in retro clothing.

In Chiado, **Ana Salazar** (Rua do Carmo 87) is still one of the leading names of local couture, while **Atelier Gardénia** (Rua Nova do Almada 96 and Rua Garrett 54) sells great clothes by nationally famous Luís Buchinho, Nuno Gama and others. The **Luvaria Ulisses** (Rua do Carmo 87A) is a glove shop from a bygone age, and **José António Tenente** (Travessa do Carmo 8) is the place if you are looking for sharp suits.

In the Baixa and around the Rossio head for **Nunes Corrêa** (Rua Augusta 250) for bespoke tailoring. Suitably for "Gold Street", **Araújos** (Rua do Ouro, also known as Rua Aurea, 261) is a top jeweller and **Azevedo Rua** (Praça Dom Pedro IV 69) is the best milliner in the capital.

ANTIQUES AND CRAFTS

Amazing religious statues are worth a look at **Galeria da Arcada** (Rua Dom Pedro V 49). **António Trindade** (Rua do Alecrim 79) has a fine range of antiques.

Casa das Velas Loreto (Rua do Loreto 53) has sold wonderful candles since 1789, and you can find delicate lead crystal at **Atlantis Cristal** (Centro Colombo and branches). **Antiga Casa do Castelo** (Rua Santa Cruz do Castelo 15) rewards most souvenir hunts with ceramics, linens and soaps.

For azulejos you're spoiled for choice: try **Ratton** (Rua Academia das Ciências 2C, São Bento) for modern designs, **Sant'Ana** (Rua do Alecrim 95, Chiado) for reproductions, **Solar** (Rua Dom Pedro V 68) for antiques, and **Viúva Lamego** (Calçada do Sacramento 29, Chiado) for made-to-order specials. If you have a few thousand Euros left, the beautiful hand-made carpets from **Arraiolos** (▶ 146), plus the shipping fee, will relieve you of them at the **Casa dos Tapetes Arraiolos** (Rua da Imprensa Nacional 116).

BOOKS AND CDs

If you're after a book about port or pousadas, **Bertrand** (Rua Garrett 73, Chiado) and **FNAC** inside the Armazéns do Chiado shopping mall are two good bookshops. For a fado CD, make for **Discoteca Amália** (Rua do Ouro 272), while **Discoteca Roma** (Avenida de Roma 20C) is better for classical and world music.

Valentim de Carvalho and the **FNAC** chain (in all the main shopping malls) are the leading music shops, selling instruments such as Portuguese guitars as well as CDs.

FOOD AND DRINK

Lisbon's quaint grocers are quite an experience. **Manteigaria Silva** (Rua Dom Antão de Almada 1C-D) is best for bacalhau, while **Manuel Tavares** (Rua da Betesga 1A-B) has an impressive array of sausages and candied fruit. A great deli is **Martins & Costa** (Rua Alexandre Herculano 34). The **Garrafeira Nacional** (Rua dos Douradores 149–157) and **Napoleão** (Rua dos Fanqueiros 70) stock incredible ranges of wines and port. Wine connoisseurs should not miss **Coisas do Arco do Vinho** (Centro Cultural de Belém) for speciality corkscrews and fine vintages. At the **Antiga Confeitaria de Belém** (Rua de Belém 84–88, ▶ 69), you can buy boxes of fresh pastéis with sugar and cinnamon.

Where to...
Be Entertained

INFORMATION

Get tickets for football matches, concerts and events at the **Agência Alvalade** (Alvalade Shopping, Praça de Alvalade 6, tel: 217 955 859), at the **ABEP booth** (Praça dos Restauradores, tel: 213 475 823/4) or **FNAC** stores in shopping malls.

ARTS AND CULTURE

There's chamber, choral and orchestral music at **Fundação Calouste Gulbenkian** (➤ 50–51). The **CCB** (**Centro Cultural de Belém**; ➤ 47) stages eclectic theatre, dance and music events, as well as exhibitions.

The Expo'98 pavilions at the **Parque das Nações** (➤ 58) have been converted into more enduring venues: the striking **Teatro Camões**

(tel: 218 923 470) is now home to the excellent Companhia Nacional de Bailado (National Ballet).

Movie fans should check out the programme at the **Cinemateca** (Rua Barata Salgueiro 39, tel: 213 596 266, box office) and the outstanding **Monumental** complex (Praça Duque de Saldanha, tel: 213 142 223), Lisbon's best art-house cinema.

SPECTATOR SPORTS

The **football**-crazy might like to try and attend a match at either of the capital's top teams' home grounds: **Sporting** (Estádio de Alvalade, Edifício Visconde de Alvalade, Rua Professor Fernando da Fonseca; tel: 217 516 000) and **Benfica** (Estadio da Luz, Avenida General Norton de Matos, tel: 217 219 500).

For a game of **roller-hockey** at weekends go to **Paço d'Arcos** (Pavilhão Gimnodesportivo, Avenida Bonneville Franco, tel: 214 432 238).

MUSIC

The tiny **Hot Clube** (Praça da Alegria 39) is still Lisbon's best jazz venue, while **Speakeasy** (Cais das Oficinas, Alcântara) has excellent jam sessions on Monday. It's carnival every night (except Sundays) at **Brazilian Bruxa Bar** (Rua São Mamede 35). The **Teatro Nacional de São Carlos** (Rua Serpa Pinto 9) has excellent acoustics.

FAMILY FUN

The best **beaches** near Lisbon are at Caparica, across the River Tagus or between Carcavelos and Guincho on the city side of the Tagus.

World **windsurfing** championships are held at Guincho.

The **golf course** at Estoril is one of Portugal's best.

NIGHTLIFE

Since **Lux** (Avenida Infante Dom Henrique, Armazém A, Santa Apolonia) became the place to be, the former nightlife temple, **Frágil** (Rua da Atalaia 126) has become less popular, but no less interesting. **Santos** and the **Avenida 24 de Julho** are home to Lisbon's club scene: **Indústria** (Rua do Instituto Industrial 6), **Kapital** (Avenida 24 de Julho 68) and **Kremlin** (Escadinhas da Praia 5) are three good haunts.

GAY NIGHTLIFE

Many of Lisbon's nightclubs are mixed, but there are gay venues in the **Príncipe Real** district.

Frágil (➤ above) is gay at weekends, while at **Harry's** (Rua São Pedro de Alcântara 57, Bairro Alto) you can witness outrageous Amalia drag-alikes.

For lesbians, the choice for nightlife is limited to **Memorial** (Rua Gustavo Matos Sequeira 42A).

Northern Portugal

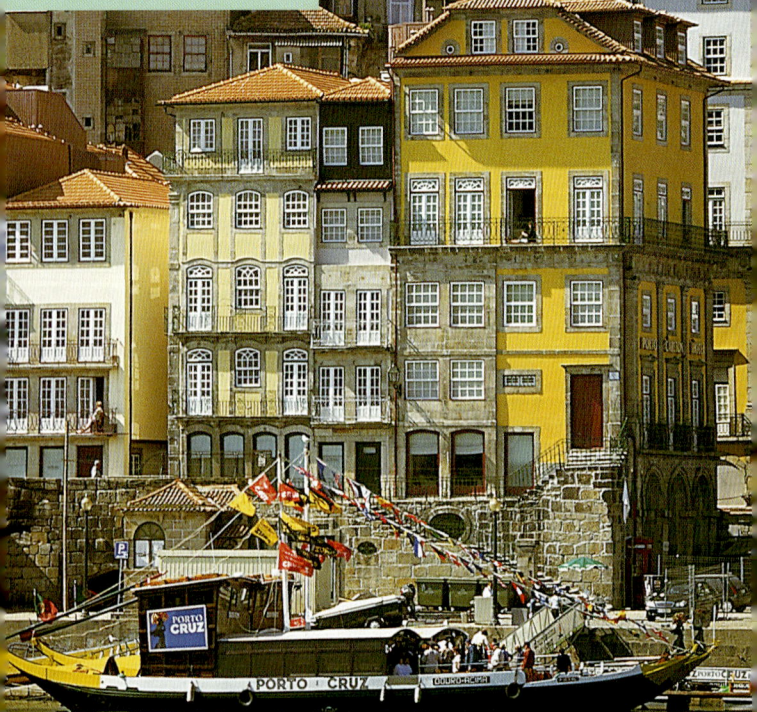

Getting Your Bearings

The north is the cradle of Portugal. It was at Guimarães that Portugal's first king, Afonso Henriques, inherited the county of Portucale, and from here that he extended it south during the Reconquest from the Moors. It was the north, too, that produced Portugal's last and longest ruling dynasty, the dukes of the house of Bragança, who came to the throne in 1640 and remained there until the foundation of the republic in 1910.

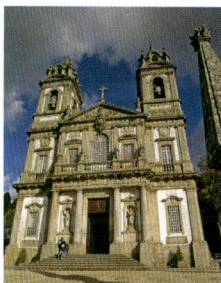

Porto, the biggest city of the north, grew rich on the Age of Discovery, when seamen and merchants travelled to Brazil, returning with gold and diamonds, which helped to finance the city's extravagant churches and palaces. Later, it gave its name to port and profited from the port wine trade, which continues to dominate Vila Nova de Gaia and the valleys of the Upper Douro.

The north is divided into two contrasting regions. The Minho, which occupies the historic boundaries of Portucale between the Douro and Minho rivers, is a land of lush, green countryside fed by the highest rainfall in Portugal. Much of the land is given over to smallholdings, though there is also a large number of manor houses, many of which take in guests. This densely populated region hosts some of Portugal's biggest country markets and fairs, with music, dancing and people in traditional costume. It also contains two important historical towns – Portugal's first capital, Guimarães, and its religious centre, Braga.

By contrast, Trás-os-Montes is a wild and rugged region of granite mountains and remote villages set in a harsh climate, which somehow manages to create the perfect conditions for producing port wine.

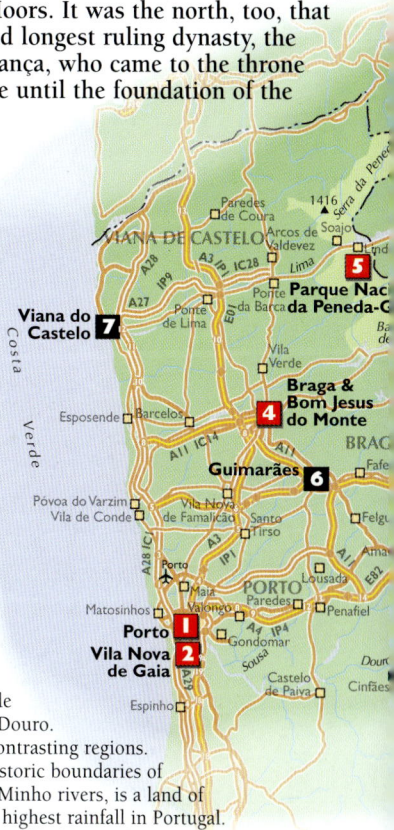

Previous page: Porto clings to a steep slope by the River Douro

Above left: The sanctuary at Bom Jesus

★ **Don't Miss**
1 **Porto** ➤ 80
2 **Vila Nova de Gaia** ➤ 84
3 **Solar de Mateus** ➤ 86
4 **Braga and Bom Jesus** ➤ 88
5 **Parque Nacional da Peneda-Gerês** ➤ 91

At Your Leisure
6 Guimarães ➤ 93
7 Viana do Castelo ➤ 93
8 Chaves ➤ 94
9 Bragança ➤ 94
10 Miranda do Douro ➤ 95

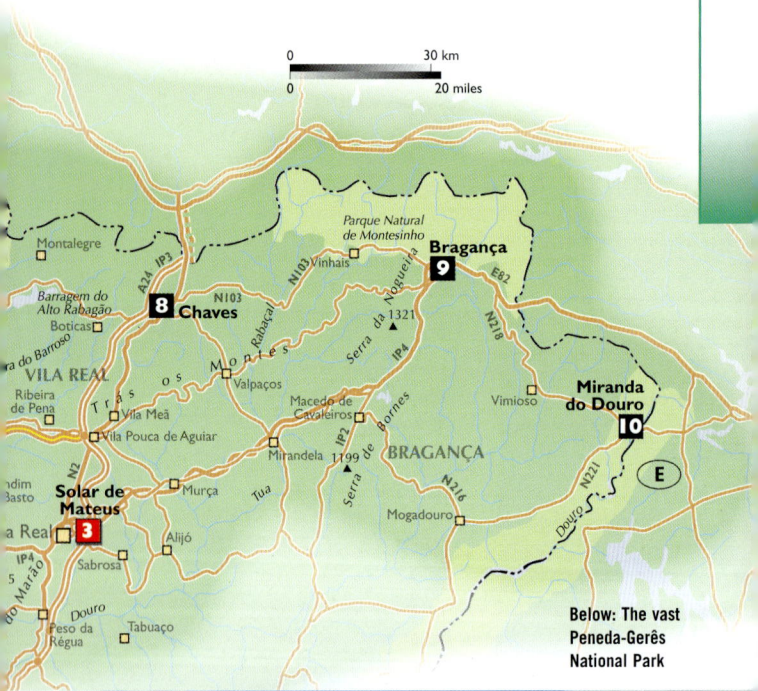

Below: The vast Peneda-Gerês National Park

This varied tour takes you from the bustling city of Porto to the vineyards of the Douro Valley and the remote villages of the Parque Nacional da Peneda-Gerês.

Northern Portugal in Three Days

Day One

Morning

Spend the morning exploring the old town of **1 Porto** (➤ 80–83). Start by climbing Torre dos Clérigos for an overview of the city, then wander around the Bolhão market and have coffee at Café Majestic (below; ➤ 98) before walking uphill to the cathedral. Drop down to the Ribeira district to admire the opulence of the Bolsa (Stock Exchange) and São Francisco church before lunch in one of the riverside cafés.

Afternoon and Evening

Walk across Ponte Dom Luís I, with great views of Porto, to reach **2 Vila Nova de Gaia** (➤ 84–85) where you can spend an enjoyable afternoon touring the wine lodges and tasting port. In summer you can also take a boat cruise on the River Douro. Return to the north bank for dinner on Cais da Ribeira (below) – perhaps *bacalhau* (salt cod) at Filha de Mãe Preta (➤ 98), overlooking the quayside.

Day Two

Morning
Leave Porto on the IP4/A4 to Amarante and Vila Real, to visit the 3 **Solar de Mateus** (► 86–87). After a stroll around the gardens, take the N2 south to Peso da Régua for lunch by the river.

Afternoon and Evening
From here you can do a shortened version of the Port Country tour (► 84), travelling through the steeply terraced vineyards (left) between Peso da Régua and Pinhão on a beautiful stretch of the Douro Valley. Returning to Vila Real, take the IP4 to Amarante and head north on the N101 to 6 **Guimarães** (► 93). Follow the signs to the castle, where Portugal's first king was born, then wander down to the old town for a drink at one of the cafés on Largo da Oliveira. Stay at Pousada de Santa Marinha (tel: 253 511 249, €€€–€€€€), in a 12th-century convent on a hill overlooking Guimarães. One of the finest of all the *pousadas*, this one has cool whitewashed corridors, fountains, and *azulejo*-tiled cloisters.

Day Three

Morning
Make an early start to visit the cathedral in 4 **Braga** (► 88–90) and the sanctuary at 4 **Bom Jesus** (► 90). From here, drive north on the IP1/A3 to the attractive town of Ponte da Lima for a walk along the river and a drink in one of the cafés by the Roman bridge. Follow the N203 along the Lima Valley to enter the 5 **Parque Nacional da Peneda-Gerês** (below; ► 91–92).

Afternoon
Allow plenty of time to explore the national park by car. You could take a tour through the villages of Soajo and Lindoso before briefly entering Spain on the way to the spa town of Caldas do Gerês. Return to Porto via Braga or take the N103 to Chaves to enter the wilds of Trás-os-Montes.

❶ Porto

Portugal's second city enjoys a magnificent position, tumbling down the steep slopes on the north bank of the River Douro. A workaday, rough-and-ready port city, frayed at the edges but wonderfully charismatic, Porto makes a good introduction to northern Portugal.

Porto (whose English name, Oporto, derives from *o porto*, "the port") has been occupied for at least 3,000 years. The Romans built a harbour here at *Portus*, an important river crossing on the route from Lisbon to Braga. The settlement on the south bank, where Vila Nova de Gaia now stands, was called *Cale*. These two towns gave their names to the county of Portucale, brought by Teresa of Castile as her dowry when she married Henry of Burgundy in 1095. When their son, Afonso Henriques, captured the rest of the country from the Moors, he named his new kingdom Portugal. In more recent history, Porto was the Cultural Capital of Europe in 2001.

The heart of the modern city is **Avenida dos Aliados**, whose central promenade, with flowerbeds and a mosaic pavement, leads up to the town hall. From the foot of the avenue, on Praça da Liberdade, you can see the baroque church and tower of **Clérigos** to the west. Designed by the Italian architect Nicolau Nasoni, this was the first oval church in Portugal. The tower, 75m (246 feet) high, is one of the tallest in the country and you can climb it for views over the city and the wine lodges of Vila Nova da Gaia (► 84–85).

East of Avenida dos Aliados, **Baixa** is the main shopping district, centred around the covered Bolhão market. Elderly women sell vegetables upstairs, while downstairs there are stalls offering maize bread, fresh fish, live chickens, pigs' ears and tripe (the people of Porto are nicknamed *tripeiros* "tripe-eaters"). Across the street are several *confeitarias* (pastry shops) featuring Porto's other speciality, *bacalhau*, large slabs of salt cod which look like cardboard and smell even worse (► 9).

Rua de Santa Catarina is lined with leather and jewellery shops and the old-world Café Majestic (► 98), and leads to Praça da Batalha. The **sé** (cathedral) is clearly visible from here, built on a rocky outcrop overlooking the Douro.

Top left: Porto may be a modern city, but it is also the capital of the traditional, rural north

Left: The neo-baroque façade of a newspaper office in Porto

Art versus Port

The **Museu Nacional de Soares dos Reis** (Rua Dom Manuel II, tel: 223 393 770; www.ipmuseus.pt, Tue 2–6, Wed–Sun 10–6, moderate; Sun 10–2 free) is Portugal's oldest national museum, dedicated to Portuguese art, including the work of the 19th-century sculptor António Soares dos Reis. The **Museu Romântico** (Quinta da Macieirinha Palace, Rua de Entrequintas 220, tel: 226 057 033, Tue–Sat 10–12:30, 2–5:30, Sun 2–5:30, inexpensive; Sat–Sun free), is a re-creation of a 19th-century aristocratic home. The same building houses the Solar do Vinho do Porto (► 71).

Below: The bustling quayside of the Ribeira district

Bottom: Traditional shops sell *bacalhau*

Begun in the 12th century as a Romanesque fortress church, it was remodelled in Gothic style. The 14th-century cloisters are decorated with *azulejos* depicting the life of the Virgin. A grand staircase by Nicolau Nasoni leads to the chapter house and an upper gallery that has fine views. There are more good views from the terrace in front of the cathedral.

The area between the cathedral and the waterfront was declared a Unesco World Heritage site in 1996. Walk down through the **Bairro da Sé**, the oldest quarter, similar to Alfama (► 54–57) in Lisbon. The daily life

of the district mingles with ancient churches and *azulejo*-tiled walls as housewives gather at the public washhouse and shop in the local market.

A statue of Henry the Navigator stands on **Praça do Infante**, near the former customs house where it is believed he was born. Also on this square is **Palácio da Bolsa**, the Stock Exchange built in 1834 over the ruins of the São Francisco convent. The highlight here is the Arabian Room, whose carved wood, gold leaf and Arabic inscriptions were modelled on the Alhambra in the Spanish city of Granada.

Behind the building, the **Igreja de São Francisco** is richly ornamented with gilded baroque carvings. At one stage there was more than 400kg (880lbs) of gold covering the chestnut-wood walls, before the church was ransacked by Napoleon's troops.

The church authorities were so shocked at this blatant display of extravagance (in contrast to the Franciscan vow of poverty) that they ordered the church to be deconsecrated. Notice the **Tree of Jesse**, in carved and gilded wood, adorning the north wall. The visit includes the **catacombs**, where there is an ossuary of human bones.

Outside the Centre

Take the bus to Serralves to visit the **Museu de Arte Contemporânea** (Rua Dom João de Castro 210, tel: 808 200 543, www.serralves.pt; Apr–Sep Tue–Thu 10–7, Fri–Sat 10–10; Sun and public hols 10–8; Oct–Mar 10–7; museum moderate; gardens inexpensive), a modern art museum that opened in 1999 in a stunning white building designed by local architect Álvaro Siza Vieira. It is situated in the gardens of the art deco Casa de Serralves, with a rose garden, arboretum, tea-house, lake and sculpture park. Continue on the bus to **Foz**, the beach at the mouth of the Douro, where you can stroll along the promenade watching waves crash against the rocks.

For Bookworms

Don't miss the wonderful art nouveau bookshop, **Lello & Irmão**, at Rua das Carmelitas 144, near the Clérigos tower, with its neo-Gothic façade, carved bookcases, spiral staircase and stained glass.

Ribeira, the fishermen's district, is the most atmospheric quarter, with narrow streets and painted houses rising above riverside arcades. A morning market is held on weekdays, but the area comes alive at night, with quayside restaurants and bars in the shadow of **Ponte Dom Luís I**. This splendid two-tier iron bridge links Porto to Vila Nova de Gaia (▶ 84–85).

TAKING A BREAK

Café Majestic (▶ 98) is all belle époque with oak-framed mirrors and soft leather banquettes, serving cakes and scones.

✚ 198 A3

Tourist Information Centre
✉ Rua Clube dos Fenianos 25 (top of Avenida dos Aliados) ☎ 223 393 470; www.portoturismo.pt

Torre dos Clérigos
✉ Rua de São Felipe Néry ☎ 222 001 729 🕐 Apr–Oct daily 9:30–1, 2–7; Aug 10–7; 10–12, 2–5 rest of year 🎫 Inexpensive

Sé
✉ Terreiro da Sé ☎ 222 059 028 🕐 Mon–Sat 8:45–12:30, 2:30–6/7, Sun 8:30–12:30, 2:30–6/7 🎫 Church free, cloisters inexpensive

Palácio da Bolsa
✉ Rua Ferreira Borges ☎ 223 399 000; www.pLciodabolsa.pt 🕐 Apr–Oct daily 9–7; Nov–Mar 9–1, 2–6 🎫 Moderate

Igreja de São Francisco
✉ Rua do Infante Dom Henrique ☎ 222 062 100 🕐 Daily 9–5:30/6/7/8 🎫 Moderate

Opposite top: The cloisters of the cathedral are lined with *azulejo* tiles

Opposite below: A baroque altar-piece in the cathedral

Below: The old-style Café Majestic

PORTO: INSIDE INFO

Top tips The best way to get around Porto is **on foot**, but you will need a good pair of shoes for all the steep hills and cobbled streets.

• Take one of the **river cruises** that depart regularly in summer from the quayside at Cais da Ribeira and also from the waterfront at Vila Nova de Gaia. Just turn up and you'll be able to get a ticket. For trips of 1 hour try Douro Acima (tel: 222 006 418) or **Rota do Douro** (tel: 223 759 042). Trips cost around €10. For longer cruises try **Douro Azul** (tel: 223 402 500; www.douroazul.com).

• For the **best views of Porto**, cross the upper level of the Dom Luís I bridge to reach the terrace of Nossa Senhora da Serra do Pilar on the south bank.

② Vila Nova de Gaia

The names of famous port shippers, Sandeman, Ferreira and Taylor, spelled out in neon letters on the hillside, draw you irresistibly across the water to Vila Nova de Gaia, the home of the port wine trade. Here, barrels of port mature in cool cellars and lodges, many of which can be visited for tastings and tours.

Although the grapes for port are grown in the Douro Valley, the ageing process takes place in Vila Nova de Gaia. It was British traders who first chose this spot at the mouth of the River Douro, whose north-facing position ensured a high level of humidity and a cool ocean breeze.

Each spring following the harvest, the barrels of new wine are transported down river, originally in square-rigged *barcos rabelos* boats, but these days in stainless steel tankers. Many of the port houses still keep *barcos rabelos* on the waterfront, loaded with barrels and sailed once a year during the annual regatta on 24 June (▶ 100).

The best way to approach Vila Nova de Gaia is by walking from Porto (▶ 80–83) across **Ponte Dom Luís I**. The lower level gives immediate access to the riverside, and the upper walkway offers a hair-raising experience and spectacular views.

The tourist office on the waterfront will give you a map and a list of **port lodges** (a corruption of the Portuguese word *loja*, meaning "warehouse"). Most people start with **Sandeman** (Largo Miguel Bombarda 3, tel: 223 740 500, moderate), founded by Briton George Sandeman in 1790 with

Visiting the Lodges
Around 20 lodges are open to visitors, and the routine at all of them is similar. Most are open weekdays (and weekends in summer) 9:30–12:30 and 2–5. Visits are usually free, though some companies make a small charge that can be redeemed against the price of a bottle. You get a tour of the cellars, a talk on the production process and a tasting, typically a glass of white and a glass of tawny port. Although they will be more than happy to sell you a bottle, there is never any pressure to buy.

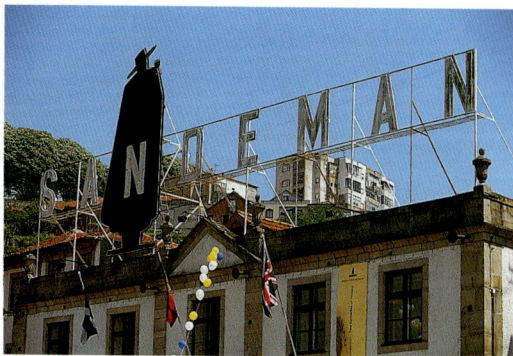

Left: The Sandeman logo features a Spanish hat and a Portuguese cape to denote the company's involvement in both sherry and port

a loan of £300 from his father. This is the slickest and most commercialised of the lodge tours, with a museum, slide show and guides.

The tour is informative, but it is interesting to compare it with one of the smaller firms. Ferreira (tel: 223 746 107, inexpensive), also on the waterfront, was founded in 1751 and is still Portuguese owned. The tasting room here is decorated with *azulejos* and there is an archive of historical exhibits relating to port.

Other lodges that can be visited include **Barros** (tel: 223 752 320), a third-generation Portuguese family firm; **Ramos Pinto** (tel: 223 775 011), with a logo of a kissing couple with a glass of port; and **Real Companhia Velha** (tel: 223 775 100), founded by Dom José I in 1756 to challenge Britain's monopoly on port.

TAKING A BREAK

There are several restaurants and cafés down by the water-front – try **Dom Luís** (➤ 98) for good-value Portuguese food.

✚ 198 A3

Tourist Information Centre
✉ Avenida Diogo Leite ☎ 223 703 735

Above: The Ponte Dom Luís I

Above left: The tasting terrace at Taylor's

VILA NOVA DE GAIA: INSIDE INFO

Top tip Let your tastebuds explore the many **different styles** of port: the aperitif, dry white, amber-coloured tawny, rich ruby and vintage, the pride of every shipper's range (➤ 10).

Hidden gem It's worth making the steep climb to **Taylor's** (Rua do Choupelo 250, tel: 223 742 800), founded in 1692 and the last surviving family-owned British port house. It is housed in an amazing old-style lodge and has a very friendly welcome. The free tour is helpful, the tastings are generous and there are wonderful views from the terrace over the Douro and Ponte Dom Luís I.

3 Solar de Mateus

The building that graces the label of every bottle of Mateus Rosé is as perfect a Portuguese manor house as you can find. With fine furniture, paintings, formal gardens and family chapel, a visit to the Solar de Mateus offers a rare glimpse into the lives of the Portuguese aristocracy.

It was built in 1745 by the third Morgado de Mateus. His descendants, the counts of Vila Real, still live in a wing of the house. The architect is unknown, but it is attributed to Nicolau Nasoni, the Italian who designed the Clérigos tower in Porto (► 80) and who was a major influence on the development of Portuguese baroque.

The façade of the house is immediately impressive, a contrast of whitewash and granite reflected in a pool that was added when the gardens were extensively remodelled in the 1930s. The forecourt is dominated by an immense double stairway, whose balustrades lead the eye up towards the pediment, flanked by classical statues and crowned by a family escutcheon.

The house can only be visited on 30-minute guided tours, and the guides tend to rush you through. You begin in the entrance hall, with its carved chestnut ceiling, 18th-century

Above and top right: The landscaped gardens and elegant façade of the Solar de Mateus

sedan chairs and family coat of arms on the wall. This leads into the **Four Seasons Room**, which takes its name from the strange paintings of seasonal vegetables in human form. On the table in the centre stands a 16th-century Hispano-Arab plate, the oldest item on display.

The neighbouring **Blue Room** features Chinese porcelain in a 17th-century Chinese cabinet, while the **Dining Room** has a Brazilian jacaranda wood dresser containing stunning Portuguese china and silver.

The highlight of the **Four Corners Room**, where ladies gathered after dinner while the men smoked and drank port, is a fine, hand-carved Indo-Portuguese ivory and wood travelling desk.

The family **museum** has several rare treasures, including the original copperplates by Jean Fragonard for a limited edition of *Os Lusíadas* (*The Lusiads*) by Portuguese poet Luís de Camões, produced in 1817 and sent by the Morgado de Mateus to 250 libraries and noble families in Europe to promote Portuguese history and culture. Some of the letters of thanks are displayed, along with religious vestments and chalices, relics of saints and martyrs, a 17th-century ivory crucifix and a statue of the Virgin carved from a single piece of ivory.

Be sure to walk around the **gardens**, with their dark avenue of cedar trees, neatly clipped box hedges and peaceful views over the surrounding countryside.

TAKING A BREAK

There is a small **café** in the gardens for snacks and refreshments, which is open in summer.

➕ 198 C4   ✉ 4km (2.5 miles) east of Vila Real   ☎ 259 323 121;
www.casademateus.com   ⓘ 🚌 Jun–Sep 9–7:30; Mar–May, Oct 9–1, 2–6;
Nov–Feb 10–1, 2–5   🚊 Vila Real   💷 House expensive, gardens moderate

SOLAR DE MATEUS: INSIDE INFO

Top tips Classical music concerts are held in the grounds at weekends during the summer.
• If you're looking for **Mateus Rosé**, don't look here – it is produced by the Sogrape company (www.sogrape.pt) from vineyards in the Beiras and has no connection with the Mateus estate, other than the label on the bottle.

In more depth The nearby town of **Vila Real** (Royal Town), dramatically perched above a gorge at the confluence of the Corgo and Cabril rivers, is the capital of the Upper Douro. The best sights are the Gothic cathedral and the house on the main street where the explorer Diogo Cão, who discovered the mouth of the Congo in 1482, was born.

4 Braga and Bom Jesus

Braga likes to describe itself as the Portuguese Rome. The largest city in the Minho has a long history as a religious capital that has left it with churches, Renaissance mansions and Portugal's most spectacularly sited sanctuary, Bom Jesus.

Braga

An old saying has it that "while Coimbra studies and Lisbon plays, Porto works and Braga prays". The Roman bishop St Martin of Braga converted the local Swabian tribe to Christianity in the 6th century AD and established the custom, still used in Portugal, of naming the days of the week in numerical order rather than after pagan gods (Monday, *segunda-feira*, is "second day", Tuesday, *terça-feira*, "third day", etc). In the 12th century, following the Christian conquest, Braga became the seat of the Portuguese archbishops and has remained that way ever since.

Start your visit at **Praça da República**, an arcaded square at the end of a long public garden with fountains and children's playgrounds. Stallholders sell Minho artefacts such as clogs and wooden toys, and there are old-fashioned cafés beneath the arches close to the 14th-century town keep. From here, walk down Rua do Souto, a pedestrianised shopping street, passing the former bishop's palace on your way to the **sé** (cathedral).

The cathedral was begun in 1070 on the site of a mosque. Originally built in Romanesque style, the subsequent Gothic, Renaissance and baroque additions give it an eclectic feel. The main Romanesque doorway survives at the western end, though it is covered by a Gothic porch that was added in the late 15th century. Among the artists who worked on the cathedral are João de Castilho, one of the architects of the Mosteiro dos Jerónimos in Lisbon (▶ 48), and the French sculptor Nicolas Chanterene, whose statue of Nossa Senhora da Leite (Our Lady of the Milk) is sheltered beneath a Gothic canopy at the cathedral's eastern end.

The cloister gives access to the **Museu de Arte Sacra**, whose junk-shop atmosphere is both fascinating and frustrating. There are amazing treasures here – gold, silver, ivory, diamonds, emeralds, pearls and jade – but it's all arranged haphazardly without labelling, and the guides do not allow you much time to linger. Among the items on display is a simple cross, used by Pedro Álvares Cabral in 1500 to celebrate the first ever Mass in Brazil.

Above: The impressive baroque organ at Braga

Right: The monumental stairway to Bom Jesus

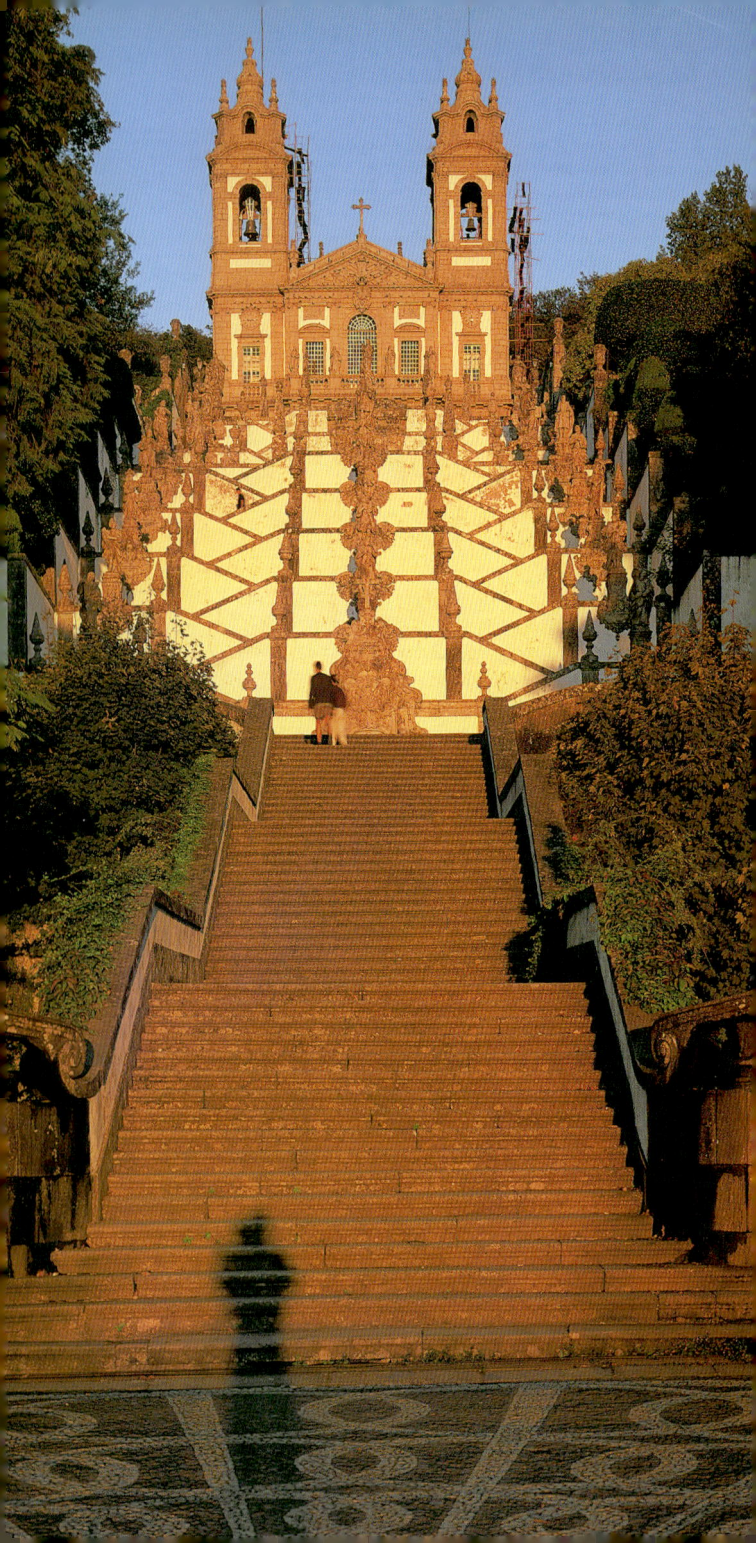

The tour of the museum also includes the **Capela dos Reis**, where Henry of Burgundy and Teresa of Castile, parents of Portugal's first king, are buried in 16th-century tombs.

Tickets also allow entry to the **Coro Alto** (upper choir), with gilded baroque organs and choir stalls carved from jacaranda wood.

Bom Jesus

Pilgrims and day trippers flock at weekends to Bom Jesus do Monte, a hilltop sanctuary 5km (3 miles) east of Braga. Although primarily a place for prayer, this is also a popular picnic spot, with gardens, woodland and a lake.

The centrepiece is the long **baroque stairway** with more than 1,000 steps. It was begun by the archbishop of Braga in 1722 and finished in the 19th century. True pilgrims ascend the stairway on their knees, but most people walk or take the old-fashioned **funicular** (daily 8–8, every 30 minutes). It's best to make the climb on foot to appreciate the symbolism of the architecture.

The stairway is lined with statues of biblical figures

Via Sacra (Holy Way) begins with a winding path lined with chapels depicting the Stations of the Cross. Each of the chapels, dripping with wax from pilgrims' candles, is filled with life-size terracotta figures evoking scenes from Christ's Passion. As you near the summit, you reach an ornamental double stairway, whose grey granite is set off against white-washed walls. Fountains depict the five human senses, with water gushing out of ears, eyes, nose and mouth, while further up, the **Staircase of the Three Virtues** features allegorical figures of Faith, Hope and Charity.

TAKING A BREAK

Visit the old-world **Café Vianna** (► 98) on Praça da República, or for a more substantial Portuguese meal, try **Inácio** (► 99) on Campos das Hortas 14.

➕ 198 B4

Tourist Information Centre
✉ off Praça da República ☎ 253 262 550

Sé/Museu de Arte Sacra
✉ Rua D. Paio Mendes ☎ 253 263 317 🕐 Sumer daily 9–6:30; winter 9–5:30 💶 Church free, museum inexpensive

BRAGA AND BOM JESUS: INSIDE INFO

Top tips Leave your car in the **underground car park** beneath Praça da República, from where everything of interest can be reached in a short walk.
• There are **regular buses** from Braga to the foot of Bom Jesus do Monte, or you can drive your car right up to the summit.

In more depth The **Palácio dos Biscainhos** (near the Arco da Porta Nova gateway, Tue–Sun 10–12:30, 2–5:30, inexpensive; Sun 10–noon, free) is a 17th-century mansion with stucco ceilings and *azulejo* tiles which has been turned into a decorative arts museum featuring Portuguese furniture, silverware and ornamental gardens.

5 Parque Nacional da Peneda-Gerês

Portugal's only national park, covering an area of 700sq km (270sq miles), is a wild and dramatic place of windswept peaks, granite crags, deep river valleys and rural villages. These are the sort of villages where the shepherds still migrate to higher ground each spring in search of pasture for their flock. The park consists of two main *serras* (mountain ranges), Serra da Peneda and Serra do Gerês, divided by the River Lima.

With few clear entry points and villages scattered around, most of the time it doesn't seem as if you are in a national park at all. Despite the presence of wildlife, such as golden eagles, wild horses and wolves, and rare varieties of Gerês lilies and ferns, it is a way of life as much as anything that is preserved here.

You can visit the park by car on a day trip from Braga or the Minho

Left: Long-horned Minho cattle

Below: The River Lima near Lindoso

Walking in the Park

Pick up a walking map from the information centres in Braga, Ponte da Barca or Caldas do Gerês to tackle some of the *trilhos* (walking trails) in the park.

Two of the best are the Trilho da Peneda, around the village of the same name, and the Trilho Castrejo from the village of Castro Laboreiro, known for its special breed of mountain dogs.

coast. The easiest approach is along the Lima Valley from Ponte da Barca. This brings you to **Soajo** and **Lindoso**, both of which have a some village houses for rent (Aldeias de Portugal, tel: 258 931 750, www.aldeiasdeportugal.pt).

Both villages are known for their *espigueiros*, communal stone granaries topped with a cross and raised above the ground as a precaution against pests. At Lindoso, a group of 60 *espigueiros* are huddled beneath the castle, resembling tombstones in a cemetery. The castle here, right next to the Spanish border, has been attacked many times. Nowadays it is a peaceful spot, with long-horned Minho cattle grazing beneath its walls.

A minor road runs north between the two villages, with views over the Lima Valley on the way to **Peneda**. This small village contains a remarkable sanctuary, **Nossa Senhora da Peneda**, modelled on Bom Jesus (► 90) and reached by a similarly long staircase. The chapel, which from below seems almost to be built into the cliff, is the focus for a huge pilgrimage each September.

Below: A typical *espigueiro* near Soajo

The most direct route between the two sections of the park means crossing the Spanish border at Lindoso and re-entering Portugal at Portela do Homem. The road dips down through a delightful wooded glade to the spa resort of **Caldas do Gerês**, where wild herbs, wildflower honey and chunky woollen sweaters are for sale and the main street is lined with spa hotels. Just outside town, a *miradouro* (viewpoint) offers fabulous views over the reservoir of Caniçada.

TAKING A BREAK

There are village-style **cafés and bars** in Soajo, Lindoso and Caldas do Gerês. Apart from that a good option would be to stock up on **picnic** provisions in any of the nearby towns.

✚ 198 B5

Park Office
✉ Avenida António Macedo, Braga ☎ 253 203 480;
www.icn.pt 🕒 Mon–Fri 9–12:30, 2–5:30

PARQUE NACIONAL DA PENEDA-GERÊS: INSIDE INFO

Top tips Allow **plenty of time** for driving within the park – the roads are steep and narrow, and the distances are greater than they look on the map.

• Arrive in **Soajo** on a Sunday morning and you will find market stalls set up on the main street selling sausages, leather boots and farming tools.

At Your Leisure

The Santa Luzia basilica

6 Guimarães

The first capital of Portugal and the birthplace of its first king, Afonso Henriques, has a special place in the heart of the Portuguese nation. Most of the sights are situated in the old town beneath the castle. Climb over the ramparts of the 10th-century fortress, and visit the Romanesque chapel of **São Miguel do Castelo**, where Afonso Henriques was baptised, and where the warriors who helped him to conquer Portugal are buried.

Near by, beside a statue of Afonso, is the **Paço dos Duques de Bragança**, built in the 15th century by the first Duke of Bragança and restored under the Salazar dictatorship as a presidential palace. It has Flemish tapestries, Persian carpets, Portuguese furniture and a gallery of paintings by local artist José de Guimarães.

A short walk along Rua de Santa Maria leads to the **old town**, with restored medieval houses. The street ends in a pair of delightful squares, where a flea market is held on Saturdays.

Praça de Santiago is surrounded by wooden-balconied houses, while **Largo da Oliveira** has a Gothic shrine outside Nossa Senhora da Oliveira (Our Lady of the Olive Tree), whose cloisters house a museum of sacred art.

✚ 198 B4
Paço dos Duques de Bragança
☎ 253 412 273; www.cm-guimaraes.pt
🕐 Jun–Sep daily 9:30–6:30; Oct–May Tue–Sun 9:30–12, 2–5 💶 Moderate (Sun 9:30–12:30 free)

7 Viana do Castelo

The capital of the Costa Verde enjoys a perfect setting on the north bank of the Lima estuary, overlooked by the pinewoods of Monte de Santa

Barcelos

The largest weekly market in Portugal takes place on Thursday mornings on a vast open square in the centre of Barcelos. Look out for the local Barcelos pottery and brightly coloured *galos de Barcelos* "Barcelos cocks" which recall the legend of an innocent Galician pilgrim, miraculously saved from the gallows when a roast cockerel began to crow. He invoked the help of St James, saying that if he were innocent the cockerel being prepared for the judge's dinner would sit up and crow.

Luzia. Once a small fishing port, Viana supplied many of the seafarers who sailed during the Age of Discovery and returned to the town to build Manueline and Renaissance mansions. The main square, **Praça da República**, is the focus of daily life, with its 16th-century fountain and Renaissance palace.

In summer it is a busy resort. You can walk or take the funicular through the pinewoods to reach a basilica and the ruins of a Celto-Iberian settlement, or take the ferry across the river to **Praia do Cabedelo**, the town's splendid beach.

✛ 198 A4
Tourist Information Office
✉ Rua do Hospital Velho
☎ 258 822 620

8 Chaves

A magnificent drive from Braga on the N103 threads through the Gerês and Barroso mountains to Chaves, famous for its smoked hams and strong red wine.

Founded by the Romans as the spa town of *Aquae Fluviae*, Chaves ("keys") was awarded by Dom João I to Nuno Álvares Pereira as a reward

for his victory against the Spanish at the battle of Aljubarrota (➤ 113).

Only 12km (7.5 miles) from the Spanish border, Chaves has a long history of conflict, most recently in 1912 when Royalist rebels attacked the town from Spain. There are two 17th-century fortresses and the keep of the 14th-century castle is now the Museu Militar.

A statue of the first Duke of Bragança, who lived in the castle, stands on **Praça de Camões**, the main square of the old town. Also here are the **Misericórdia** church, with a gilded altar-piece, painted ceiling and *azulejo*-tiled walls, and the **Museu da Região Flaviense**, devoted to archaeology and local crafts.

✛ 199 D4
Tourist Information Office
✉ Terreiro de Cavalaria
☎ 276 340 661; www.rt-atb.pt

Museu da Região Flaviense/ Museu Militar
✉ Praça de Camões ☎ 276 340 500
🕐 Daily 9–12:30, 2–5:30
💲 Inexpensive

9 Bragança

The remote capital of Trás-os-Montes is closely identified with Portugal's last ruling dynasty, descendants of an illegitimate son of João I who became the first Duke of Bragança – though later dukes preferred to live in their palace at Vila Viçosa (➤ 136).

The city is built around a 12th-century **citadel**, a walled village and museum where ancient monuments

What to Do With the Kids
• Douro boat trips at Porto (➤ 83).
• The climb to Bom Jesus, either on foot or by the funicular railway (➤ 90).
• Shopping for clay cockerels at Barcelos market (➤ above).
• The beaches of the Costa Verde around Viana do Castelo (➤ 93–94).

sit side by side with whitewashed houses and cobbled streets. The castle contains a small military museum, and there are great views from the tower. Near here is a medieval pillory, an ancient stone pig on its pedestal (▶ 24), and the five-sided **Domus Municipalis**, Portugal's only surviving example of Romanesque civic architecture, where public meetings were held and the *homens bons* (good men) would gather to settle disputes.

Just beneath the citadel, on the way to the cathedral, the **Igreja de São Vicente** is where Dom Pedro is believed to have secretly married Inês de Castro (▶ 111).

The **Museu do Abade de Baçal** in the old bishop's palace contains religious art, archaeological finds and folk costumes collected by an abbot.

Bragança is a good base for excursions into the Montesinho natural park (▶ 23–24).

➕ 199 E5
Tourist Information Office
✉ Avenida Cidade de Zamora
☎ 273 381 273

Castelo and Museu Militar
☎ 273 322 378 🕐 Sep–Jun Tue–Sun 9–12, 2–5; Jul 9–6; Aug 9–6:30
💰 Inexpensive (Sun 9–noon free)

Museu do Abade de Baçal
✉ Rua Conselheiro Abílio Beça 27
☎ 273 331 595 🕐 Tue–Fri 10–5, Sat–Sun 10–6 💰 Inexpensive (Sun 10–2 free)

🔟 Miranda do Douro

Set on a cliff overlooking a deep gorge in the River Douro, Miranda is a medieval border town whose inhabitants speak their own particular dialect, *mirandês*. The 16th-century sé (cathedral) includes the **Menino Jesus da Cartolinha**, a statue of the child Jesus in 17th-century costume and a top hat, who is said to have appeared to rally the Portuguese forces during a Spanish siege in 1711.

The excellent **Museu da Terra de Miranda** features a reconstruction of a farmhouse kitchen and folk costumes such as those worn by the *pauliteiros* (stick dancers) at festivals.

➕ 199 F4
Tourist Information Office
✉ Largo do Menino Jesus da Cartolinha ☎ 273 430 025

Museu da Terra de Miranda
✉ Largo Dom João III ☎ 273 431 164 🕐 Tue 2–5:30, Wed–Sun 9–12:30, 2–5:30 (6:30 in summer)
💰 Inexpensive (free Sun)

Right: The citadel at Bragança

Where to... Stay

Prices

Expect to pay for a double room with bathroom in high season

€ = under €60 €€ = €60-€120 €€€ = €121-€180 €€€€ = over €180

Hotel da Bolsa €€

Excellently located between the Ribeira and the Baixa districts, this 3-star hotel sits alongside the fine Stock Exchange building and is a mere 50m (55 yards) from the Portwine Institute. Built on the site of the São Francisco monastery, its 19th-century façade conceals a modern interior and although the rooms are a little dated, they offer standard facilities. There is a public car park next to the hotel.

🚹 198 A3
☒ Rue Ferreira Borges 101
☎ 222 026 768, fax: 222 058 888;
www.hoteldabolsa.com

Infante de Sagres €€€-€€€€

This centrally located hotel is regally luxurious on the inside. Chinese porcelain from the 17th century and Tabriz rugs adorn the public rooms while the bedrooms have retro bathrooms and antique furniture. Sculpted wood and stained glass underscore the aristocratic appearance and oriental salons give the place an exotic air. Don't miss the buffet breakfast in the dining room where regional specialities are also served at lunch and dinner.

🚹 198 A3
☒ Praça Dona Filipa de Lencastre 62
☎ 223 398 500,
fax: 223 398 599;
bookings@hotelinfantesagres.pt;
www.hotelinfantesagres.pt

Residencial dos Aliados €-€€

The pleasantly appointed en suite rooms in this imposing stone building are soon snapped up, so it is wise to book ahead. The bedrooms overlooking the avenue are noisy, despite double-glazing, so you might ask for an interior room. Most of the hotel was renovated in the late 1990s so the bathrooms are modern. A very good breakfast is included in the room price.

🚹 198 A3
☒ Rua Elísio de Melo 27
☎ 222 004 853/4,
fax: 222 002 710;
www.residencialaliados.com

Casa da Quinta de São Martinho €€

You will need to book ahead to stay at this tiny, popular guesthouse. It is a 200m (218 yards) hop across the main road from the Solar de Mateus (► 86-87), a short way east of Vila Real. A lovely swimming pool in the quiet grounds is the only luxury at this home-from-home country house. The two rooms inside the house and two self-contained flats are charmingly decorated and the resident family is very welcoming. They also have a well-stocked cellar of port.

🚹 198 C4 ☒ Mateus, Vila Real
☎ 933 202 326/933 437 291;
geral@quintasaomartinho.com;
www.quintasaomartinho.com

Albergaria da Sé €

A recent addition, on a quiet street right in the city centre by the sé (cathedral), this scrupulously clean guesthouse offers the best budget accommodation in town, with smart, bright rooms, all with en suite facilities. The staff are friendly and helpful. Fish dishes and Minho specialities are served in the pleasant restaurant.

🚹 198 B4 ☒ Rua Gonçalo Pereira 39-51 ☎ 253 214 502, fax: 253 214 501; www.albergaria-da-se.com.pt

Hotel do Parque €€

Like its sister hotel, Hotel do Elevador, run by the same company and situated at the top of the funicular, this renovated 19th-century hotel is located right alongside the Bom Jesus sanctuary (▶ 90), in well-manicured parkland. The plush, slightly old-fashioned rooms have all the modern comforts – TV, air-conditioning and mini-bar. The Restaurante Panorâmico lives up to its name and serves well-prepared regional dishes backed by an extensive cellar stocked with *vinho verde* and Dão red wines.

✚ 198 B4 ⌂ Monte do Bom Jesus, Braga ☎ 253 603 470, fax: 253 603 479; www.hoteisbomjesus.pt; hbj@hoteisbomjesus.pt

GUIMARÃES

Casa de Sezim €€

Despite an enviable collection of paintings and artefacts, this exquisite salmon-pink and stone 16th-century *solar*, surrounded by a huge wooded estate, retains a lived-in ambience. All but one of the nine rooms have their own bathrooms and all are furnished with family heirlooms. It has been in retired diplomat António Pinto de Mesquita's family for generations. Dinner can be requested and horses are available for riding.

✚ 198 B4 ⌂ Santo Amaro, Nespereira (off Santo Tirso road), Guimarães ☎ 253 523 000, fax: 253 523 196; www.sezim.pt

VIANA DO CASTELO

Estalagem Casa Melo Alvim €€–€€€

Next to Viana do Castelo's railway-station, this delightful Manueline *solar*, built in 1509 by the Conde da Carreira, was successfully extended in the 17th and 19th centuries. In the 1990s it was turned into a first-class inn, fully respecting the appearance of the imposing stone building. Furnishings and décor, including superb carpets and bedsteads, are a subtle blend of traditional styles with a modern preference for sobriety and sleek lines. Each of the 20 bedrooms is different. Alto Minho cuisine is the cuisine on offer at the exemplary Conde do Camarido restaurant.

✚ 198 A4 ⌂ Avenida Conde da Carreira 28, Viana do Castelo ☎ 258 808 200, fax: 258 808 220; hotel@meloalvimhouse.com; www.meloalvimhouse.co,

TRÁS-OS-MONTES

Estalagem do Caçador €€

The open fire is as welcome in winter as the swimming pool in summer at this cosy country inn. Hunting motifs abound, and hare, rabbit and venison often end up on the excellent menu in the restaurant. Antlers, stuffed birds, prints and hunting scenes in the spacious rooms continue the theme, and the cabinets full of Toby jugs and other knick-knacks lend the place the air of an eccentric museum.

✚ 199 E4 ⌂ Largo Manuel Pinto de Azevedo, Macedo de Cavaleiros ☎ 278 426 354/6, fax: 278 426 381; www.estalagensdeportugal.com ⊘ Closed 24–26 Dec

Forte de São Francisco €€€–€€€€

Housed in an expertly converted 17th-century fortress dominating the town centre, this luxurious hotel with tastefully decorated rooms has a swimming-pool terrace that commands amazing views of the surrounding hills. The bright modern restaurant, specialising in *transmontano* cuisine, is also one of the best in Chaves (open to non-patrons). There's even a baroque church, in pristine condition, within the complex. It's undoubtedly the most impressive place to stay in the region.

✚ 199 D4 ⌂ Forte de São Francisco, Alto da Pedisqueira, Chaves ☎ 276 333 700, fax: 276 333 701; www.forte-s-francisco-hoteis.pt

Where to...
Eat and Drink

Prices

Expect to pay per person for a three-course à la carte meal, excluding drinks and tips
€ = under €12   **€€** = €12–€24   **€€€** = €25–€36   **€€€€** = over €36

PORTO

PORTO

Café Majestic €

Arguably the most beautiful café in Portugal, this intellectuals' haunt dating from the 1920s has miraculously survived intact, complete with stucco cherubs and mouldings. Magnificent chandeliers, leather upholstery, marble-top tables and huge art deco mirrors complete the picture, along with a grand piano sometimes used for concerts. Ideal for coffee or tea and *pastéis*, though they do snacks and simple meals at lunchtime, too, served by liveried waiters.

➕ 198 A3 ✉ Rua de Santa Catarina 112 ☎ 222 003 887 ⓦ Mon–Sat 9:30am–midnight

Escondidinho €€€

Attentive service, perfectly prepared food and a sound wine list bolster this traditional restaurant's reputation – book ahead. In a quaint dining room you can sample all manner of fish, in soup, grilled or sometimes cooked in wine. Save room for dessert, for example the *folhada de maçã* (apple tart).

➕ 198 A3 ✉ Rua Passos Manuel 144 ☎ 222 001 079 ⓦ Mon–Sat noon–3, 7–10

Filha de Mãe Preta €€

You should try at least one of the many restaurants along the atmospheric Cais da Ribeira, down at the riverside overlooking the port warehouses in Gaia. Grilled sardines and mackerel are the favourites among the seafood-dominated menu at Filha de Mãe Preta, perhaps the best of all the restaurants, with its gorgeous *azulejos* and arched windows. Despite its popularity with tourists and Porto people alike, it maintains high standards.

➕ 198 A3 ✉ Cais da Ribeira 40 ☎ 222 086 066 ⓦ Mon–Sat noon–3, 6:30–10

VILA NOVA DE GAIA

Dom Luís €€

The views from the upper floor across the River Douro to Porto are fabulous, as is the house special, *tripas à moda do Porto* (tripe) – if that's your thing. Otherwise the menu is varied enough to suit all tastes, making it a useful place to

soak up all the port you may have sampled in the nearby *adegas*. The *ementa turística* (set daily menu) is good value and you can trust the house wine, an excellent Douro.

➕ 198 A3 ✉ Avenida Ramos Pinto 264–266 ☎ 223 751 251 ⓦ Tue–Sun noon–3:30, 7–midnight Closed 25 Dec–1 Jan

BRAGA

Café Vianna €

Like its equally atmospheric neighbour, the Astória, this low-key art nouveau coffee-house is great for people-watching over a drink and snack, either inside or on the *esplanada* (terrace). The coffee, cakes and *pregos* (bread rolls filled with a sliver of sizzling steak) are excellent. Some of the delicious local pastries to sample are *rabanadas* (cinnamon-flavoured French toast) and *charutos de chila* (pumpkin-filled pastry rolls).

➕ 198 B4 ✉ Praça da República ⓦ Daily 9–7

Where to...
Shop

A triangle between the Estação São Bento, the University and the City Hall forms the main trading area, with stationers, grocers and clothes and shoe shops along **Rua de Santa Catarina**. **Via Catarina** is a shopping mall with nearly 100 shops.

Behind its ornate neo-Gothic façade, art nouveau **Lello & Irmão** (Rua das Carmelitas 144, tel: 222 018 170) must be one of the most beautiful bookshops in the world, with its beguiling double staircase leading up to exquisite reading rooms and a cosy café-bar.

For crafts go to the **Centro Regional de Artes Tradicionais** (Rua da Reboleira 33–37, tel: 223 320 076) and for design items head up to the **Casa de Ferrágens**

---

tano delicacies. The *javali estufado com repolho e maçã* (wild boar with cabbage and apple) is especially delicious and enough for two. Wood-panelled rooms, crisp white linen and attentive service make this a delightful experience.

➕ 199 E5 ✉ Praça da Sé 34 ☎ 273 323 875 🕐 Daily noon–3:30, 6:30–11

BARCELOS

Bagoeira €€

A cavernous place on the Campo da Feira (marketplace), this typical inn has been catering to merchants and visitors since the 19th century. Minho dishes and gargantuan roasts are served in traditional style, with pottery jugs of refreshing *vinho verde*. *Bacalhau à Bagoeira* is the house variation on *à minhota*, with onions and potatoes. It has a few en suite rooms too (€).

➕ 198 A4 ✉ Avenida Sidónio Pais 495 ☎ 253 811 236 🕐 Daily noon–2:30, 7–10:30

Inácio €€€

Just outside the city centre, this traditional restaurant, with a rustic interior, has a limited but well-prepared menu. The emphasis is on *bacalhau (à Ignácio)* (sic) and roast lamb or pork. Lamprey (*lampreia*) is served in season, while *rojões à moda do Minho* (casseroled pork) is another house special.

➕ 198 B4 ✉ Campos das Hortas 4 ☎ 253 613 235 🕐 Wed–Mon noon–3:30, 7–10:30. Closed Christmas, Easter and first 2 weeks in Sep

GUIMARÃES

Solar do Arco €€

Situated near a stone arch along Guimarães' prettiest street, this is not the tourist trap you might think, despite the multilingual menu (try the good-value *ementa turística* – tourist menu). Roast *bacalhau* and *tamboril* (monkfish) are regular specials, but seafood, veal and pork are equally well prepared.

➕ 198 B4 ✉ Rua de Santa Maria 48–50 ☎ 253 513 072 🕐 Mon–Sat noon–3, 7–11, Sun noon–3

VIANA DO CASTELO

Os Três Potes €€

With its traditional granite walls and dark wooden furniture, this place can seem a little sombre, but the menu is varied with many Minho specialities on offer. Try the wood-oven-roasted kid (*cabrito*) or the chargrilled octopus (*polvo na brasa*). There are folkloric shows on Saturday evenings.

➕ 198 A4 ✉ Beco dos Fornos 7/9 ☎ 258 829 928 🕐 Daily noon–3:30, 7–10:30

BRAGANÇA

Solar Bragançano €€

In an 18th-century manor house, with a bar, right in the heart of the city, you can have chestnut soup, game or trout and other *transmon-*

Carvalho e Baptista (Rua Almada 79–83).

Garrafeira do Carmo (Rua do Carmo 17, tel: 222 003 285), a charming wine merchant, also sells *bacalhau*. For a spectacular display of the latter, there's Casa Oriental at Campo Mártires da Pátria 111/112 (tel: 222 002 530).

Visiting the various lodges across the river at Vila Nova de Gaia (▶ 84–85) is an experience in itself, but it's impossible to take them all in. If limited for time, go to Sandeman's (▶ 84) or Taylor's (▶ 85).

BARCELOS

Every Thursday the Campo da Feira in Barcelos has stalls selling sausages, cheese, breads and crafts.

The "Barcelos cock" (▶ 94) and distinctive Barcelos pottery – a rich brown with cream dots – originated here. The Ramalho family have handed down the skill from grandmother to granddaughter – their items are signed RR or JR.

Where to...
Be Entertained

FESTIVALS

São João (St John's Day), 23–24 June, is celebrated across the country. In Porto there is folk music, doll displays and general revelry. It ends with fireworks, and there is a *barcos rabelos* regatta (▶ 84).

Palácio da Bolsa holds regular concerts throughout the year as part of its Festival de Música. And for the young at heart there is Ritual Rock at the Palácio de Cristal in August.

The Igreja Matriz at Freixo de Espada à Cinta is the starting point for a famous Good Friday procession, the Romaria de Sete Paços. Viana do Castelo is famous for its *romaria* (Nossa Sra da Agonia) a three-day carnival held around 20 August.

SPORT AND OUTDOOR PURSUITS

You can hire surfing gear at Viana do Castelo. The Surf Club de Viana (Rua José Espregueira 62, tel: 258 826 274)) teaches beginners.

Amigos do Mar (tel: 258 829 028) does sailing and canoeing.

Hiking is the main activity inland, especially in the national parks such as Peneda-Gerês (▶ 91–92) – where you can also practise watersports on the Caniçada reservoir, hiring canoes, motorboats and windsurfing gear. Contact AML (tel: 253 391 779; www.aguamontanha.com).

You might prefer a river trip on the Douro: contact Douro Acima (tel: 222 006 418) or Douro Azul (Rua de São Francisco 4, tel: 223 402 500) for one- or two-day cruises.

MUSIC AND NIGHTLIFE

For classical music, there's Porto's Auditório Nacional Carlos Alberto (Rua das Oliveiras 43, tel: 223 401 900, geral@tnsj.pt) or the futuristic Casa da Música at the Rotunda da Boavista, built to mark Porto's year as European Capital of Culture (Avenida da Boavista 604-610, tel: 220 120 298). *Fado* is performed regularly at Mal Cozinhado (Rua do Outeirinho 13, tel: 222 081 319).

Aniki-Bóbó (Rua da Fonte Taurina 36, Porto, closed Sun) is packed with fans of jazz and drum 'n' bass in the early hours.

For nightclubs there's River Café (Calçada João do Carmo 31, Masarelos) or Indústria (Avenida Brasil 843, Foz do Douro). Swing (Praceta Engeniero Amaro da Costa 766), is a disco with bars – one is gay. In Braga the good clubs are around Praça da República – try Sardinha Biba (Lugar dos Galos, Carandá). Viana do Castelo's Viana Sol (Rua dos Manjovos), is open late.

Central Portugal

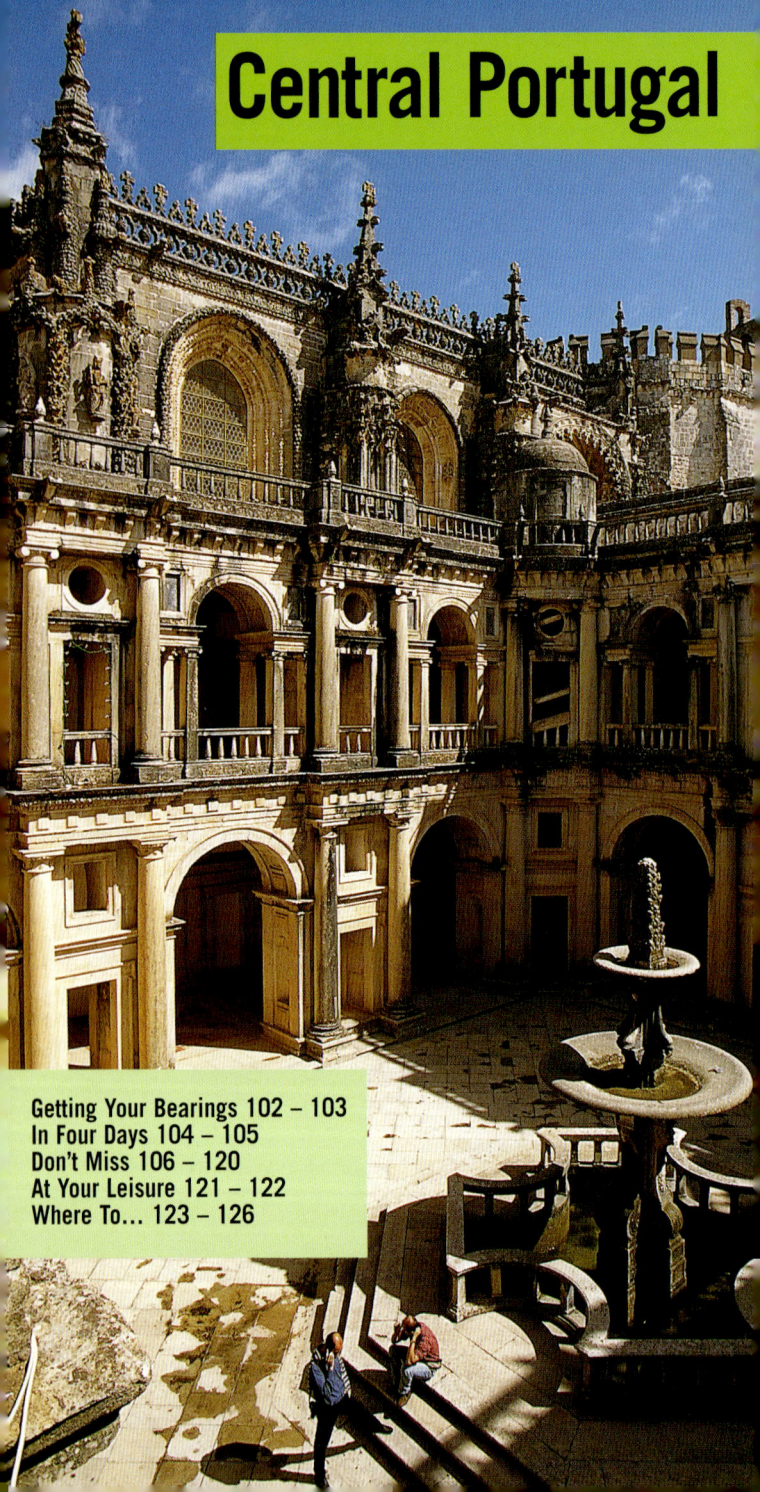

Getting Your Bearings

Central Portugal stretches almost from Lisbon to Porto and from the Spanish border to the Atlantic coast – yet apart from the charming university city of Coimbra and the fascinating pilgrimage town of Fátima it receives few visitors and is little known outside the country.

The heart of central Portugal is the Beira (border) region, a group of three provinces between the Douro and the Tagus rivers. This was the historic homeland of the *Lusitani* tribe, Celto-Iberians who resisted the Roman invasion of Portugal, whose leader Viriatus, killed in 139BC, remains a national hero. Coimbra, which takes its name from the Roman settlement at Conímbriga, was capital of Portugal for more than 100 years. These days it is the capital of Beira Litoral, a seaside province of sandy beaches, pine forests and dunes, which is popular with Portuguese holidaymakers in summer.

Further inland, Beira Alta is a region of solid towns and granite villages, where Dão wines and Serra cheese are made, the latter by the sheep farmers of the highlands of Serra da Estrela, while remote Beira Baixa is the setting for Monsanto, one of Portugal's most spectacular hilltop villages.

The twin provinces of Estremadura and Ribatejo are dotted with castles and monuments recalling the time when the Christian armies marched south through this region, reconquering land from the Moors. This is where you will find the holy trinity of great Portuguese churches, at Alcobaça, Batalha and Tomar, as well as the moving modern shrine at Fátima, attracting pilgrims from across the Catholic world.

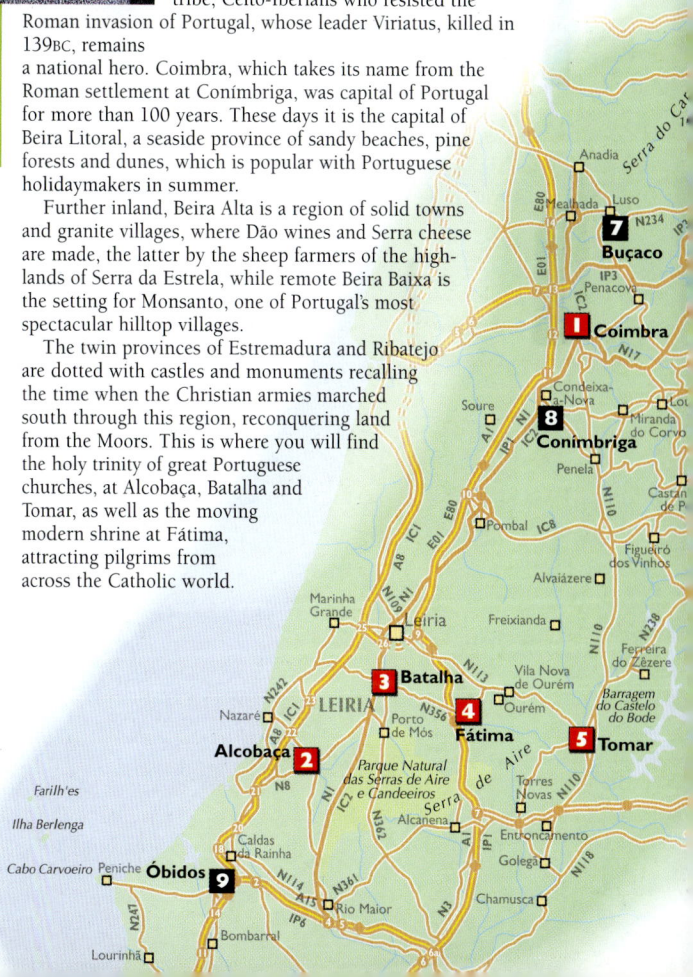

Left: A villager in Monsanto

Above: Serra da Estrela, the rooftop of Portugal

Page 101: The cloisters of the Convento do Cristo, Tomar

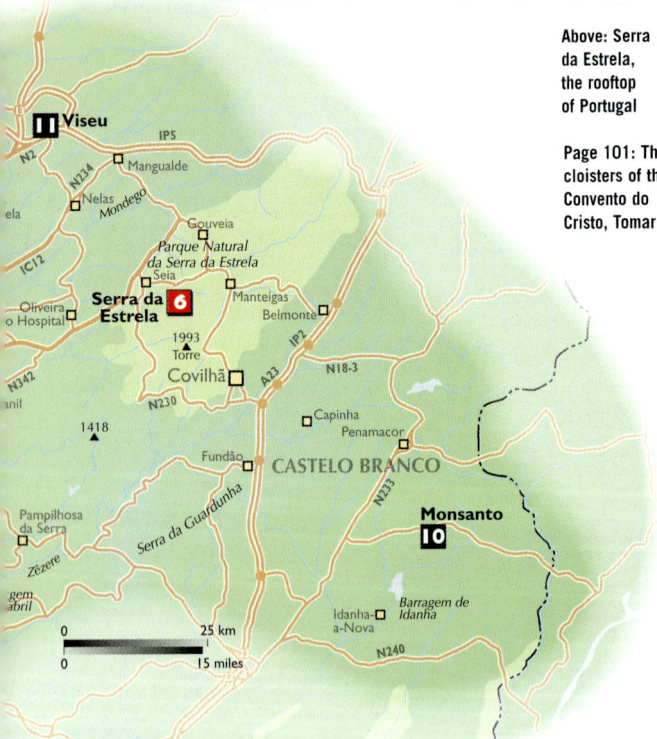

★ Don't Miss

At Your Leisure

From historic churches and Roman remains to majestic mountain heights and Coimbra's venerable university, central Portugal has some varied highlights.

Central Portugal in Four Days

Day One

Morning

Start by exploring ⒈Coimbra (► 106–109) on foot. Climb the hill to the university (right) to visit the library, chapel and graduation halls, then drop down through the old town, passing the old cathedral on the way to the church of Santa Cruz. Have lunch in the neighbouring Café Santa Cruz (► 124).

Afternoon and Evening

Cross the river and drive south on the N1 to see the Roman remains at ⒏Conímbriga (► 121). Continue on this road as far as Leiria, then pick up the A8/IC1 motorway to ⒐Óbidos (below; ► 121). Book ahead to stay in the old castle, now a *pousada* (► 124) and enjoy the sunset walk around the walls.

Day Two

Morning

Spend some time in Óbidos, admiring its whitewashed houses and views, then go north on the A8/IC1 and take the exit to **2 Alcobaça** (➤ 110–111) to visit the monastery and wine museum before lunch.

Afternoon and Evening

From Alcobaça it is a short drive to the superb abbey of **3 Batalha** (Capela do Fundador, right; ➤ 112–113). Afterwards, for a complete contrast, head east on the N356 to the sanctuary at **4 Fátima** (➤ 114–115). Stay at the *pousada* in the walled town of Ourém, 10km (6 miles) from Fátima (➤ 123). Climb the hill to the castle for views across the plain.

Day Three

Morning

Drive to **5 Tomar** (➤ 116–118) to visit the Templar church-fortress, then wander down to the town centre to see Portugal's oldest synagogue before enjoying lunch by the river.

Afternoon and Evening

You need to allow three hours for the drive to the **6 Serra da Estrela** (below; ➤ 119–120). Go east on the IP6 and then north on the IP2, bypassing Castelo Branco or taking a diversion to the hilltop village of **10 Monsanto** (➤ 122). If you are getting a taste for *pousadas*, stay at Pousada de São Lourenço (tel: 275 980 050), in a stone-built house above Manteigas with views over the Zêzere Valley. Alternatively, stay outside the natural park at Solar de Alarcão in Guarda (➤ 123) and eat at one of the restaurants along Rua Francisco dos Passos, which specialise in hearty mountain cuisine (➤ 125).

Day Four

Spend a full day exploring the mountains. Visit the information centre in Manteigas for walking maps, then take a picnic to Poço do Inferno (➤ 119). If you don't want to walk, drive the circuit from Penhas da Saúde (➤ 119) to Torre (➤ 120) for spectacular views of the high sierra.

⬤ Coimbra

Portugal's oldest university sits on the crown of a hill overlooking the River Mondego. With historic buildings and churches, parks and gardens, and a lively student feel, Coimbra is one of the most enjoyable Portuguese cities in which to spend some of your time.

The first king of Portugal, Afonso Henriques, moved the capital here from Guimarães, but it was his successor, Dom Dinis, who founded the university that is today synonymous with Coimbra. Established in 1290 by papal decree to teach medicine, arts and law, the university moved back and forth between Lisbon and Coimbra before settling in João III's royal palace at Coimbra in 1537. Despite clinging to traditions, the students here are known for their liberal outlook. During the 20th century, Coimbra was a focus for radical opposition to the Salazar régime.

Below: Cross the water for the best views of Coimbra

Across the River

Walk across Ponte de Santa Clara for the best view of the old town and the university buildings rising above the river. On the south bank, the Gothic convent of **Santa Clara-a-Velha**, where Inês de Castro (➤ 110–111) once lived, has been sinking into the sand for centuries but is slowly being recovered and stands behind a new riverside park. Near here is **Portugal dos Pequenitos** (Rossio de Santa Clara, tel: 239 801 170; Mar–May, 16 to 30 Sep 9–7; Jun to 15 Sep 9–8; Feb, Oct–Dec 10–5; moderate), an enjoyable but politically dated theme park where children can clamber over miniature models of Portuguese houses and buildings from Portugal's former colonies. Behind the park, the peaceful gardens of **Quinta das Lágrimas** (Villa of Tears) mark the spot where Inês de Castro was murdered after a tryst with Dom Pedro at the Fonte dos Amores (Lovers' Spring). The palace at the centre of the gardens is now a luxury hotel (➤ 123).

Left: The
venerable
Coimbra
university

Below: The
library has
shelf upon
shelf of
ancient tomes

University

The university is in the
upper town, on the summit
of Alcáçova hill. Despite
the steep gradients, Coimbra
is best explored on foot and
it is easiest to start by climbing to the top of the hill and
working your way back down.

From the river, head for the **Pátio das Escolas**. This handsome quadrangle, with buildings on three sides and a terrace
overlooking the Mondego, is at the heart of the old university.
A statue of João III stands at the centre and in one corner is a
baroque bell-tower.

You can visit most of the buildings, but you need a ticket
to enter the **Biblioteca Joanina** (library) and **Sala dos
Capelos** (ceremonial hall). The ticket office for both of these
is in the main university building, at the left end of the colon-
naded walkway on the north side of Pátio das Escolas. The
baroque library, named after its benefactor, João V, is the main
attraction, decorated in gilded wood and lacquered in green,
red and gold. The Sala dos Capelos, where investitures and
degree ceremonies take place, occupies the grand hall of the
Manueline palace, with a panelled ceiling and portraits of
Portuguese monarchs.

A corridor, offering superb views over the Coimbra rooftops,
leads to the private examination hall, with a painted ceiling,
tiled walls and portraits of former rectors.

On the east side of the square, the **Porta Férrea** (iron gate),
built in 1634, contains carved figures representing the original
faculties and statues of Dom Dinis and João III. This leads to
the modern university buildings, including the faculties of
medicine, science and technology. Most of these date from the

1960s, when the dictator António Salazar, a former economics professor at Coimbra, destroyed Manueline and Renaissance buildings in the name of modernisation.

Two Cathedrals

From the statue of Dom Dinis, steps lead down to **Praça da República**, with its student cafés. Behind the aqueduct, is the **Jardim Botânico** (tel: 239 855 233, Mon–Fri 9–5:30, Sat, Sun only if booked in advance, gardens: free, greenhouses: inexpensive), Portugal's largest botanical garden.

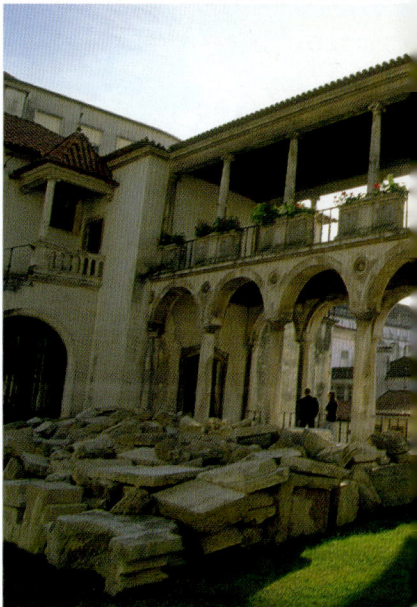

Go back up the steps and turn right to explore the rest of the upper town. The **Sé Nova** (New Cathedral) was actually built in 1598 and includes the choir stalls and font from the old cathedral. Just down the hill, the **Museu Nacional Machado de Castro**, named after a famous Coimbra sculptor, is housed in the 16th-century bishops' palace. It includes medieval painting and sculpture and the cryptoporticus in the basement, a series of underground galleries and part of the old Roman forum.

Further downhill, the **Sé Velha** (Old Cathedral) is a Romanesque church-fortress on the site of the first cathedral in Portugal. Of interest here are the 13th-century cloisters and the Hispano-Arab tiles covering the walls.

Mosteiro de Santa Cruz

From here you can walk down to **Arco de Almedina**, the 12th-century gateway to the city.

Go through the arch and turn right along a busy pedestrian street to reach the **Mosteiro de Santa Cruz**. Many of the leading artists of the Coimbra school, such as Jean de Rouen, worked on pieces for the monastery in the 16th century. The Renaissance porch, complete with trumpet-ing angels over a double doorway, is by Diogo de Castilho and Nicolas Chanterène, who also designed the pulpit and was responsible for the tombs of Portugal's first kings, Afonso Henriques and his son, Sancho I, behind the high altar. Buy a ticket to visit the **Sala do Capítulo** (chapter

Left: A statue of a medieval knight in the Museu Nacional Machado de Castro

house) by Diogo de Boytac, with its fine Manueline ceiling, and the beautiful **Claustro do Silêncio** (Cloister of Silence), one of the purest examples of Manueline art.

Below: The courtyard at the Museu Nacional Machado de Castro

Turn left on coming out of the church to return to the river at Largo da Portagem.

TAKING A BREAK

Try the **trendy student cafés** around Praça da República. **Trovador** (➤ 125), by the Sé Velha, is good for lunch.

✚ 198 B1

Tourist Information Centre
✉ Largo Dom Dinis ☎ 239 832 591

Universidade Velha (Biblioteca Joanina and Sala dos Capelos)
✉ Paço das Escolas ☎ 239 859 843
🕐 Apr–Oct 8-30–7 (tickets), 9–7:30 (visits); Nov–Mar 9:30–5 (tickets), 10–5:30 (visits) 💶 Moderate

Museu Machado de Castro
✉ Largo Dr José Rodrigues ☎ www.ipmuseus.pt 🕐 Closed until 2009

Sé Velha
✉ Largo da Sé Velha ☎ 239 825 273
🕐 Sat, Mon–Thu 10–1, 2–6, Fri 10–1, Sun only for services 💶 Church free, cloisters inexpensive

Mosteiro de Santa Cruz
✉ Praça 8 de Maio ☎ 239 822 941
🕐 Mon–Sat 9–noon, 2–5, Sun 4–5
💶 Church free, cloisters inexpensive

COIMBRA: INSIDE INFO

Top tips Parking in central Coimbra is difficult – it is generally easier to park across the river and walk across Ponte de Santa Clara.
• To avoid the climb to the university, take **tram No 1** from Largo da Portagem.
• In summer there are **river trips** from a jetty in the park beside the Santa Clara bridge on the north bank.
• Look out for the chance to hear the **Coimbra version of** *fado*, sung by students in long black capes and less melancholy than its Lisbon counterpart. You are mostly likely to hear this in bars and restaurants and in the streets during student festivities. Or try to catch it at Trovador (➤ 125) or Diligência (➤ 126).

Hidden gem Following signs from Praça Dom Dinis, walk upstairs and ring the bell to be let into the **Museu Académico** (tel: 239 827 396, Mon–Fri 10–12:30, 2–5, inexpensive), with costumes, photos and artefacts describing university traditions such as *bedels* (beadles), *repúblicas* (communally run student houses) and the Queima das Fitas (Burning of the Ribbons) in May.

2 Alcobaça

The largest church in Portugal is a supreme example of Gothic architecture and would be worth a visit to Alcobaça for the building alone. What makes it even more special is that the church has become a shrine to one of the most tragic love stories in Portuguese history.

The **Mosteiro de Santa Maria** (more commonly known as the Mosteiro de Alcobaça) was founded by Afonso Henriques in 1153 to give thanks for victory over the Moors at Santarém. The baroque façade dates from the 18th century, but once you are inside everything is pure Gothic. Unlike many Portuguese churches, which drip with ornamental detail, the clean lines and soaring columns of the central nave create a simple, harmonious feel. The only exception to the almost complete absence of decoration is the richly sculpted sacristy portal behind the high altar, designed by João de Castilho in 16th-century Manueline style and arrayed in floral motifs.

The **tombs of Dom Pedro I and Inês de Castro**, richly carved in limestone with scenes from the Bible and the lives of Pedro and Inês (► box), face one another across the aisle.

Opposite: The tomb of Dom Pedro

Below: The baroque façade of the monastery at Alcobaça

ALCOBAÇA: INSIDE INFO

Top tip Climb the hill to the ruined castle above the town for the **best views** of the monastery.

In more depth The **Museu Nacional de Vinho** (on the road to Batalha; tel: 262 582 222; Mon–Fri 9–12, 2–5; inexpensive) explains the history of wine making for which the region is famous and has a fascinating collection of old wine bottles, wine-making equipment and decorative posters.

The reclining figure of Inês de Castro is supported by six angels, while the dead, including her assassins, are thrown into hell at her feet. On Pedro's orders, the lovers were buried foot to foot, so that they could feast their eyes on one another when they rise on the day of judgement. The tombs are inscribed with the motto *Até ao fim do mundo* ("Until the end of the world").

The entrance to the cloisters is through the **Sala dos Reis**, with statues of Portuguese kings carved by the monks and tiled walls telling the story of the monastery. The peaceful **Claustro de Silêncio**, added in the 14th century by Dom Dinis, has orange trees at the centre and a lovely Renaissance *lavabo* where the monks would wash their hands before entering the refectory.

Alongside here are the **kitchens**, once famed for the extravagance of their banquets, with huge conical chimneys, and a stream that flowed straight from the River Alcôa, providing a plentiful supply of fish. A staircase from the cloister leads to the 13th-century dormitory.

TAKING A BREAK

Café Dom Pedro, across the square from the monastery, has snacks such as *bifanas* (roast pork sandwiches) and *pregos* (steak sandwiches).

➕ 200 B4

Mosteiro de Santa Maria
☎ 262 505 120; www.ippar.pt ⏰ Daily 9–5, Oct–Mar; daily 9–7, rest of year 💶 Church free, cloisters moderate

Dom Pedro I and Inês de Castro

Visitors crowd into the transept to see the tombs of Dom Pedro I and his lover, Inês de Castro. Inês was lady-in-waiting to Pedro's wife, Constanza of Castile, but Pedro's father, Afonso IV, had her banished from court to put an end to the affair. After Constanza died, Inês returned to live with Pedro at Coimbra, where she was murdered in 1355 on the orders of Afonso IV who feared Spanish influence over the Portuguese throne. Two years later, when Pedro assumed the throne, he wreaked revenge on the killers by having their hearts torn out and eating them himself. He also revealed that he and Inês had been secretly married at Bragança; her corpse was exhumed and he ordered the court to pay homage to their dead queen by kissing her decomposed hand.

3 Batalha

As you round a corner on the busy N1, a great church comes into view, with pinnacles, turrets and flying buttresses in honey-coloured limestone. This is Batalha (Battle Abbey), a masterpiece of Gothic architecture that has become a symbol of Portuguese history and of independence from Spain.

The **Mosteiro de Santa Maria da Vitória**, commonly known as the Mosteiro da Batalha (Abbey of the Battle), was built to celebrate the Portuguese victory over the Spanish at the Battle of Aljubarrota in 1385. Three years after King João I's victory work on the abbey began.

Admire the worn exterior of the abbey and the **statue of Nuno Álvares Pereira** (▶ box opposite) on horseback on the square in front of the church. The main portal, beneath a Gothic window, features carved statues of Christ and the apostles, together with angels, saints and João I's coat of arms. The long, tall nave is beautifully simple, with Gothic pillars and vaulting and 16th-century stained glass.

Immediately to the right as you enter is the **Capela do Fundador** (Founder's Chapel), where João I and his wife, Philippa of Lancaster, are buried beneath an octagonal lantern, their tombs carved with effigies of the couple lying hand in hand. Also buried here are their four

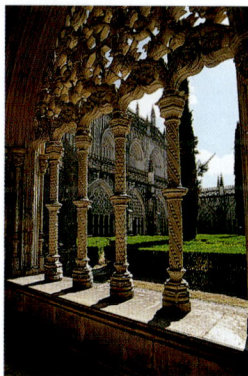

The Battle of Aljubarrota

King Fernando I of Portugal died in 1383 without leaving a male heir. King Juan I of Castile claimed the throne from his marriage to King Fernando's daugher, Beatriz, but was opposed by Fernando's illegitimate half-brother, João I. Heavily outnumbered by Spanish troops, João promised to build a magnificent church to the Virgin if he was successful, and with the help of his faithful lieutenant Nuno Álvares Pereira, and 500 English archers supplied by King Richard II, his supporters won the day. João's victory ushered in a new era for Portugal, with 200 years of independence under the rule of the House of Avis.

younger sons, including Henry the Navigator.

The original **Claustro Real** (Royal Cloister) was embellished with rich Manueline tracery by Diogo de Boytac, architect of the monastery at Belém (▶ 48). All the main symbols of Manueline art are here, including armillary spheres, crosses of Christ, twisted branches and exotic foliage.

On one side of the cloister, the **Sala do Capítulo** (chapter house) contains Portugal's two Unknown Soldiers, one from World War I and the other a victim of Portugal's wars in Africa. They are permanently watched over by military guards. A museum dedicated to them is in the former refectory.

A second cloister leads to the **Capelas Imperfeitas** (Unfinished Chapels), begun by João I's eldest son Dom Duarte as a royal mausoleum and containing the tombs of Duarte and his queen, Leonor of Aragón. The chapels, which can also be reached from behind the main abbey, are perhaps the highlight of the entire complex, with an Indian-inspired Manueline portal and a roofless octagonal rotunda.

Left: The church is full of space and light

Below left: Manueline tracery can be seen in the Claustro Real

TAKING A BREAK

There are a few cafés on the square behind the abbey, and the **Estalagem Mestre Afonso Domingues** (next to the abbey, tel: 244 765 260) has Portuguese food.

➕ 200 B4

Right: Batalha, built to celebrate victory in battle

Mosteiro de Batalha
☎ 244 765 497 ◉ Apr–Sep daily 9–6; Oct–Mar 9–5 ⛪ Church free, cloisters moderate

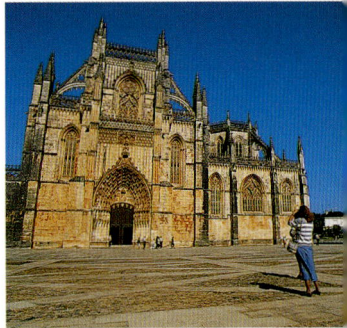

4 Fátima

The so-called "altar of Portugal", Fátima is Portugal's greatest Roman Catholic shrine. The story of what happened to three shepherd children in 1917 has moved millions, and made the town one of the biggest centres of pilgrimage in the Roman Catholic world.

The Vision

It was on 13 May, 1917 that the Virgin Mary appeared in an oak tree to 10-year-old Lúcia dos Santos and her cousins Jacinta and Francisco as they were tending their family's sheep in the village of Cova da Iria, near Fátima. The children spoke of a lady "brighter than the sun" who called them to return at the same time each month for six months. Although their story was greeted with much scepticism, the children returned and the visions continued.

On the final occasion, 13 October, a crowd of 70,000 people witnessed the sun dancing in the sky like a ball of fire and countless miracles occurred – the blind could see, the sick were cured and the lame walked.

On the same day, the Virgin revealed to Lúcia the "three secrets of Fátima", which are said to have foretold World War II, Russian communism and the assassination of a pope.

The Children

Jacinta and Francisco died of pneumonia in 1920, but Lúcia entered a Carmelite convent in Coimbra in 1928, where she died in 2005, age 97. Jacinta and Francisco, who are buried inside the basilica, were beatified in 1989 by Pope John Paul II, the first step on the path to sainthood.

The Basilica

A vast, neo-classical basilica was completed in 1953, and accommodates the pilgrims who flock here. The esplanade in front of the basilica can hold a million people and is

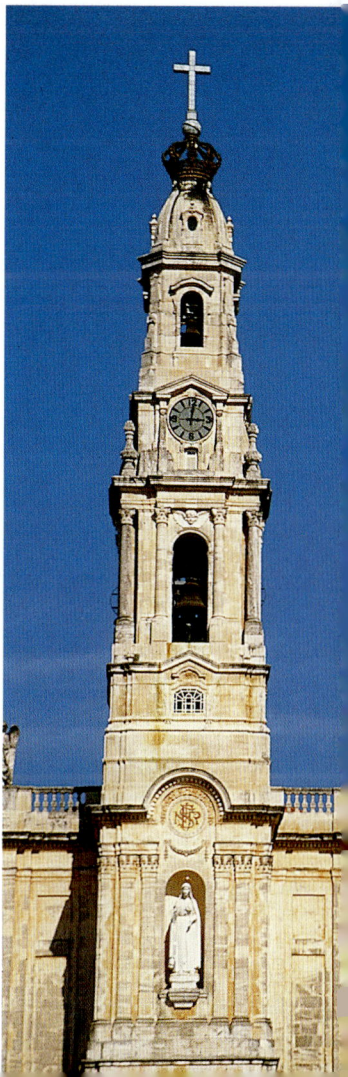

Far left: The three children of Fátima

Centre: A giant statue of Christ stands in front of the basilica

Left: The Monument to the Pilgrims, on a round-about at the edge of town

Below: Pilgrims light candles for Our Lady of Fátima

twice the size of St Peter's Square in Rome. In a corner of the square stands the **Capela das Aparicões** (Chapel of the Apparitions), on the site of the original visions, where pilgrims pray and light candles to a statue of the Virgin.

Visits and pilgrimages to Fátima take place all year, and particularly on 13 May and 13 October, when millions come here, many of them making their way to the basilica on their knees.

TAKING A BREAK

The *pousada* at Ourém (► 123), built on a hilltop 10km (6 miles) northeast of Fátima, makes a good night's stop and there are bars selling the local *ginja* (cherry brandy).

✚ 200 C4

Tourist Information Centre
✉ Avenida Dom José Alves Correia da Silva ☎ 249 531 139

FÁTIMA: INSIDE INFO

Top tips From Easter to October there are **candlelit processions** in front of the basilica at 9:30 each evening. The procession is largest on 12th of the month.
• You should be **silent** around the basilica and the Chapel of the Apparitions.

In more depth You can visit the village of **Aljustrel**, outside Fátima, to see the Casa Museu de Aljustrel where Lúcia dos Santos grew up, and the ethnographic museum next door (tel: 249 532 828, May–Oct Mon, Wed–Fri 10–1, 3–7, Sat–Sun 10–1, 2–7; Nov–Apr Mon, Wed–Fri 10–1, 2:30–7, Sat–Sun 9:30–1, 2:30–6; house free, museum inexpensive).

5 Tomar

The third in the trio of medieval churches, the Convento de Cristo stands in the grounds of a castle on a wooded slope overlooking Tomar. Once a powerful military and religious capital, Tomar is now a peaceful town on the banks of the River Nabão and makes a pleasant base for exploring the surrounding area.

Below and bottom: The Convento de Cristo contains many hidden corners, such as this staircase which leads to the cloister roof

The Monastery

The Knights Templar castle dominates the town. Within its walls stands the **Convento de Cristo**, one of Portugal's Unesco World Heritage Sites. It was begun in 1160 but has Gothic and Manueline additions.

The tour of the monastery begins in a pair of cloisters, **Claustro da Lavagem** and **Claustro do Cemitério**, both added by Henry the Navigator, whose ruined palace can be seen through the arches.

Next you come to the **Charola** (or Rotunda), the spiritual heart of the complex, a 12th-century round church that was modelled on the Holy Sepulchre of Jerusalem, with an octagonal chapel where the knights are reputed to have held services on horseback. The columns are richly painted with 16th-century frescoes. The Charola now forms the eastern end of a Manueline church, built under the reign of Manuel I.

From here you move into the **Claustro Principal** (Great Cloister), added in 1557 in neo-classical and Renaissance style. Climb onto the roof for the best views of the **great western window** by Diogo de Arruda and the **south portal** by João de Castilho, two of the most sumptuous examples of Manueline art in Portugal. The window in particular contains all the familiar symbols

of the Manueline era, including anchors, cables, twisted ropes, an armillary sphere and the Cross of the Knights of Christ. From here you can wander along corridors of monks' cells and step onto the rooftop terrace before finishing with the walkway around the castle walls.

The Town

The old town, to the west of the river, is centred around the elegant **Praça da República**, where a statue of Gualdim Pais stands in front of the town hall. On one side of the square, the church of **São João Baptista** has an elegant Manueline portal and a pulpit carved with the Templar cross and the royal coat of arms.

Just south is the oldest surviving **synagogue** in Portugal, lovingly maintained by one of two remaining Jewish families in Tomar. Built around 1430, and abandoned after the expulsion of the Jews in 1497, it has been used as a prison, chapel, hayloft and cellar, but is now a museum containing 13th- and 14th-century Jewish tombstones as well as sacred items donated by members of Jewish communities across the world.

Tomar's other museum, **Museu dos Fósforos**, is housed in a wing of a 17th-century convent. An eccentric display features more than 40,000 matchboxes, the largest collection in Europe, beginning with Queen Elizabeth II's coronation in 1953

The Knights and Tomar

Tomar was founded in 1157 by Gualdim Pais, the first Grand Master of the Knights Templar of Portugal, a military force with powerful religious overtones. The town was created on land donated by Afonso Henriques in return for the knights' help in the reconquest of Portugal from the Moors. Tomar subsequently became the knights' base. In 1314 the order was deemed too powerful and was suppressed by Pope Clement V, but it was reconstituted in Portugal by Dom Dinis under the name the Knights of Christ. Henry the Navigator became "governor" in the 15th century and tapped the order's wealth to fund his explorations, while the Knights of Christ were given spiritual control over all Portuguese conquests.

and continuing with Portuguese politicians, Spanish bullfighters and Japanese topless models.

A warren of narrow streets leads down to the River Nabão, where the shady Parque do Mouchão, on an island in the middle of the river, has open-air cafés and a waterwheel, said to date from Roman times.

TAKING A BREAK

Churrasqueira Mendes (behind the market, tel: 249 315 393, daily 8–3), serves huge portions of barbecued chicken and pork at wooden tables. **Bela Vista** (➤ 125), by the old bridge, is another option.

✚ 200 C4

Tourist Information Centre
✉ Avenida Dr Cândido Madureira ☎ 249 329 000; www.rttemplarios.pt

Convento de Cristo
✉ 15-minute walk above the town ☎ 249 313 481 🕐 Sun 9–2; Oct–May Mon–Sat 9–5; Jun–Sep Mon–Sat 9–6 💷 Moderate

Sinagoga
✉ Rua Dr Joaquim Jacinto 73 ☎ 249 322 427 🕐 Daily 10–1, 2–6 💷 Free

Museu dos Fósforos
✉ Varzea Grande ☎ 249 329 829 🕐 Daily 10–5 💷 Free

TOMAR: INSIDE INFO

Top tip Come here on Friday when the riverbanks are taken over by a **large market**, with fresh food and flowers on the east bank, and clothes, shoes and household goods on the west bank.

Hidden gem Cross the Ponte Velha (Old Bridge) to reach the chapel **of Santa Iria** (Tue–Sun 10–6, free), Tomar's patron saint, a young nun who was murdered and thrown into the river after a 7th-century feud between two rival suitors, a nobleman and a monk. One gave her a potion to make her appear pregnant and the other killed her in a fit of rage. The church, built in the 16th century, features a stone-carved calvary, a coffered painted ceiling and rich 17th-century *azulejos*.

In more depth Pick up the series of tourist office leaflets detailing **historical walks**, each of which is designed to last a leisurely half day.

6 Serra da Estrela

Rocky hillsides are carved up by glacial valleys in the Serra da Estrela, Portugal's highest mountain range. In summer you can walk across carpets of scented grasses and wild flowers, and in winter the peaks are covered in snow. Much of the area has been designated a natural park.

Opposite: Manueline carving in Tomar

The Serra da Estrela forms a 60km by 30km (37 miles by 19 miles) range, with a summit of 1,993m (6,537 feet). This is a land of hardy shepherds, long-horned sheep and related industries, cheese-making and wool. The mainstays of the economy are farming and forestry, though outdoor tourism is becoming ever more important. In winter, there is skiing and hunting for partridge, rabbit and wild boar; in summer there is trout fishing in the rivers and walking in the hills.

There is good access to the mountains from Covilhã, a busy textile town to the south of the natural park. From here, the N339 climbs through **Penhas da Saúde**, Portugal's only ski resort, on its way to the high sierra. This is a good starting point for a circular tour, allowing at least half a day. Soon after Penhas da Saúde, turn right on the N338 for a beautiful drive along the Zêzere Valley, a deep glacial gorge formed during the Ice Age.

Top right: Serra cheese, *queijo da Serra*

Below: The glacial scenery of the Zêzere Gorge

All along the valley, there are distant views of **Manteigas**, the small town at the centre of the park. Here you can pick up information on walking and hiking in the mountains, including the half-day circular walk from Manteigas to the **Poço do Inferno** ("Hell's Well") waterfall.

From Manteigas you can follow the twisting N232 towards Gouveia, climbing ever higher with wonderful views over the

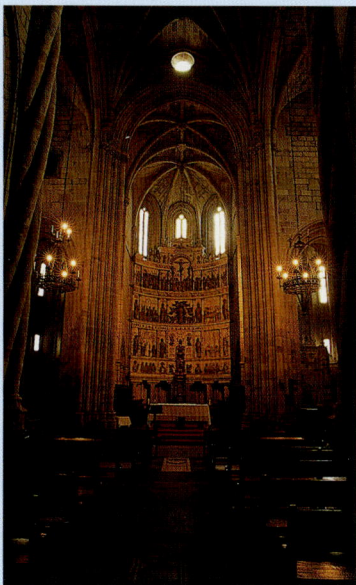

Above: The cathedral of Guarda

Zêzere Valley. You pass a *pousada* and the source of the River Mondego, which empties into the sea near Coimbra. The scenery here is stunning, with weird rock formations of wind-sculpted granite such as the Cabeça do Velho (Old Man's Head).

A minor road leads to **Sabugueiro**, Portugal's highest village, where cheese, ham, sausages and woollen blankets are on sale. Turn left on the N339 for the slow climb to **Torre**. The highest mountain in Portugal (1,993m/6,537 feet) takes its name from the stone tower erected here in the 19th century so that the peak would top 2,000m (6,560 feet). On winter weekends, families flock here to go sledging in the snow. On the way down to Penhas da Saúde, look out for the statue of **Nossa Senhora da Boa Estrela**, carved into a niche in the rock.

Two towns that make good bases for visiting the park are **Guarda**, the highest town in Portugal (1,056m/3,464 feet), with a 14th-century Gothic cathedral, and **Belmonte**, birthplace of the explorer Pedro Álvares Cabral, who discovered Brazil. Belmonte was once home to a large population of *marranos* (Jews who fled here after their expulsion from Portugal in 1497) and it still has a large Jewish community.

TAKING A BREAK

There are **cafés** in all the main villages offering *queijo da serra*, sandwiches made with the local cheese.

✚ 198 C1/D1

Park Tourist Information Office
✉ Rua 1 de Maio, Manteigas ☎ 275 980 060; www.icn.pt

SERRA DA ESTRELA: INSIDE INFO

Top tips Try *queijo da serra*, a strong cheese made from sheep's milk and curdled with thistle flowers. The runny, ripe cheese, usually scooped out with a spoon, is at its best in winter.
• These are serious mountains and they need to be **treated with respect**. The weather can change quickly – it can be sunny in Manteigas while Torre is obscured in mist, or you might drive through the mist to emerge in bright sunshine above the clouds. Be prepared for anything, even in summer, and allow plenty of time.

At Your Leisure

7 Buçaco

Buçaco is a place where you can still believe in fairies. The walled **Mata Nacional** (National Forest) is a magical landscape of sylvan glades and cedar-scented woods. Once a monastic retreat from which women were banned by papal decree, the forest is dotted with fountains, hermitages and shady walks. At the centre is the bizarre neo-Manueline **Buçaco Palace**, designed as a royal hunting lodge and now one of Portugal's top hotels (► 124). The Carmelite convent next door has cork-lined cells and mosaic walls with a plaque recalling the battle of Buçaco, when the Duke of Wellington spent a night in the convent after his victory over Napoleonic troops in 1810.

➕ 198 B1
Mosteiro dos Carmelitas
☎ 231 939 226 🕐 Tue–Sun 9–12:30, 2–5:30. Closed Sun Oct–May
💰 Inexpensive

8 Conímbriga

The best-preserved Roman remains in Portugal are situated 15km (9 miles) south of Coimbra. The site stands on either side of the old Roman road from Lisbon to Braga, parts of which are still visible. Some of the houses have detailed mosaics, with images of birds, fish, horses and dragons. Note the **Casa das Fontes**, a 2nd-century villa with ornamental gardens and pools. The excavations here have uncovered evidence of a forum, aqueduct, shops, taverns and public baths. A museum contains archaeological finds, some of which date from a Celto-Iberian settlement before the arrival of the Romans in the 1st century BC.

➕ 200 C5 ✉ Condeixa-a-Nova ☎ 239 941 177; www.conimbriga.pt 🕐 Jun–Sep daily 9–8 (museum Tue–Sun 9–8); Oct–May daily 10–6 (museum Tue–Sun 10–6) 💰 Moderate (Sun 9–1 free)

9 Óbidos

This walled town of whitewashed houses was traditionally given as a wedding gift by the Portuguese kings to their queens, a custom begun by Dom Dinis for Isabel of Aragón in 1282 and continued for 600 years. **Porta de Vila**, the gateway to the town, is lined with 18th-century tiles and leads to **Rua Direita**, the main street, with its souvenir shops and *ginja* (cherry brandy) bars. Halfway

What to Do With the Kids

• **Portugal dos Pequenitos**, Coimbra (► 106), a theme park of Portugal in miniature.
• **Museu dos Fósforos**, Tomar (► 117), a mad display of 40,000 matchboxes.
• **Forest walks** in Buçaco (► above), which occupies a special place in the hearts of the Portuguese.
• The beaches of the **Costa da Prata**, the coastline running along Central Portugal.

up the street, the church of **Santa Maria** has *azulejo* walls and there is a striking Manueline pillory in the church square. The **castle**, at the top of town, was converted into a royal palace in the 16th century and is now one of Portugal's finest *pousadas* the **Pousada do Castelo** (▶124). From here, climb onto the ramparts to make a circuit of the walls, which should take around 45 minutes.

✚ 200 B4

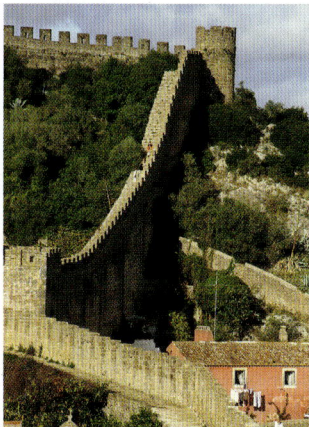

Above: You can walk around the walls at Óbidos

🔟 Monsanto

One of the oldest settlements in Portugal, inhabited in pre-Roman times, Monsanto is perched on the side of Monte Santo (Sacred Mountain), with houses built into the mountainside between huge granite boulders. Climb to the **ruined castle**, built in the 12th century, for magnificent views stretching as far as the Serra da Estrela. On 3 May during the Festa das Cruzes, the younger village women throw flowers from the ramparts in memory of a famous

siege when the starving inhabitants threw their last calf from the castle walls in a successful attempt to fool their attackers into thinking that they were able to last out for a long time. There are a few signs of tourist development – a small *estalagem*, a couple of restaurants and craft shops – but mostly life goes on as it always has in this remote, quintessential hilltop village.

✚ 201 F5

🔟 Viseu

The capital of the Beira Alta and the Dão wine region, Viseu is an attractive town. At the heart of the old town is **Largo da Sé**, with two churches facing one another across the square. The larger and more imposing façade is that of the baroque church of Misericórdia; the Sé (cathedral) has lovely Renaissance cloisters and a Manueline knotted ceiling.

The main attraction is the **Museu de Grão Vasco**, named after Vasco Fernandes (1480–1543), a leading figure in the 16th-century Viseu school of painting. It includes his painting, *St Peter Enthroned*.

✚ 198 C2

Tourist Information Office
✉ Avenida Calouste Gulbenkian
☎ 232 420 950; www.cm-viseu.pt

Museu de Grão Vasco
✉ Paço dos Três Escalões ☎ 232 422 049; www.ipmuseus.pt 🕐 Tue 2–6, Wed–Sun 10–6 💰 Moderate (Sun 9:30–12:30 free)

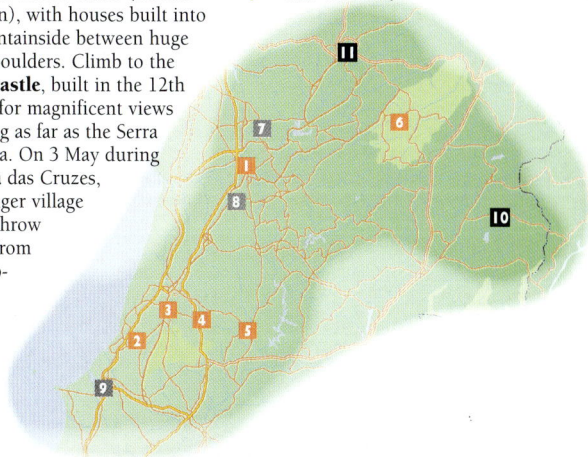

Where to... Stay

Prices

Expect to pay for a double room with bathroom in high season

€ = under €60 €€ = €60–€120 €€€ = €121–€180 €€€€ = over €180

Casa Pombal €

By the university and commanding views across the rooftops to the river, this guesthouse is a delightful place to stay. You feel as though you are staying at one of the famous *repúblicas* or student houses. A steep staircase leads to a number of antiquated but very comfortable rooms, some with bathrooms. A hearty Dutch-style breakfast (eggs, cheese, cold meats and bread) is served in the dining room where delicious meals can be prepared to order.

✚ 198 B1 ☒ Rua das Flores 18
☎ 239 835 175, fax: 239 821 548;
www.casapombal.com

Quinta das Lágrimas €€€–€€€€

Famous for having received the Duke of Wellington in 1808, this luxurious hotel is set in 10 hectares (25 acres) of wooded parkland. In addition to a pool, luxury spa and tennis courts there's a golf academy with a 9-hole pitch-and-putt and driving range. Inside the main house the décor is elegant and the bedrooms are huge, in the modern spa wing rooms are minimalist-chic. Meals are served in the Arcadas da Capela restaurant, and the cellar offers more than 200 vintages.

✚ 198 B1 ☒ Rua António Augusto
Gonçalves, Santa Clara ☎ 239 802
380, fax: 239 441 695;
www.quintadaslagrimas.pt

Pousada Conde de Ourém €€–€€€

This charming modern *pousada*, converted from medieval houses, is a good base from which to visit Fátima and Tomar. Climb to the castle for distant views of Fátima. Rooms are spacious and comfortable, and there is a pool open in summer. Spend the evening in the *pousada's* restaurant enjoying local specialities like fried rabbit with cabbage "Conde de Ourém" and a buffet of cheeses and desserts.

✚ 200 C4 ☒ Largo João Manso
☎ 249 540 920; **www.pousadas.pt**

Estalagem de Santa Iria €–€€

As Tomar's *pousada* is a long way out of town, this is the best choice, especially if charm and tranquillity are your criteria. Even the early 20th-century writer Somerset Maugham has signed the visitors'

book. This unpretentious inn, with 14 bright, spacious rooms, is idyllically located on a wooded island in the middle of the town. The dining room serves delicious dishes.

✚ 200 C4 ☒ Parque do Mouchão
☎ 249 313 326, fax: 249 321 238;
www.estalagemiria.com

Solar de Alarcão €€

This 17th-century granite manor house just inside the city ramparts enjoys fabulous views across to the back of the squat cathedral. The interior courtyard is overlooked by an impressive *loggia*. The three double bedrooms, each with its own bathroom, are full of character and extremely comfortable, with period furnishings. Breakfasts are copious, just the thing if you're setting off into the Serra da Estrela. Book ahead in the high season.

✚ 199 D2 ☒ Rua Dom Miguel de
Alarcão 25 ☎ 271 211 275, fax: 271
214 392

Where to...
Eat and Drink

Prices

Expect to pay per person for a three-course à la carte meal, excluding drinks and tips
€ = under €12 €€ = €12–€24 €€€ = €25–€36 €€€€ = over €36

COIMBRA AND ENVIRONS

Café Santa Cruz €

University students keep this wonderfully atmospheric café-bar alive, especially in the evening. It's housed in the former sacristy of the 16th-century Igreja Santa Cruz. Coffee, wine and beer are served with inexpensive snacks in a fabulous vaulted room – stone walls, leather benches and a generally decadent appearance. The *esplanada* (terrace) is packed out in summer.

🚏 Praça 8 de Maio
☎ 239 833 617 🕐 Mon–Sat
7am–11:30pm (1:30am in summer)

A Cozinha €

Rua das Azeiteiras is a quiet narrow alleyway in the Baixa, lined with interesting traditional eateries that it's hard to choose between. This place, with its mock *azulejos* jostling for space with an almost clinical décor, is a favourite with locals. *Chanfana* (goat in a wine sauce) and *carne de porco à dente-jana* (pork simmered with clams and fresh coriander), are typical dishes, served in huge helpings (this is definitely a place to ask for *meia dose* – half portions), along with decent house wine, dished up by no-nonsense staff and with the

---

BUÇACO

Hotel Palace do Bussaco €€€€

The Buçaco Forest (► 121), where Napoleon suffered a major defeat in the Peninsular Wars, benefits from a microclimate and is a holy place, under papal protection since the 17th century. The hotel was built as a royal hunting lodge just before the monarchy was abolished in 1910, but it's still fit for a sovereign. The mock-Manueline palace houses 34 luxurious rooms, a fabulous dining room and some impressive *azulejos*. There are also tennis courts. The cellar is one of the best in Portugal.

🚏 198 B1 🚏 Mata do Buçaco, Luso
☎ 231 937 970, fax: 231 930 509;
www.almeidahotels.com

ÓBIDOS

Pousada do Castelo €€€–€€€€

The magnificent site – commanding fantastic views – alone justifies splashing out to stay here. It's one of the most prestigious *pousadas*, if

---

only because there are only nine rooms, a couple of them in the eyrie-like tower. Exuberant tapestries enhance the romantic atmosphere in the impeccably restored medieval interior. Traditional meals are served in the charming refectory – or you could drop by for afternoon tea.

🚏 200 B4 🚏 Rua do Castelo
☎ 262 955 080, fax: 262 959 148;
www.pousadas.ot

MONSANTO

Estalagem de Monsanto €€

Monsanto's *estalagem* is set in a modern building that blends in with the fine houses in this hilltop town. With only ten rooms it gets booked up in summer, but if possible get the corner room upstairs, which has fantastic views in two directions across the verdant Beira-Baixa landscapes. The food is hearty and the service friendly.

🚏 201 F5 🚏 Rua da Capela 3
☎ 277 314 471, fax: 277 314 481;
www.estalagemdemonsanto.pt

inevitable TV for atmosphere. It's certainly an authentic experience.

➕ 198 B1 ⌖ Rua das Azeiteiras 65–67 ☎ 239 827 115 🕐 Mon–Sat noon–3, 7–10:30

Ramalhão €€

Wild rabbit, duck and free-range chicken feature on the slightly unusual menu, while *ensopado de enguias* (eel stew) draws customers from a wide radius. This goldmine of a restaurant (30km/18½ miles west of Coimbra), with its rustic décor and charming *patio*, is renowned for its locally grown or caught produce and expert Bairrada cooking. It gets packed on market day (every other Wednesday).

➕ 198 B1 ⌖ Rua Tenente Valadim 24, Montemor-o-Velho ☎ 239 689 435 🕐 Tue–Sat 12:30–3, 7:30–10, Sun 12:30–3. Closed Oct

Trovador €€–€€€

Not only is the food good, but this is one of the rare places in Coimbra where you can be sure to hear the local version of *fado*, sung by men instead of women, and more important for the lyrics than the tune. All kinds of regional specialities can be tasted, with *chanfana* (goat in a wine sauce) leading the way. The wine list is top notch, including local Bairradas, but also vintages from all over Portugal. The delightful décor, with wood panelling and crisp white linen, plus charming service, make this restaurant, near the old cathedral, the best in the old town.

➕ 198 B1 ⌖ Largo da Sé Velha 17 ☎ 239 825 475 🕐 Mon–Sat noon–3, 7:30–10. Closed 15–31 Dec

TOMAR

Bela Vista €€

The fantastic location by Tomar's Old Bridge, overlooking the ducks (cooked with *arroz de pato*, a kind of rice, they're a house special) on the River Nabão, is only part of the appeal. This is the locals' favourite haunt. A reliable but expertly executed menu of family-style dishes, deft service and a homelike interior keep them coming. In good weather try and get a table on the shady front terrace under the vines. The *ementa turística* (tourist menu) is unbeatable value.

➕ 200 C4 ⌖ Rua Marquês de Pombal 68 ☎ 249 312 870 🕐 Wed–Sun noon–3, 7–9:30; Mon noon–3. Closed 1–15 Nov

GUARDA

Solar da Beira €–€€

Just off Guarda's central square, this rustic little restaurant is popular with locals for Sunday lunch. Roasts and grills, with emphasis on locally reared lamb (*borrego*) plus hearty dishes like *arroz de pato* and all kinds of sausages are on the menu. The décor is simple in the extreme, with paper tablecloths and few concessions to modernity. The *arroz doce* (rice pudding with cinnamon) is really delicious.

➕ 199 D2 ⌖ Rua São Francisco dos Passos 9 ☎ 271 211 563 🕐 Daily 11–4, 6–midnight (closes Sun pm in winter)

ÓBIDOS

A Ilustre Casa de Ramiro €€€

Despite the voguish pink ochre interior walls, Ramiro's "illustrious house" (as the name translates) is steadfastly old-fashioned and proud of its noble tradition of polite service and family fare. Choose from a wide range of wood-fired grills and *bacalhau* dishes – omelettes being the only concession to vegetarians. The house specialities are *arroz de pato* (succulent duck baked with rice, a vast dish, enough for two) and *trouxas de ovos* (a dessert of egg yolks and syrup). The wine list, including rare local vintages, is extensive but expensive.

➕ 200 B4 ⌖ Rua Porta do Vale ☎ 262 959 194 🕐 Fri–Wed 12:30–3, 7–10:30. Closed Jan and Feb

Where to... Shop

MARKETS

Every Tuesday **Viseu** stages a magnificent regional market at Largo Castanheiro dos Amores. A covered market near the Rossio is held every weekday.

In the **Serra da Estrela**, Gouveia's Thursday markets are worth seeing, as is the busy **Montemor-o-Velho**, 30km (18.5 miles) west of Coimbra, every other Wednesday.

The daily market in **Coimbra** itself is held in an impressive hangar behind the City Hall.

CRAFTS

Obidos has a number of shops along Rua Direita selling ceramics and crafts – try the **Centro de Artesanato**. In **Alcobaça**, quality glazed earthenware is on sale at **Raul da Bernarda** (Ponte Dom Elias). In **Coimbra** you can pick up earthenware goods at several shops along Rua Quebra Costas. **Rua Ferreira Borges** and **Rua Visconde da Luz** are Coimbra's main shopping arteries, lined with boutiques, grocers, bookshops and tobacconists.

Just outside, at Condeixa-a-Nova, factories sell hand-painted ceramics directly to customers.

FOOD AND DRINK

In **Coimbra**, **A Camponesa** (Rua da Louça) is the best-known grocers, excellent for wines and spirits. In **Viseu**, **Pastelaria Horta** (Rua Formosa) has delicious pies and cakes.

Snap up good bottles of Dão wine in Viseu's grocers. Queijos da serra (mountain cheeses) can be outstanding – the covered market in Guarda on Rua D Nuno Álvares Pereira, best on Saturday mornings, is the place to find them.

Where to... Be Entertained

SPORT AND OUTDOOR PURSUITS

Surfing is first class at **Buarcos**, near Figueira da Foz. At **Aveiro**, hire **bikes** to explore the lagoon from **Agência de Viagens Culturália** (Rua João Mendonça 31, tel: 23 442 3142) or make use of **BUGA**, Aveiro's free bicycle service. **Hiking** in the **Serra da Estrela** is great, and trails are well marked (▶ 119–120).

Several **spas** are located in this region – **Termas de Monfortinho**, enjoys a stunning location and you can play tennis and hire mountain bikes – ask at the **Hotel Fonte Santa** (tel: 277 430 300).

FESTIVALS

The **Queima das Fitas** ("ribbon burning") enlivens **Coimbra** in May. Don't miss **Aveiro's Festa da Ria**, in the second half of August, when the distinctive *moliceiro* boats are decorated. "Holy Bathing" can be witnessed at **Figueira da Foz**, along with other partying, on and around **St John's Day** (24 June).

MUSIC AND NIGHTLIFE

Nightlife is focused on **Coimbra** and **Figueira da Foz**, where there's also a good **film festival** in September. A good nightclub is **Bergantim** (Rua Dr Lopes Guimarães 28, Figueira da Foz). In Coimbra, **Diligência** (Rua Nova 30) is the best place for local *fado*, while **Boémia** (Rua do Cabido 6) is a beautiful venue for jazz. **Scotch Club** (Quinta da Insua) and **Via Latina** (Rua Almeida Garrett 1) are Coimbra's liveliest discos.

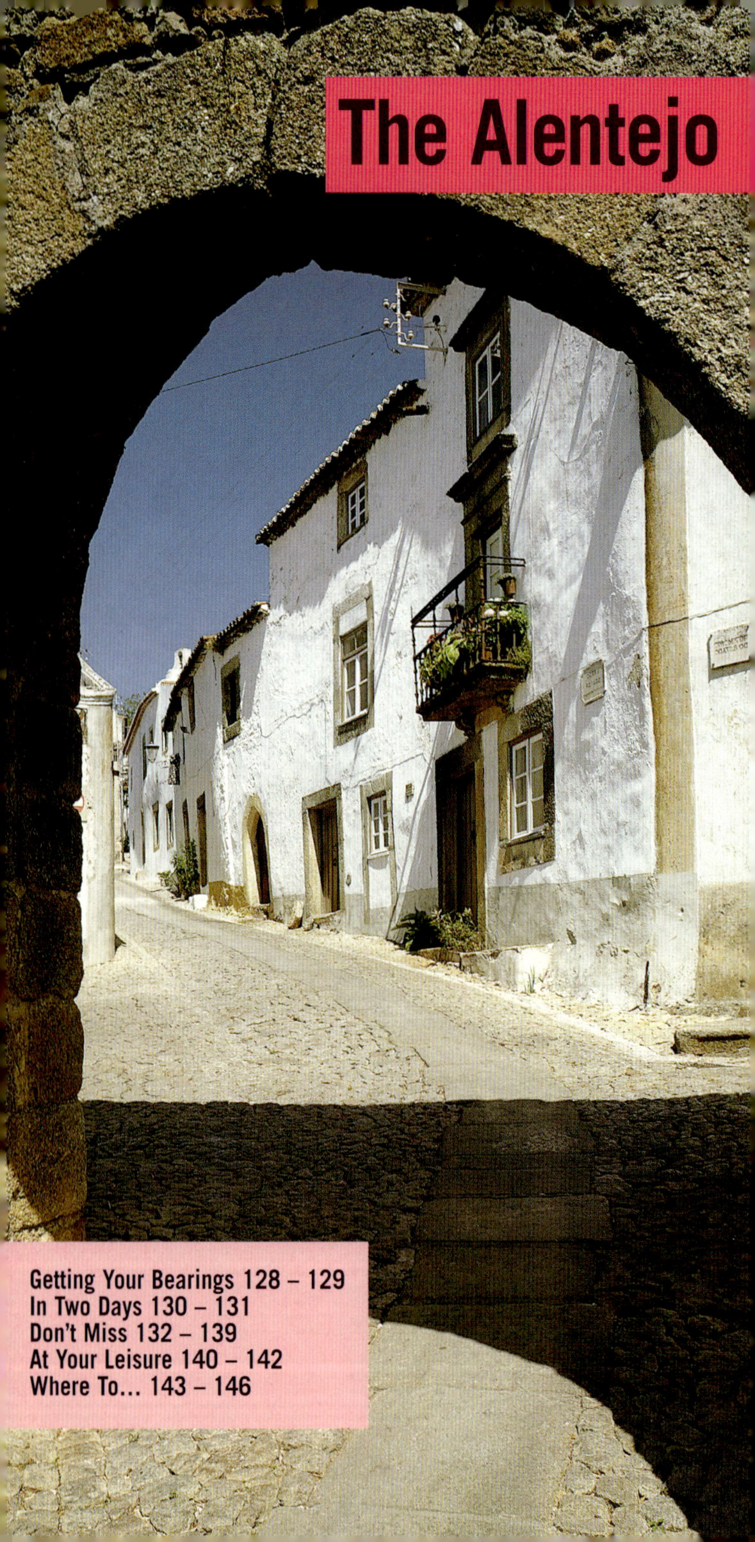

The Alentejo

Getting Your Bearings

The Alentejo ("Beyond the Tagus") is a sun-baked plain that stretches across southern Portugal, occupying land between the River Tagus and the Algarve. This is both the largest and the most sparsely inhabited region of Portugal, where just 12 per cent of the population are scattered across a third of the country in isolated hamlets and small market towns. It is a proud region whose people share a strong sense of identity, expressed through their music, rural traditions and hearty peasant cuisine.

The landscape of the Alentejo is almost entirely man-made and agricultural. The Romans established vast feudal estates (*latifúndios*) to grow olives, vines and wheat, many of which survived right up to the 1974 revolution. Even today, when many of these estates have become co-operatives, the white-washed *monte* (farmhouse) surrounded by vineyards is still a familiar sight. Wine and wheat are still important products, but the region is best known for its cork oaks, which provide more than half of the world's cork, used in everything from aircraft insulation to bottle stops.

Some people find the endless expanse of farmland tedious, but others are inspired by the wide open spaces and the strong elemental colours of the landscape – red earth, yellow wheat and big blue skies. Upper Alentejo in particular has several interesting sights, from the Renaissance city of Évora to the marble towns of Estremoz and Vila Viçosa, and the hilltop villages of Monsaraz and Marvão. The Moorish history of the region is more evident in Lower Alentejo, in towns like Mértola and Serpa, with their low, whitewashed, blue-trimmed houses.

Above: The lonely hills and valleys of the Serra de São Mamede

Previous page: Whitewashed houses and cobbled streets in Marvão

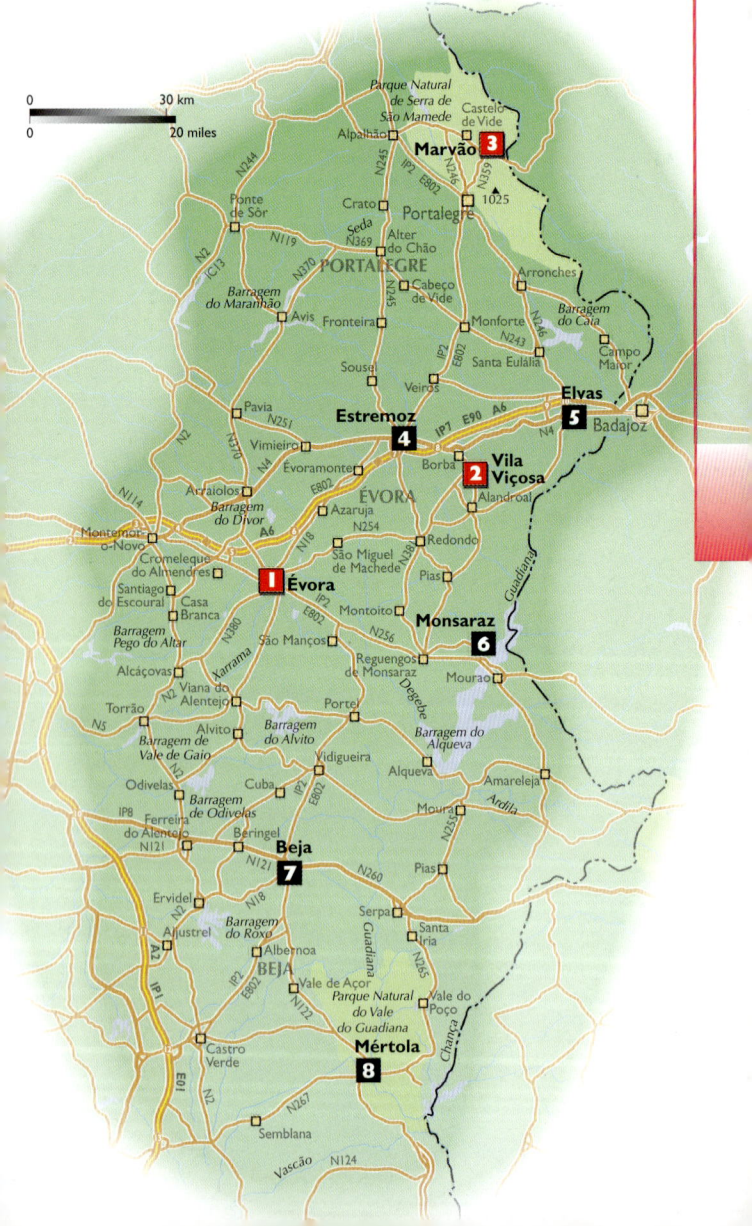

0 ——— 30 km
0 ——— 20 miles

Parque Natural de Serra de São Mamede
Alpalhão
Castelo de Vide
Marvão **3**
Crato
Portalegre
Ponte de Sôr
N244
N245
IP7 E802
N246
N359
1025
N2
N119
Seda
N369
Alter do Chão
PORTALEGRE
IC13
N245
Cabeço de Vide
Arronches
Barragem do Maranhão
Avis
Fronteira
Monforte
N243
Santa Eulália
Campo Maior
Barragem do Caia
Sousel
Veiros
IP2
E802
N370
N251
Pavia
Vimieiro
Estremoz **4**
IP7 E90 A6
Elvas **5**
Badajoz
N2
N4
N4
Evoramonte
Borba
Vila Viçosa **2**
Arraiolos
E802
ÉVORA
Alandroal
N114
Barragem do Divor
A6
Azaruja
N254
Montemor-o-Novo
N18
Redondo
Guadiana
Cromeleque do Almendres
São Miguel de Machede
Santiago do Escoural
Casa Branca
N380
Évora **1**
Pias
N381
IP1
Montoito
Barragem Pego do Altar
São Manços
Xarrama
E802
N256
Monsaraz **6**
Alcáçovas
Reguengos de Monsaraz
Mourão
N2
Viana do Alentejo
Degebe
Torrão
Portel
Barragem do Alqueva
N5
Alvito
Barragem do Alvito
Barragem de Vale de Gaio
Vidigueira
Alqueva
Amareleja
Odivelas
Cuba
IP2
E802
Moura
Ardila
IP8
Barragem de Odivelas
Ferreira do Alentejo
N121
Beringel
Beja **7**
N260
Pias
Ervidel
Serpa
Aljustrel
N18
Barragem do Roxo
Santa Iria
Albernoa
N265
BEJA
Guadiana
IP1
E802
Vale de Açor
Parque Natural do Vale do Guadiana
Vale do Poço
Castro Verde
Mértola **8**
N122
N2
N267
Chança
Semblana
Vascão
N124

Spend your days in historic towns and cities and your
nights in dramatic mountain villages on this two-day tour
of Upper Alentejo.

The Alentejo in
Two Days

Day One

Morning

Spend the morning walk-
ing around the walled city
of **1** **Évora** (right;
► 132–135). Start by
climbing to the Roman
temple, then visit the
cathedral, museum and
Capela dos Ossos (Chapel
of Bones) before lunch at
one of the pavement cafés
on Praça do Giraldo.

Afternoon

Leave Évora on the N18 in the direction of **7** **Beja** (► 142). When the road
to Beja turns right, keep straight ahead on the N256 to Reguengos de
Monsaraz. Turn left here, following signs to Monsaraz across a landscape of
vineyards and olive groves. Just beyond the pottery-producing village of
São Pedro de Corval, look out for Rocha dos Namorados (Lovers' Rock),
a prehistoric *menhir* beside the road. Continue on this road to **6** **Monsaraz**
(below; ► 141), visible on its hill across the plain.

Evening

Spend the night in the sleepy village of Monsaraz and wake to magnificent views. Book ahead for a room at Dom Nuno (► 144) or look for village houses along Rua Direita advertising rooms for rent.

Day Two

Morning

Retrace your route to Reguengos de Monsaraz and follow signs north to Alandroal and Vila Viçosa on the N255. Arriving in **2** **Vila Viçosa** (► 136–137), leave your car outside the old royal palace and take a guided tour of the palace before wandering up to the castle and down to the town centre for lunch beside the orange trees and marble fountain on Praça da República.

Afternoon

The road from Vila Viçosa to Borba leads past the quarries that are the source of the local marble. Turn right in Borba to reach the N4, passing more quarries on your way to **4** **Estremoz** (► 140). Drive up to the castle at the top of the town for a drink at the Pousada da Rainha Santa Isabel (right; ► 144) and visit the municipal museum to admire the pottery (left). Leave Estremoz on the IP2, go north to Portalegre, bypass Portalegre and turn right to **3** **Marvão** (► 138–139), whose hilltop castle (below) dominates as you approach. Leave your car outside the village and walk up to the castle in time to enjoy the sunset walk around its ancient walls.

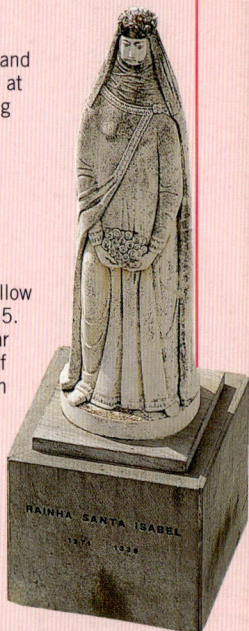

Evening

Ask at the tourist office (► 139) about rooms in private houses in Marvão, or stay the night at the delightful Pousada Santa Maria (► 143) and celebrate your arrival with a hearty Alentejan meal of roast lamb or goat.

RAINHA SANTA ISABEL
1271 1336

❶ Évora

With its Moorish alleys, shady squares, fountains and Renaissance mansions, the largest city in the Alentejo makes a good place for a stroll. Founded by the Romans, strengthened by the Moors and recovered from them for Afonso Henriques by Geraldo Sempavor (Gerald the Fearless), Évora rose to prominence in the 15th and 16th centuries as a centre of arts and learning – a reputation that survives to this day.

The Romans built their walled city of *Ebora Cerealis* high on a hill above the Alentejo plain. At the summit of the town, they erected the temple of Diana, now the **Templo Romano** and the best-preserved Roman monument in Portugal.

Used as a slaughterhouse during the 19th century, the granite columns and marble capitals of this 2nd-century AD temple have only recently been restored. Floodlit at night, it makes a spectacular sight.

Left: The compact old town is a good place for walking

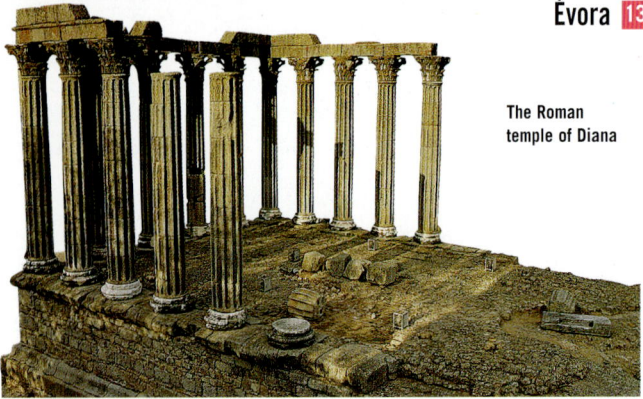

The Roman
temple of Diana

Convento dos Lóios

All the main sights are within the walled town, made a World
Heritage Site by UNESCO in 1986. Directly behind the
temple, the **Convento dos Lóios** is a 15th-century monastery
that has been converted into an appealing *pousada* (► 143),
where you dine in the cloisters and sleep in the monks' cells.
Even if you're not staying here, it's worth going in to admire
the Gothic cloisters and the Manueline chapter-house door.

   The attached church, **Igreja dos Lóios**, was the private
chapel of the dukes of Cadaval, who are buried beneath
marble tombstones. The nave is lined with floor-to-ceiling
azulejos depicting the life of a former patriarch of Venice.
You can peek through a pair of grilles in the floor to see a
medieval cistern and an ossuary of human bones.

The Cathedral

The **sé** (cathedral), completed in 1250, has a fortress-like
Romanesque appearance similar to that at Coimbra (► 108).
A Gothic portal, carved with figures of the apostles, stands
between two strangely unmatched towers. Inside, there is
marble everywhere, in the lectern, pulpit and high altar.
The entry to the **Museu de Arte Sacra** also gives access to the
Coro Alto, where the carved oak choir stalls feature scenes
of rural life such as grape-picking and pig-sticking (hunting wild boars with spears), and the **Gothic cloister**,
where you can climb onto the roof for views over Évora
and a close-up look at the cathedral lantern and towers.

Detail: Carved
apostles on
the door of
the cathedral

Below: The
cathedral at
Évora

In the museum there is an extraordinary 13th-century figure of the Virgin, whose innards open up to reveal biblical scenes.

Museu de Évora

The **Museu de Évora** is housed in the former archbishop's palace. It contains Roman tombstones and funerary inscriptions, medieval and Renaissance sculpture and 17th-century *azulejos* from Lisbon.

Among the paintings on the first floor, look for *Holy Virgin with Child* by Alvaro Pires de Évora, painted around 1410. Pires is the earliest identified Portuguese artist, and although a number of his paintings are on show in Pisa and Florence, this is the first to be permanently exhibited in Portugal.

Also here is a 16th-century Flemish polyptych of 13 panels depicting the *Life of the Virgin*, which was previously the cathedral altarpiece. The museum is closed until 2009.

The Town

A staircase beside the cathedral leads down towards **Largo da Porta de Moura**, one of Évora's most attractive squares, with a Renaissance fountain and 16th-century houses which have Manueline-Moorish arcades. Alternatively, take Rua 5 de Outubro (lined with souvenir and craft shops), opposite the cathedral, to reach **Praça do Giraldo**, a handsome square with arches, a marble fountain and café terraces. During the Inquisition this was an execution ground, but it is now a lively meeting place for students and tourists.

A short distance away, the **Igreja de São Francisco** is home to one of Portugal's most macabre sights. To the right of the façade, with its unusual portico of pointed, rounded and horse-shoe arches, a separate entrance leads to the cloister and the **Capela dos Ossos** (Chapel of Bones), whose walls and columns are entirely covered with the skulls, femurs, tibias and other bones of 5,000 monks. Grinning skulls stare down from the ceiling and a grisly corpse hangs on one wall (which some children might find upsetting). Above the entrance, an inscription reads: *Nós ossos, que aqui estamos, Pelos vossos esperamos* ("We bones here are waiting for your bones").

For a change, walk across the square to the **Jardim Público**, and the remains of a 16th-century Moorish- style palace.

TAKING A BREAK

There are **outdoor cafés** on Praça do Giraldo, in the Jardim Público and the gardens by the Templo Romano. If you are looking for something more substantial, there's **O Forcado** (► 145), popular with the locals, or **O Fialho** (► 144), famous across Portugal for its excellent traditional dishes.

Below: Terrace cafés on Praça de Giraldo

➕ 201 D2

Tourist Information Centre
✉ Praça do Giraldo ☎ 266 777 071

Igreja dos Lóios
✉ Largo do Conde de Vila Flor ☎ 266 704 714
🕐 Tue–Sun 9–noon, 2–5 💷 Moderate

Museu de Évora
✉ Largo do Conde de Vila Flor ☎ 266 702 604
🕐 Closed for refurbishment until early 2009; main exhibits now on display at Igreja do Convento de Santa Clara (tel: 266 708 095)

Sé
✉ Largo Marquês de Marialva ☎ 266 769 800
🕐 Jul to mid-Sep Tue–Sun 9–5; mid-Sep–May 9–noon, 2–4:30 💷 Museum inexpensive

Igreja da São Francisco/ Capela dos Ossos
✉ Praça 1 de Maio ☎ 266 704 521 🕐 Daily 9–12:30, 2:30–5:15 💷 Inexpensive

ÉVORA: INSIDE INFO

Top tips The gardens in front of the Templo Romano are a good place to **watch the sun set**.
• Évora's medieval appearance does not lend itself to modern transport. If you are driving, it is best to **park on the outskirts** and walk in.

Hidden gem A steep hill behind the cathedral and Museu de Évora leads to the **old Jesuit university**, founded by Cardinal Henrique, the future king, in 1559. The university was closed down in 1759 by the Marquês de Pombal, but is now open, so you can wander around its beautiful tiled courtyard.

In more depth Take a walk through the old Moorish quarter, **Mouraria**, with its whitewashed houses and lamplit, cobbled streets. From beneath the gardens in front of the Roman temple, Rua dos Fontes drops steeply through Mouraria to Largo do Avis, beside the only remaining medieval gateway to the walled town. From the pretty square of Largo do Chão das Covas, Rua do Cano follows the course of the old aqueduct, parts of which can still be seen outside the walls.

2 Vila Viçosa

The power and wealth of the Portuguese kings is on display in Vila Viçosa, the seat of Portugal's last ruling dynasty, the dukes of Bragança. Built of marble, this is a prosperous town whose shining "white gold" can be seen everywhere.

Begin at **Terreiro do Paço**, the vast square in front of the Paço Ducal. A statue of João IV on horseback stands at the centre. The palace, fronted with marble, dominates the square. To one side is the royal chapel; to the other, Convento das Chagas, the mausoleum of the duchesses of Bragança, now a *pousada*. Across the square is the Mosterio dos Agostinhos, where the dukes are buried.

The **Paço Ducal** can only be visited on a guided tour, with additional charges to see the armoury, treasury, Chinese porcelain and Museu dos Coches. There are Flemish tapestries, Portuguese furniture and portraits of former kings in the Sala dos Duques. Most interesting are the private apartments of Dom Carlos (Portugal's penultimate king) and Dona Amelia, abandoned on the day of Carlos' assassination in 1908, with the table still set for dinner, family portraits and Dona Amelia's sketches on the walls.

The **Museu dos Coches** (Coach Museum), in the Royal Stables, contains beautifully maintained coaches, landaus and state carriages, including the one in which Dom Carlos and Crown Prince

The Dukes of Bragança

Although the town was given a royal charter as early as 1270, it was the dukes of Bragança who made Vila Viçosa. The title of Bragança was created in 1442 for an illegitimate son of João I of Avis; the second duke, Dom Fernando, moved his court to Vila Viçosa, and the fourth duke, Dom Jaime, began the building of the Paço Ducal (Ducal Palace) in 1501. Vila Viçosa became the finest address in Portugal, with banquets, balls and bullfights held in the palace for the leading families of the day. All that changed in 1640 when the eighth duke, João IV, reluctantly accepted the throne, ending 60 years of Spanish rule. The Braganças ruled Portugal until the fall of the monarchy in 1910 and continued to live in the palace, though many of its treasures were taken to Lisbon and the royal palaces at Mafra (► 66) and Sintra (► 60–61).

Above: The modern town centres on Praça da República

Right: Vila Viçosa is built out of marble from the local quarries

Opposite: A statue of Dom João IV, the first of the Bragança kings, stands before the Paço Ducal

Luís Felipe were travelling when they were shot.

From the Terreiro do Paço, the **Avenida dos Duques de Bragança** leads towards the old walled town, dominated by a 13th-century *castelo* (castle). This was the original residence of the dukes of Bragança and has a small archaeological museum.

TAKING A BREAK

Café Restauraçao, Praça da República, serves sandwiches and snacks.

🞣 201 E2

Tourist Information Office
✉ Praça da República ☎ 268 881 101

Paço Ducal
✉ Terreiro do Paço ☎ 268 980 659
🕐 Tue–Sun, phone for times 💷 Moderate
(expensive if additional charges are included)

VILA VIÇOSA: INSIDE INFO

Top tip Accommodation in Vila Viçosa is not plentiful, although the tourist office should be able to help you find somewhere.

Hidden gem What looks like a pair of red garage doors at the end of a row of houses on Avenida dos Duques de Bragança opens up to reveal a **Passo**, one of a series of 16th-century Stations of the Cross remodelled in the 18th century with a marble portal and *azulejo* tiles depicting scenes from the life of Christ.

❸ Marvão

The most spectacular of all Portugal's hilltop villages perches like an eagle's nest on a rocky ridge 862m (2,827 feet) up in the Serra de São Mamede. The castle and medieval walls seem to grow out of the rock, and it is clear that this must have been a near-impregnable fortress. During the 16th century, Marvão had a population of more than 1,400, but today fewer than 200 people live here.

The Romans came here, and so did the Moors – the village takes its name from Ibn Maruán, the 9th-century Islamic Lord of Coimbra (Marvão comes from Maruán). After the Christian conquest, it was Dom Dinis who fortified the castle here at the end of the 13th century. It was to become one of a long chain of defensive outposts protecting the border with Spain.

Unless you are staying the night, it is best to park outside the village and enter on foot through the main gate, **Porta de Rodão**. From Praça do Pelourinho, with its 16th-century pillory, Rua do Espírito Santo, known for its whitewashed houses with wrought-iron balconies, leads into Rua do Castelo, which leads to the castle. Rua do Castelo is like a living museum of Gothic and Renaissance architecture, preserved untouched during the centuries of Marvão's decline and only now being rediscovered and restored.

You can climb onto the walls, with their battlements, turrets and towers, and make a complete circuit, but it is

Below: Looking down over the village from the castle walls

Above: Marvão was one of a chain of fortified towns and villages along the Portuguese border with Spain

easier to walk up to the castle along the village streets. The **castle**, rebuilt in the 17th century, is magnificent. Two fortified gates lead to a courtyard where you can climb onto the parapet for views over the village. Breaching a second line of defence, you come to another courtyard, which contains the armoury (now a military museum) and the castle keep. The views from here are impressive. To the north, in the distance, are the snow-capped peaks of the Serra da Estrela (► 119–120); to the south, the rugged mountains of the Serra de São Mamede; to the west, the Alentejo countryside; to the east, Spain. If you are lucky you might spot eagles circling overhead.

Just outside the castle walls, the **Museu Municipal**, in the 13th-century church of Santa Maria, displays folk costumes, baptismal outfits, religious art and archaeological finds.

TAKING A BREAK

Casa do Povo, in Rua de Cima, offers well-prepared, filling Alentejan cuisine.

➕ 201 E4

Tourist Information Centre
✉ Largo de Santa Maria ☎ 245 909 131

Museu Municipal
✉ Largo de Santa Maria ☎ 245 909 132 🕐 Daily 9–12:30, 2–5:30
💰 Inexpensive

MARVÃO: INSIDE INFO

Top tips Try to stay overnight to watch the **sunset** from the castle walls and enjoy the evening peace of the village.
• As well as the **Pousada Santa Maria** (► 143), there are several **private houses** with rooms to let – ask at the tourist office.

Hidden gem Walk down the steps to your right just inside the castle entrance to see a **monumental cistern**, built by Dom Dinis, and capable of storing six months' water for the villagers.

In more depth The surrounding **Serra de São Mamede** is a natural park with Roman and neolithic remains and wildlife including griffon vultures, red deer and Europe's largest colony of bats. Also here is the spa town of **Castelo de Vide**, with a 14th-century castle and a synagogue in the old Jewish quarter.

At Your Leisure

4 Estremoz

The largest of the Alentejo "marble" towns seems to have an extra sheen of white as marble from the local quarries is used as an everyday building material. Life here centres on the **Rossio Marquês de Pombal**, a huge square where one of Portugal's biggest markets is held on Saturdays.

Other sights of interest are in the upper town, around the 13th-century **castle** built by Dom Dinis for his future wife, Isabel of Aragón (and now one of the most famous *pousadas* in Portugal – ► 144). As queen, Isabel became known for her devotion to the poor and she was sainted after her death. Her story is told in *azulejos* in the **Capela da Rainha Santa Isabel**, including that of the Miracle of the Roses. Her husband disapproved of her giving alms to the poor, so she hid the bread which she was carrying for the poor in the folds of her skirt where he would not see it. When he became suspicious and challenged her she opened her skirt and the bread had miraculously turned into roses to prevent him from finding out. A marble statue of the saint stands on the castle terrace, from where there are views to Évoramonte.

Estremoz pottery, famous since the 16th century

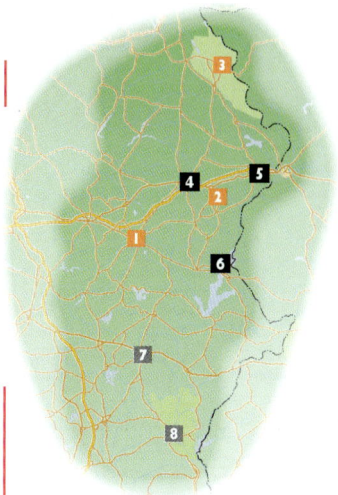

The **Museu Municipal** features folk art in cork, oak and marble, and *bonecos* (terracotta figurines for which Estremoz is famous).

✚ 201 E2
Tourist Information Office
✉ Praça da República
☎ 268 339 200

Museu Municipal
✉ Largo Dom Dinis ☎ 268 333 608
🕐 Tue–Sun 9–12:30, 2–5:30 (May–Sep to 6:30) 🎟 Inexpensive

5 Elvas

One of the most heavily fortified frontier towns in Europe sits just 12km (7.4 miles) from Portugal's border with Spain and 15km (9.3 miles) from the Spanish citadel at Badajoz. Captured by Afonso Henriques in 1166, retaken by the Moors, and finally seized by Christian forces in 1226, Elvas has been besieged many times but only once taken by Spanish troops.

The star-shaped fortifications that surround the town, built according to the designs of the French military engineer, Vauban, date largely from the 17th century. They are

supplemented by two fortresses, one of which, **Forte de Santa Luzia**, can sometimes be visited (check at the tourist information office).

The streets of the old town radiate from Praça da República. At one end stands the **Igreja de Nossa Senhora da Assunção**, which had cathedral status until 1882, when the town lost its bishopric.

Behind the church, **Largo de Santa Clara** is an attractive triangular "square" with a Manueline marble pillory, still with its original iron hooks to which prisoners were tied.

On one side of the square, the **Igreja de Nossa Senhora da Consolação** looks plain from the outside but the interior is extraordinary, an octagonal chapel with painted marble columns and blue-and-yellow *azulejos* lining the walls.

Ask the caretaker to take you up to the roof for views of the nearby castle, the fortresses and the remarkable five-tiered **Aqueduto Amoreira** (1498–1622), that runs for 7km (4 miles) before ending in the fountain in the Largo da Misericórdia.

✚ 201 F2
Tourist Information Office
✉ Praça da República
☎ 268 622 236

Igreja de Nossa Senhora da Consolação
✉ Largo de Santa Clara
🕐 Tue–Sun 9–12:30, 2–5:30

What to Do With the Kids
• **Capela dos Ossos**, Évora (for older children, ► 134): Grisly corpses and grinning skulls at the Chapel of Bones.
• **The castle at Marvão** (► 139): Fabulous views across the Serra da Estrela and magnificent fortifications.

🏃 Monsaraz

Monsaraz would be just another attractive hilltop village were it not for the famously fantastic views enjoyed by hordes of day trippers, and the plaques on the Porta de Vila recalling visits by Portuguese presidents Soares and Sampaio.

There are two parallel streets – **Rua Direita**, with a tourist office, the parish church, Igreja Matriz and 16th-century houses, and **Rua de Santiago**, which has a more lived-in feel, with shops, restaurants and crafts. Rua Direita leads to the 13th-century **castle**, once a Knights Templar fortress. The ramparts have unparalleled views over the village and the Alentejo countryside. The courtyard is sometimes the bullring.

✚ 201 E2
Tourist Information Office
✉ Largo Dom Nuno Alvares Pereira
☎ 266 557 136

Below: The peaceful countryside around the attractive village of Monsaraz

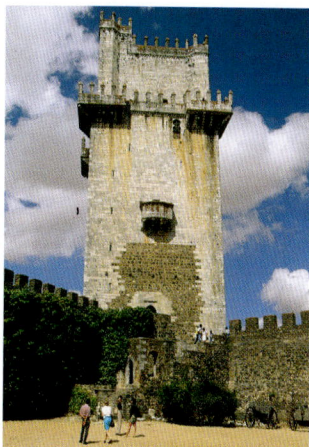

You can climb the 40m (131-foot) high walls of the castle keep at Beja

7 Beja

The capital of Lower Alentejo is a pleasing town of whitewashed houses, founded by Julis Caesar as *Pax Julia* to commemorate a peace (*pax*) treaty between the Romans and the Lusitani tribe. The most striking monument is the 13th-century **castelo** (castle); you can climb the keep for views over the Alentejo wheatlands.

Beja is best known as the home of Mariana Alcoforado, the nun whose (possibly fictional) love letters to a French cavalry officer were published in France in 1669 as *Lettres Portugaises*. The convent where she lived, Nossa Senhora da Conceição, is now the **Museu Regional**, with prehistoric and Roman finds, and a Flemish painting from the 16th century, *Our Lady of the Milk*, showing the Madonna breastfeeding.

Of more interest are the convent buildings, especially the baroque chapel, tiled cloisters and 16th-century Hispano-Arab *azulejos* in the chapter house.

Another convent is now the **Pousada de São Francisco** (▶ 144).

➕ 201 D1

Tourist Information Office

✉ Rua Capitão João Francisco de Sousa ☎ 284 311 913

Castelo

✉ Largo do Lidador ☎ 284 311 912
🕐 Summer Tue–Sun 10–1, 2–6; winter, Tue–Sun 9–noon, 1–4 💷 Inexpensive (Sun free)

Museu Regional

✉ Largo da Conceição ☎ 284 323 351 🕐 Tue–Sun 9:30–12:30, 2–5:15 💷 Inexpensive (Sun 9:30–12:30)

8 Mértola

This pretty little walled town at the confluence of the Guadiana and Oeiras rivers has a long history as a trading port at the highest navigable point on the Guadiana.

These days, Mértola promotes itself as a *vila museu* (museum town), with small museums scattered around the town devoted to its Roman, Islamic and Portuguese history. You can visit all of them on one ticket, including access to the castle keep for views over the rooftops. Don't miss the parish church, converted from a mosque at the end of the 12th century, whose *mihrab*, facing east to Mecca, is still visible behind the altar and whose horseshoe arches and columns retain a strong Islamic feel.

➕ 202 D2

Tourist Information Office

✉ Rua da Igreja 1 ☎ 286 610 109; www.cm-mertola.pt 🕐 Daily 9–12:30, 2–5:30 💷 Museums moderate

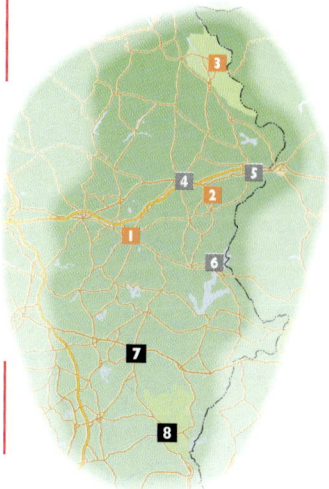

Where to... Stay

Prices
Expect to pay for a double room with bathroom in high season
€ = under €60 €€ = €60–€120 €€€ = €121–€180 €€€€ = over €180

ÉVORA

Pensão Policarpo €

Tucked away behind the cathedral, this modest, comfortable guest-house deserves its glowing reputation. Traditional brightly painted furniture lends a splash of colour to the sober rooms, most of which have small bathrooms. Breakfast, in a dining room decorated with *azulejos*, is self-service. Parking is free.
➕ 201 D2 ✉ Rua da Freiria de Baixo 16 ☎ 266 702 424, fax: 266 703 474; www.pensaopolicarpo.com

Pousada dos Lóios €€€–€€€€

The fabulous monastery of the Lóios, dedicated to John the Evangelist, was built in the 15th century. With an excellent restaurant in the ornate cloisters, it's one of the country's leading *pousadas*. The majestic rooms are furnished and decorated with valuable antiques, in particular the "presidential" suite, which has Indo-Portuguese furniture. There is also a good-sized swimming pool.
➕ 201 D2 ✉ Largo Conde de Vila-Flor ☎ 266 730 070, fax: 266 707 248; www.pousadas.pt

Pousada Nossa Senhora da Assunção €€€–€€€€

One of Portugal's leading young architects, José Paulo dos Santos, worked magic when he turned a 16th-century monastery into a modern luxury hotel in the 1990s. Just outside the "model" village of Arraiolos (famous for its hand-knotted rugs; ▶ 146), amid luxuriant pastures and cork-oak groves, its location and architectural beauty make it one of the most desirable of all the *pousadas*. White and blue are the key colours, softened by traditional carpets, clay jars, parquets and the different coloured marbles used in each dazzling bathroom. There's also a magnificent swimming pool and superb church.
➕ 201 D2 ✉ Pousada Nossa Senhora da Assunção, Convento dos Lóios, Arraiolos ☎ 266 419 340, fax: 266 419 280; www.pousadas.pt

VILA VIÇOSA

Casa dos Peixinhos €€–€€€

Behind the castellated whitewashed portal stands the noble façade of this stylish eight-room guesthouse. Inside the 16th-century house, the family coat of arms over the fire-place further reminds you of its aristocratic past and present. The bathrooms are all lined with locally quarried marble while the rooms have vivid but tasteful colours. Meals, in addition to the breakfast included, may be ordered.
➕ 201 E2 ✉ 7160–285 Vila Viçosa (signposted from centre) ☎ 268 980 472, fax: 268 881 348; www.casadospeixinhos.pa-net.pt

MARVÃO

Pousada Santa Maria €€–€€€

Cool in summer and warm in the winter, like the other whitewashed houses in this picturesque hilltop village, this *pousada* is a delight. The large spacious rooms and simple dining room look across the olives and cork-oaks of the Alentejo. Enjoy the views while sampling local specialities, including excellent cheeses and well-chosen wines.
➕ 201 E4 ✉ Rua 24 de Janeiro 7 ☎ 245 993 201, fax: 245 993 440; www.pousadas.pt

Where to...
Eat and Drink

ESTREMOZ

Pousada da Rainha Santa Isabel €€€

Generally regarded as the most prestigious *pousada* of all, this one is contained in an austere-looking medieval castle. Details such as four-poster beds, tapestries fit for a museum, entire walls of *azulejos* and the long vaulted refectory earn the whole ensemble the epithet of "grandiose". Relax by the swimming pool and dine on Alentejo specialities, sampling fine wines from the extensive cellar.

➕ 201 E2 ⊠ Castelo de Estremoz, Largo Dom Diniz ☎ 268 332 075, fax: 268 332 079; www.pousadas.pt

MONSARAZ

Casa Dom Nuno €

Along the main street near the church, this popular guesthouse has charming small rooms and serves a very good breakfast. The main attraction, apart from the prime location, is the terrace, which offers guests stunning views for miles across the Alentejo. This guesthouse is often closed in winter, and you need to book well ahead in the summer.

➕ 201 E2 ⊠ Rua do Castelo 66 ☎ 266 557 146, fax: 266 557 400 Ⓘ Closed part of Dec

BEJA

Pousada de São Francisco €€€

The cells of this ancient Franciscan monastery have become comfortable rooms. Don't be put off by the impersonality of the huge entrance hall and mammoth staircase – the guest areas are intimate and cheery. A cool 13th-century chapel in the complex has been carefully restored, and a pool installed in the grounds – much needed in a city where summer temperatures can top 40°C.

➕ 201 D1 ⊠ Largo Dom Nuno Alvares Pereira, 7801-901 Beja ☎ 284 313 580, fax: 284 329 143; www.pousadas.pt

ÉVORA

Cozinha de Santo Humberto €€€

Évora probably has more reliably excellent restaurants than any city outside Lisbon and this is one of them. When you go down into the pristine white cellar (used to store wine), you'll note a sideboard loaded with delicious starters and desserts. Another trademark is the row of blackened kettles hanging from the ceiling. In season go for the game – the wild boar ragout is exceptional – or try *chispe assado* (roast pork).

➕ 201 D2 ⊠ Rua da Moeda 39 ☎ 266 704 251 Ⓘ Fri–Wed noon–3, 7–10. Closed third week Nov

O Fialho €€€–€€€€

Justly famous – gourmets even come especially from Lisbon – O Fialho is surprisingly simple to look at and calls itself a *cervejaria* (beer house). A few hunting trophies and simple *azulejos* are the only ornaments. This is not a place to turn down the *acepipes* (➤ 38), even though the starters are fabulous. What sets the food apart is the use of herbs and spices, for example in the *bacalhau carpaccio*, sprinkled liberally with

capers. *Lombos de javali* (medallions of wild boar) are set off with a hint of rosemary. Attentive service, outstanding wines and home-made liqueurs complete the experience.

🖽 201 D2 🖾 Travessa das Mascarenhas 16, near Praça Joaquim António de Aguiar ☎ 266 703 079, fax: 266 744 873 (for reservations) 🕓 Tue–Sun noon–midnight. Closed 1–21 Sep

O Forcado €–€€

If you're having trouble choosing from the row of humble eateries along this delightful street, take the locals' advice and plump for O Forcado. For an amazingly low cost you can have soup, *bacalhau* and almond tart with wine or sparkling water and coffee included. The menu is limited but the food is fresh, wholesome and more than enough to keep you fuelled for a day's sightseeing.

🖽 201 D2 🖾 Rua dos Mercadores 26 ☎ 266 702 566 🕓 Mon–Sat noon–2, 8–10:30

VILA VIÇOSA

A Bolota Castanha €€€

This is a tastefully decorated roadhouse famed for miles around – it's visible and well signposted from the N4 Elvas to Estremoz road. There's an interesting selection of regional dishes with the emphasis on local lamb, pork and fish, with a French or Italian touch, such as herbs, pepper or cream. The wine list is impressive and there are lovely views if you're by a window.

🖽 201 E2 🖾 Quinta das Janelas Verdes, Terrugem (halfway between Elvas and Vila Viçosa) ☎ 268 657 401 🕓 Tue–Sat noon–3:30, 7–10:30, Sun noon–3:30

ESTREMOZ

Adega Típica do Isaías €€

Huge, age-old amphorae tell you this has long been a wine cellar, and jugs of red are plonked onto every table. This wonderfully down-to-earth place attracts locals from every walk of life interested only in the delicious food, from *pimentos assados* (roast red peppers) to *bolo de mel* (honey cake), via *borrego no forno* (roast lamb) or *estufado de lebre* (hare stew). Meat and fish are barbecued out on the street, doing a good job to tempt passers-by.

🖽 201 E2 🖾 Rua do Almeida 21 ☎ 268 322 318 🕓 Mon–Sat noon–2, 7–10:30. Closed public holidays and 2nd and 3rd weeks in Aug

ELVAS

A Coluna €–€€

This is a discreet but popular restaurant with a whitewashed interior and white table linen. The menu is simple, and everyone swears by the *cabrito* (goat), the *bacalhau* dishes and the *cataplana* (▶ 57). It's slightly hidden away from the central square, but soon fills up with locals.

🖽 201 F2 🖾 Rua do Cabrito 11 ☎ 268 623 728 🕓 Wed–Mon noon–3, 7–10

MONSARAZ

O Alcaide €€

Breathtaking views across the open plains from the picture window are a wonderful backdrop for simple home cooking. *Migas de pao con carne de porco* (pork with croutons) and *borrego* (roast lamb) are just two of the regional specialities on offer.

🖽 201 E2 🖾 Rua de Santiago 18 ☎ 266 557 168 🕓 Fri–Wed noon–3, 7–9. Closed first half of Jul and all Oct

BEJA

Café Luís da Rocha €–€€

This bustling café-bar is not a beautiful place, but if you linger long enough you'll see a cross section of the city as people pop in for a coffee or beer or a chat. The *queijadas* (cheese-filled cakes) are excellent.

🖽 201 D1 🖾 Rua Capitão João Francisco de Sousa 63 ☎ 284 323 179 🕓 Dining room daily noon–3:30, 7–10. Café daily 8–11pm. Closed Sun Jul–Sep.

Where to...
Shop

MARKETS

Try to see the market in **Évora**, every second Tuesday morning. Every week, Tuesday to Friday you can bargain for ceramics on **Praça Primeiro de Maio**.

Estremoz holds an impressive market every Saturday on the Rossio – the cheeses are fabulous. Earthenware is a speciality of the town, especially the oddly shaped *moringues* (water jars), some of which are set with marble.

CRAFTS

The best place to check out Arraiolos carpets is... **Arraiolos**, 20km (12.5 miles) north of Évora. The nationally famous beautiful rugs, hand-knotted and with colourful designs, are sold at workshops just outside the town, at Ilhas; or at several shops on Rua 5 Outubro, where prices are far lower than in Lisbon.

Flôr da Rosa, west of Portalegre, is renowned for its pottery, sold at traditional *olarias* near the convent.

Fine crafts can be found at **Milflores** (Rua Dr Matos Magalhães 1, Marvão). Unusual goods in wood, wicker and cork are crafted by **Joaquim Canoas Vieira** (Largo de Nossa Senhora do Passo, Barbacena, near Elvas, tel: 268 662 151).

FOOD AND DRINK

Tour the wine co-operative (*adega*) at **Rossio de Cima**, Borba (tel: 26 889 4264) before buying some of the produce. The office, Praça Joaquim Antonio de Aguiar (tel: 266 746 498, rota@vinhosdoalentejo.pt) can fill you in about the Alentejo Wine Route, and supply a list of *adegas*.

Picnic provisions can be bought at Évora's covered market.

Where to...
Be Entertained

FESTIVALS

The last third of June is Évora's **Feira de São João**, a festival of pagan origin. It combines music and crafts with food. May is festival month for **Beja** – like Évora's *feira*, but with bullfights. In the last week of September it's the turn of **Elvas** – the Festa de São Mateus features a large procession through the town. **Monsaraz** holds a *vacada* (bloodless bullfight) in the castle on the second weekend of September. During the second week of July there's a crafts and folk festival.

SPORT AND OUTDOOR PURSUITS

The Atlantic beaches on the west coast are some of the least spoiled and most dramatic in the country – head for **Zambujeira** and **Odeceixe**. One of the best places for **horse-riding** is run by **Miguel Palha** at Rua da República, Chança, near Alter do Chão.

The 18-hole **golf** course at Marvão, in the lee of the castle, has a spectacular location – **Ammaia**, Quinta do Prado, San Salvador da Aramenha 7330-330 (tel: 245 993 755; www.portugalgolf.pt).

NIGHTLIFE

Évora is about the only town in the region with any nightlife. *Titeres* (puppet shows) at the theatre on Praça Aguiar are worth checking out. Or seek out the **Bar Casa do Vinho** (Praça 1 de Maio) or **Desassossego Bar** (Travessa do Janeiro).

The Algarve

Getting Your Bearings

Sandy beaches and sunny skies. White-washed villas with geraniums around the door. Fishing boats and the scent of freshly grilled sardines. These are the classic images of Portugal, and they are also the images of the Algarve.

For many people, the Algarve *is* Portugal, yet this small region at the southwest corner of Europe is in fact the least typical of all. The climate is more Mediterranean than Atlantic, the landscape more north African than Portuguese. This was *al-gharb*, the western outpost of Moorish Spain, which held out against the Christian reconquest for a century after the fall of Lisbon. Reminders of the Arab presence are every-where, from latticed chimneys with geo-metric designs to the almond trees that carpet the ground with a "snowfall" of white blossom in January.

The Algarve shoreline is neatly divided in two by the provincial capital, Faro. East of here the *sotavento* (leeward) coast, sheltered by the barrier islands and lagoons of the Ria Formosa. To the west, the *barlavento* (windward) coast is battered by the Atlantic, producing the

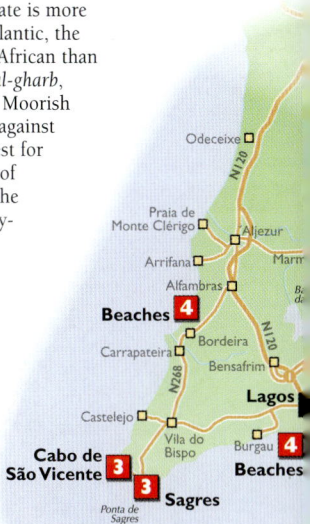

Odeceixe

Praia de
Monte Clérigo

Aljezur

Arrifana

Alfambras

Beaches 4

Carrapateira

Bordeira

Bensafrim

Castelejo

Lagos

Vila do
Bispo

Burgau 4

**Cabo de
São Vicente** 3

3 **Sagres**

*Ponta de
Sagres*

Beaches

**Top left:
Fishing boats
at Albufeira**

**Left: Sand-stacks dot
the beach at
Praia de Dona
Ana, Lagos**

Page 147: Sun, sand and sea, the Algarve dream

typical rock formations of sandstacks, grottoes, cliffs and coves to be found on the Algarve. Henry the Navigator had his school at Sagres, and towns like Tavira and Lagos played a key role in the *descobrimentos* (discoveries) (➤ 7).

Later, the entire region was levelled by the 1755 earthquake, which had its epicentre near Lagos. But the greatest influence on the Algarve has been the arrival of mass tourism, bringing eight million visitors a year. High-rise resorts, golf courses and waterparks have mushroomed from Faro to Lagos, and the development shows no sign of ending. To escape it, head inland to the villages of the Barrocal and the mountains of Monchique, or spend some time in the charming town of Tavira.

This busy tour sweeps across the Algarve, taking in castle ruins, sunbathing and swimming on some of the best beaches in Portugal, a spa village, and on to the "End of the World".

The Algarve in Three Days

Day One

Morning
Explore the old town of 🚌 **Tavira** (➤ 152–153). Climb to the castle ruins for the excellent views, then wander down to the riverside for a picnic in the gardens or lunch at Bica, a no-frills café (➤ 167).

Afternoon and Evening
Walk, drive or take the bus to Quatro Águas, 2km (1.2 miles) east of Tavira, and catch the ferry to Ilha de Tavira (above) for a lazy afternoon on the beach, sunbathing and swimming in some of the warmest waters in Portugal. The Portas do Mar seafood restaurant, on Quatro Águas beside the jetty, is a good place for dinner.

Day Two

Morning
Leave Tavira on the N125 towards Faro. Stop in Luz da Tavira to admire its 16th-century parish church and platibanda

houses, with windows and doorways framed in floral and geometric motifs. Continue to Quinta de Marim for a walk around the **6 Parque Natural da Ria Formosa** (➤ 162). Try to arrive in **7 Faro** (➤ 162) to visit the archaeological museum before lunch by the harbour.

Afternoon and Evening
Continue west on the N125. Just before Almansil, pull off the road to see the astonishing church of São Lourenço, whose interior is completely covered in blue-and-white *azulejos*. Arrive at **11 Albufeira** (➤ 164) in time for a quick dip in the sea or a bracing walk along the beach (right). Albufeira has restaurants to suit every taste and budget, from fresh fish at A Ruina, overlooking the beach, to roast chicken and pizzas in a variety of places in the back streets around Rua 5 de Outubro.

Day Three

Morning
Make an early start and head inland towards Paderne and Portela in the foothills of the Barrocal region. You can take a brief diversion east on the N124 to see the pretty village of **10 Alte** (➤ 164) before returning on the same road to **12 Silves** (below; ➤ 165). Drive up to the castle and visit the cathedral before a seafood lunch at Rui Marisqueira (➤ 169).

Afternoon and Evening
Continue west on the N124 and right on the N266 to climb to the **2 Serra de Monchique** (➤ 154–155). Drive up to the summit of Fóia for great views, then explore the spa village of Caldas de Monchique. Next take a scenic drive through eucalyptus and pinewoods to Aljezur, and follow the N268 south along the wild west coast. You should arrive in **3 Sagres** (➤ 156–157) in time to visit the fortress before watching the sun set from **3 Cabo de São Vicente** (➤ 157–158).

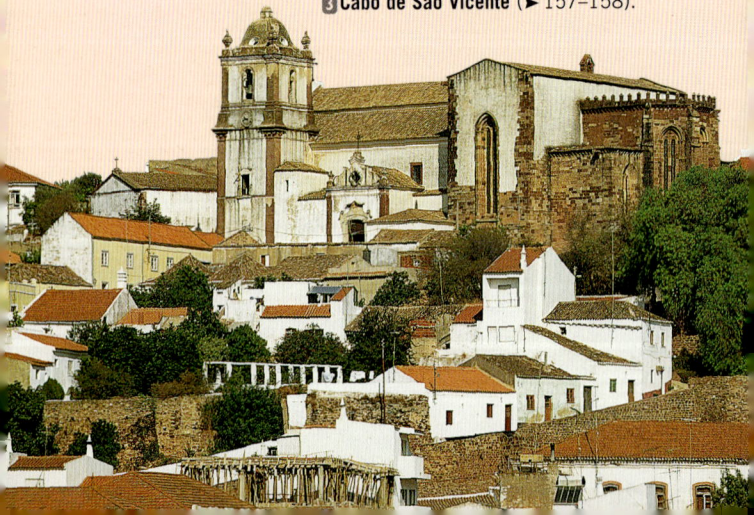

❶ Tavira

This elegant riverside town has somehow managed to escape the tourist tide sweeping the Algarve. It straddles the River Gilão and is close to some of the area's best beaches. A seven-arched bridge, dating from Roman times, joins one side of the town to the other, and its noble houses are adorned with wrought-iron balconies and latticework doors.

Above: Tavira is a world away from some of the bigger resorts

Tavira is the most beautiful town of the Algarve's *sotavento* (leeward) coast. It has palm-lined gardens, fine churches and handsome 18th-century mansions overlooking the river.

During the Islamic era this was one of the three biggest towns in *al-gharb*, and it continued to flourish up to the 16th century as a port providing support for the Portuguese garrisons overseas. Tuna fishing became a major industry until it was ended by the 1755 earthquake, which silted up the harbour, but the town now has a new lease of life as a low-key, low-rise resort.

The best place to start is **Praça da República**, the arcaded square on the west bank of the River Gilão. Climb the steps to **Igreja da Misericórdia**, with its 16th-century portal featuring carvings of Our Lady of Mercy flanked by saints Peter and Paul and the coats of arms of Tavira and Portugal.

A short climb to the left ends at **Castelo dos Mouros**, a ruined Moorish castle fortified by Dom Dinis, where you can walk around the walls for

TAVIRA: INSIDE INFO

Top tip Try the local speciality, *bife de atum cebolada* (tuna steak with onions) at one of the riverside restaurants.

Hidden gem Cacela Velha, 10km (6 miles) east of Tavira, is a tiny village with a fort, church and houses perched on a cliff overlooking a sandy beach on the edge of the Ria Formosa. It is one of the few unspoiled Algarve coastal spots.

Above: Café life beside the River Gilão

Below: The waterfront is lined with grand houses and balconies

great views over Tavira and its distinctive *telhadas de tesouro* (treasure roofs), hip-gabled, pyramid shaped rooftops, which each cover a single room.

Behind the castle, the **Igreja de Santa Maria do Castelo**, built on the site of an old mosque, contains the tombs of Dom Paio Peres Correia, who captured the city from the Moors in 1242, and of seven Christian knights murdered three years earlier.

Further down the hill, the **church of Santiago**, on the edge of the old Mouraria (Moorish quarter), has a plaque on its façade depicting St James the Moor-Slayer, who, according to tradition, helped Dom Paio to conquer the town.

From Praça da República, shady **waterfront gardens**, with an iron bandstand at the centre, lead to the **old fish market**, reopened in 2000 with craft shops and cafés clustered around a central courtyard.

Ilha de Tavira

From the jetty at Quatro Águas, 2km (1.2 miles) east of town, ferries depart (regularly in summer and occasionally in winter) for Ilha da Tavira, an offshore island that forms part of the **Parque Natural da Ria Formosa** (► 162).

Walk across the mudflats to reach the magnificent 11km (6.8-mile) **beach**, backed by sand dunes and lapped by the warmest waters in the Algarve. With beach bars and a campsite, this is hardly a deserted spot, but it is a world away from the big resorts to the west. You can also reach the island by boat from the village of Santa Luzia, or by walking across the causeway and taking the miniature train from the nearby holiday village of Pedras d'el Rei.

TAKING A BREAK

Veneza, on Praça da República, is a popular café and pastry shop. **Portas do Mar** (► 167), one of the fish restaurants by the jetty at Quatro Águas, has an excellent reputation too.

✚ 202 D1

Tourist Information Office
✉ Rua da Galeria 9 ☎ 281 322 511

② Serra de Monchique

The green hills of the volcanic Monchique mountain range provide a welcome respite from the summer heat of the Algarve coast. A trip into the mountains offers the chance to experience a different Algarve, far removed from the overcrowded beaches and busy resorts of the south.

The mountains provide a natural barrier between the Alentejo and the Algarve, soaking up the Atlantic mist and sheltering the coastal region, helping to ensure its famous mild climate. Cork oaks, chestnut and eucalyptus trees grow on wooded hillsides, and the meadows come alive with wild flowers such as rhododendron and mimosa in spring.

The easiest approach to the mountains is to drive north from **Portimão**, one of the Algarve's largest towns and not a place to linger. After 20km (12.5 miles) you reach **Caldas de Monchique**, a spa village since Roman times when it was known as *Mons Cicus*, from which the name Monchique is derived. Nestling in a verdant valley, this is a delightful spot, made more attractive by the recent renovation of the 19th-century spa buildings and neo-Moorish casino.

Above left: Bright local pottery is on display in many of the craft shops in Monchique

Below: The spa town of Caldas de Monchique is set in a verdant valley

You can taste the water at **Fonte dos Amores** (Lovers' Spring), then walk up through the woods to a pretty picnic area beside a stream. Bear in mind that the most famous visitor to the spa, João II, died soon after taking the waters in 1495.

The road continues for 6km (3.7 miles) to **Monchique**, the main town of the region. Climb the steps to the old town to see the 16th-century parish church, Igreja Matriz, whose Manueline portal features columns carved into knotted ropes.

Keep going and eventually you come to a ruined convent, with gardens of lemon and magnolia trees and views across the town to the peak of Picota (773m/2,535 feet).

The highest summit in the Algarve, **Pico da Fóia** (902m/2,960 feet), is reached by a short drive from Monchique. The peak is often shrouded in mist, but on clear days the views stretch to Portimão, Lagos (▶ 165) and Cabo de São Vicente (▶ 157).

Return to Portimão the same way you came, or follow the N267 on a scenic mountain road to Aljezur and the **beaches of the west coast** (▶ 159–161).

Above: The restored spa buildings at Caldas de Monchique

TAKING A BREAK

There are several **inns** on the road to Fóia offering chicken *piri-piri* and rustic mountain cuisine. For a snack, have a *presunto* (cured ham) sandwich and a bottle of Monchique mineral water at **O Tasco** (open all year, tel: 282 910 910, €–€€), a wine bar set beneath the arches in a former stables in Caldas de Monchique.

✚ 202 B2

Tourist Information Office
✉ Largo de São Sebastião, Monchique ☎ 282 911 189

SERRA DE MONCHIQUE: INSIDE INFO

Top tips Look out for *medronho*, a local firewater spirit made from the fruit of the arbutus (wild strawberry) tree.
• Skirting Monchique on the road back down to the coast, stop to look at the handmade **folding wooden chairs**, a design brought to Monchique by the Romans and kept alive by the "Chair Man of Monchique" at a workshop halfway down the hill.

In more depth Ask at the tourist information office in Monchique for information about **walking in the mountains**. A popular walk is the climb to the summit of Picota, the second highest in the range, which takes around 1.5 hours from Monchique.

③ Sagres and Cabo de São Vicente

This wild and windswept cape at the southwest tip of Europe was once known as *O Fim do Mundo* (The End of the World). Standing on the headland and gazing out into the ocean as the waves crash against the cliffs, it is difficult not to feel the excitement of the medieval explorers who set off from Sagres into the great unknown, wondering what perils lay ahead and whether they would ever return.

School of Navigation

It was here in the 15th century that Prince Henry the Navigator founded his School of Navigation, gathering together the greatest cartographers, astronomers, mariners and shipbuilders in Europe. Great advances were made, including the design for a new type of ship, the caravel, a lateen-rigged sailing vessel that was later used by Christopher Columbus for his Atlantic crossings. It was the invention of the caravel that paved the way for Portugal's era of maritime discovery (► 9). Among the explorers who studied at Sagres were Vasco da Gama, Pedro Álvares Cabral and Ferdinand Magellan.

Henry's school was pillaged in 1587 by the British buccaneer Sir Francis Drake, and his precious library was burned to the ground. It probably stood on the site of the **Fortaleza de Sagres**, a 17th-century fortress on a windy promontory on the edge of town. All that remains from an earlier age are the simple chapel of **Nossa Senhora da Graça** and the huge **Rosa dos Ventos** (Wind Compass), 43m (47 yards) in diameter, possibly dating from Henry's time.

Above left: A cannon at the Fortaleza de Sagres

The Town

Sagres is an end-of-the-road sort of town, attracting surfers and backpackers in summer, as well as more upmarket visitors who stay in the **Pousada do Infante** (► 168).

The real attraction of the town lies in its **beaches**, which are some of the best in the Algarve – as long as you can put

up with freezing water and strong ocean winds. The more sheltered beaches are to the east of the fortress.

Praia da Mareta is the most accessible, just below the main square. **Praia da Baleeira** is right beside the harbour, from where it is a short walk to the windsurfing beach of **Praia da Martinhal**.

Cabo de São Vicente

From the *fortaleza*, the road continues for 6km (3.7 miles) across the headland to Cabo de São Vicente, named *Promontorium Sacrum* (Sacred Promontory) by the Romans, who thought the sun sank into the water here every night. Later it became a Christian shrine, based on the legend that the body of St Vincent had been washed ashore here in the 4th century AD after a boat carrying his remains ran aground

at the cape. Later still, in the 12th century, the relics were said to have been transferred to Lisbon in a boat piloted by ravens, and St Vincentis now the patron saint of the capital.

Henry the Navigator is thought to have built his palace on the headland, roughly where the lighthouse now stands. This is one of the most powerful

lighthouses in Europe, its 3,000-watt bulb visible up to 100km (62 miles) out at sea. The waters around the cape have been the site of numerous naval battles, but these days there is not much to disturb the peace. The gusts up on the 60m (197 feet) cliffs can be fierce, and fishermen risk their lives by dangling oversize rods into the sea from the edge of the rock face. Come up here at sunset for magical views.

Below: The lighthouse at Cabo de São Vicente – possibly the first sight of home for the explorers

TAKING A BREAK

The best places to eat are at the **Pousada do Infante** (where you can also stay; ➤ 168) or head down into Sagres town to one of the several eateries on the Praça da República. Try **Cochina** (€) with its extensive menu, or one of the beachfront café/restaurants (**Nortada**, tel: 282 624 147, €).

✚ 202 B1

Tourist Information Centre
✉ Rua Comandante Matoso, Sagres ☎ 282 624 873

Fortaleza de Sagres
✉ Ponta de Sagres
☎ 282 620 140
🕐 Oct–Apr daily 9:30–5:30; May–Sep 9:30–8
💷 Moderate

SAGRES AND CABO DE SÃO VICENTE: INSIDE INFO

Top tips Take a **sweater** to the cape even in summer. If you forget, stalls by the lighthouse sell chunky cardigans and rugs.
• You can walk from Sagres to Cabo de São Vicente along a **clifftop path**. It's a good way of admiring the wild flowers that burst into life on the rocky cape in spring.

Hidden gem Praia do Beliche is a secluded, sheltered cove beneath the cliffs on the way from Sagres to Cabo de São Vicente.

In more depth If Sagres has given you a taste for wild Atlantic beaches, continue up the west coast on the **Costa Vicentina** (➤ 161).

4 Algarve Beaches

You could spend your entire holiday searching for the perfect beach. Everyone has their favourite, from long stretches of golden sand to tiny coves hidden beneath grottoes and ochre cliffs. There are beaches for families, watersports or for a sheltered, away-from-it-all feeling – just take your pick.

Good for Families

Praia Verde
✚ 202 D1

The "green beach" is reached by crossing a valley of pine trees and walking down through the dunes. The sea here is calm and warm and perfect for small children. This is one of a chain of beaches that stretch from Cacela Velha to Monte Gordo, 2km (1.2 miles) east.

Ilha de Tavira
✚ 202 D1

Take the ferry from Tavira to reach this popular island beach (▶ 153). The main beach is suitable for families, but there are some nudist sections further along. Praia do Barril, 4km (2.5 miles) away at the island's western end, is usually less crowded – you can get there by crossing the footbridge from Pedras d'el Rei.

Albufeira
✚ 202 C1

Walk through the rock tunnel to reach this classic Algarve beach, with sandstacks beneath the cliffs. West of Albufeira is a series of attractive cove beaches, such as Praia de São Rafael and Praia da Galé.

Armação de Pêra
✚ 202 B1

The biggest and possibly the most famous beach in the Algarve has sandstacks at one end and flat sands stretching towards Albufeira at the other, with plenty of sunbathers and

At Albufeira the sand just goes on and on

just about every kind of beach activity in between. The resort is popular with Portuguese families.

Praia da Rocha
✠ 202 B1

This was the first tourist town to be developed in the Algarve, giving it a certain time-worn appeal. From the old fortress there are views over the wide beach of golden sand, with strangely eroded rocks sheltering beneath 70m (230-foot) cliffs.

Sheltered Coves
Praia da Marinha
✠ 202 B1

The largest of the cove beaches around the fishing village of Carvoeiro, now a growing resort with a small beach tucked between tall cliffs. In summer, you can take boat trips from Carvoeiro to other nearby cove beaches, including Praia do Benagil and Praia Senhora da Rocha.

Praia de Dona Ana
✠ 202 B1

This perfect cove beach is just outside Lagos, which means it can get crowded on summer weekends. You can

take a boat trip in summer to see the grottoes and caves of Ponte da Piedade (► 185).

Good for Watersports
Meia Praia
✠ 202 B1

Stretching for 4km (2.5 miles), the long crescent beach at Meia Praia, on the east side of Lagos, is popular with windsurfers. Children like it, too, as there are lots of shells washed up on the sand. Watch the strong currents.

Praia da Luz
✠ 202 B1

The largest resort as you head west, this beach has windsurfing and diving schools and a splendid beach backed by cliffs at its eastern end. A clifftop path leads past Ponte da Piedade to Lagos (► 185).

Praia de Odeceixe
✠ 202 B2

This sheltered, dark sandy cove on the borders of the Alentejo and the Algarve sits at the mouth of the Seixe estuary 4km (2.5 miles) from a village of white houses. The beach is especially popular with surfers.

ALGARVE BEACHES: INSIDE INFO

Top tips Beware of **dangerous currents** on the west coast beaches (Arrifana, do Amado, Bordeira, Castelejo, Cordoama and Odeceixa). On calm days the sea can seem almost benevolent, but only experienced swimmers should go in.
• The easiest **access** to the west coast beaches is from Lagos to Arrifana or Sagres to Bordeira.

Off-The-Beaten-Track

Boca do Rio
➕ 202 B1

Halfway between Burgau and Salema on the edge of the Budens wetland reserve, this small beach is situated at a river mouth inside the Costa Vicentina natural park. You can walk along the cliffs to the sandy beach at Cabanas Velhas.

Ilha da Armona
➕ 202 D1

Boats depart from the fishing port of Olhão for this attractive holiday island. There are sand dunes on the sheltered, landward side, or you can escape the crowds by walking across to the other side of the island to a magnificent ocean beach.

Praia da Cordoama
➕ 202 A1

This remote beach is reached by following a dirt track across moor-land from Vila do Bispo. The beach stretches for ever beneath grey slate cliffs. The nearby beach of **Praia do Castelejo** is slightly more accessible on a tarmac road.

Praia da Bordeira
➕ 202 B1

This huge, curving beach, backed by sand dunes, is situated around a lagoon at the mouth of the Bordeira River near Carrapateira.
   Praia do Amado, 4km (2.5 miles) south on the other side of the head-land, is just as impressive.

Praia da Arrifana
➕ 202 B1

This beautiful crescent of sand shelters between cliffs about 10km (6 miles) outside Aljezur. There are good views along the coastline from the ruined fortress above the beach. **Praia de Monte Clérigo**, about 8km (5 miles) from Aljezur, is good for families.

TAKING A BREAK

Most of these beaches have summer **restaurants and bars** offering grilled fish and other snacks. If you are visiting remote beaches like Cordoama and Odeceixe out of season, take a **picnic**.

Praia da Bordeira on the wild west coast feels the full force of the Atlantic

At Your Leisure

The sleepy village of Alcoutim

5 Alcoutim

A giant casuarina tree stands by the harbour in the sleepy village of Alcoutim, looking across the River Guadiana to the Spanish village of Sanlúcar de Guadiana. Here you are close enough to Spain to hear dogs barking, children playing and the church clock chiming the hour on the far bank. Local fishermen will ferry you across, and in summer you can take river trips as far south as Vila Real. Climb to the 14th-century castle at the top of the village for the best views, then follow the beautiful drive along the valley on a twisting road to Foz de Odeleite.

✚ 202 D2
Tourist Information Office
✉ Rua 1° de Maio
☎ 281 546 179

6 Parque Natural da Ria Formosa

The Ria Formosa nature reserve covers 60km (37 miles) of coastline, sheltered from the ocean by partly submerged sand dunes and a network of salt marshes and lagoons.

The best introduction to the ecology and human history of the park is to follow the 3km (2-mile) **self-guided trail** at the Quinta de Marim educational centre near Olhão. The trail leads through pinewoods and

along the shore, passing a working tide mill on the way to a freshwater lake where you might spot herons, storks and purple gallinule (a relative of the moorhen). Also here is a bird hospital for injured wild birds and a kennel where you can see web-footed Portuguese water dogs. You can pick up a map at the reception gate.

✚ 202 C1 ✉ 3km (2 miles) east of Olhão, signposted off the N125 ☎ 289 700 210; www.icn.pt ① Daily 9–12:30, 2–5:30 (office); 10:30–6 (park) 🖐 Inexpensive

7 Faro

The capital of the Algarve is one of the most underrated cities in the country, known mainly for its airport through which millions pass on their way to the south coast beaches.

Starting at the marina, you enter the old town through **Arco da Vila**, a handsome gateway usually topped by a pair of nesting storks – just

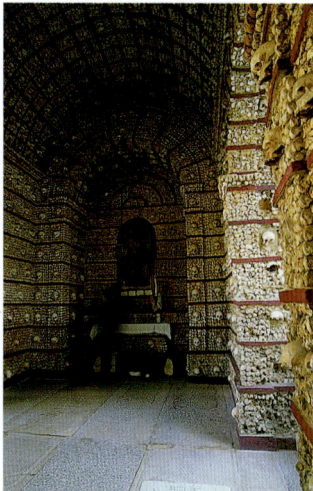

Grim reminders of mortality in the bone chapel at Faro

inside the gateway, an 11th-century horseshoe arch is all that remains of the Moorish walls. Climb to the cathedral square, cobbled and lined with orange trees, then make your way to the **Museu Municipal**, housed in a former convent. Besides the lovely Renaissance cloisters, the chief attraction here is a 3rd-century Roman mosaic depicting the head of Neptune surrounded by the four winds.

It's worth making the short stroll through the new town to the Igreja do Carmo, best known for its chilling **Capela dos Ossos** (Chapel of Bones), whose walls are covered with more than 1,200 skulls and assorted body parts – though this is not as impressive as the similar chapel in Évora (▶ 134).

🕂 202 C1

Tourist Information Office
✉ Rua da Misericórdia 8–12
☎ 289 803 604

Museu Municipal
✉ Praça Dom Afonso III ☎ 289 897 400
🕒 Oct–May Tue–Fri 10–6, Sat–Sun 10:30–5; Jun–Sep Tue–Fri 10–7, Sat–Sun 11:30–6. Last entry 30 mins before closing 💷 Inexpensive; Sun free entry until 2pm

Capela dos Ossos
✉ Largo do Carmo ☎ 289 824 490

🕒 Apr–Oct Mon–Fri 10–1, 3–5, Sat 10–1; Nov–Mar Mon–Fri 10–1, 3–6, Sat 10–1 💷 Inexpensive

8 Estói

The pink rococo palace that dominates the village of Estói was begun in 1840 for the Conde de Cavalhal. It is due to be restored and opened as a *pousada*, but in the meantime it is a romantic ruin and no date has been given for its opening. Just down the hill from the village are the Roman ruins at **Milreu**, which include fine dolphin mosaics.

🕂 202 D1

Milreu
☎ 289 997 823 🕒 Tue–Sun 9–12:30, 2–5:30 (2–6 Apr–Oct) 💷 Inexpensive

The classical gardens at Estói

🄰 Loulé

The Algarve's second city is also a thriving crafts centre and market town. The best time to come is for the busy Saturday market, when local produce and pottery is sold in and around a neo-Moorish market hall. In the streets beneath the castle, you can watch craftspeople at work, carving wood, weaving baskets and making lace in tiny workshops. Loulé is known across Portugal for its Carnival celebrations, the biggest in the country, which take place each February before Lent. Look out for two contrasting churches – the parish church of **São Clemente**, its bell tower housed in a 12th-century minaret, and the space-age **Nossa Senhora da Piedade**, beside an 18th-century chapel on a hill overlooking the town.

✚ 202 C1

Tourist Information Office
✉ Avenida 25 de Abril 9 ☎ 289 463 900

🄸 Alte

This charming village of whitewashed houses is found in the foothills of the Barrocal, a fertile region north of Loulé, which produces almonds, oranges and figs. You could easily spend an hour pottering around the village, admiring the parish church with its Manueline portal and 16th-century *azulejos*, then walk up to the Fonte Pequena and Fonte Grande to drink water from the springs at this well-known beauty spot by the River Alte.

✚ 202 C1

🄸 Albufeira

What was once a quiet fishing village has been transformed over the last 50 years into Portugal's biggest seaside resort. Yet the old town has also survived. Here is a maze of medieval alleyways on a cliff overlooking the beach, its Moorish archway and whitewashed houses lit by old-fashioned lanterns at night. A tunnel carved through the cliff face leads to the main beach, with its curious sandstacks; a second beach,

Sandstacks on the beach at Albufeira, a classic Algarve scene

Praia dos Barcos, has fishing boats on the sand. Beyond here is the nightlife area known as "the Strip", which has good restaurants and lively bars.

➕ 202 C1
Tourist Information Office
✉ Rua 5 de Outubro ☎ 289 585 279

Silves makes a good day out from the Algarve beaches

🔢 Silves

The Moorish capital of *al-gharb* was once a magnificent city, a place of poets, princes and splendid bazaars described in Islamic chronicles as ten times greater than Lisbon. The modern town is dominated by the red sandstone walls of its castle, which you can walk around. Near here is the 13th-century **cathedral**, the pink granite columns of its Gothic nave delightfully uncluttered by the extravagant baroque decoration that affects so many Portuguese churches. The tombstones are those of medieval crusaders who helped capture the town in 1242.

Walk downhill to the **Fábrica do Inglês**, a museum and leisure complex inside an old cork factory.

➕ 202 B1
Castelo
☎ 282 445 624 🕐 Mid-Jul to mid-Sep daily 9–6:30; Mid-Sep to mid-Jul 9–5:30 💰 Inexpensive

Fábrica do Inglês
✉ Rua Gregório Mascarenhas ☎ 282 440 480 🕐 Museum daily 9:30–12:45, 2–6:15 (May–Sep to 8:45). Closed Oct–Jun Sun). Fábrica daily 9am–midnight. Closed Oct–Jun Sun and first 2 weeks Jan 💰 Museum inexpensive, Fábrica free

🔢 Lagos

The port at the mouth of the Bensa-frim River played an important role during the Age of Discovery, when ships departing for Africa sailed from here. A **statue of Henry the Navigator** stands on Praça da República, facing the harbour. On a corner of the same square is a darker reminder of those seafaring days, the site of the first European *mercado de esclavos* (slave market, now an art gallery). A walk along the riverfront can conjure up powerful images of those days. In the backstreets, the **Museu Municipal** has an eclectic collection of Bronze Age *menhirs*, Roman mosaics, African artefacts, Algarve fishing nets, pickled animals, weapons, coins and a gilded chapel.

➕ 202 B1
Tourist Information Office
✉ Rua Belchoir Moreira de Barbudo ☎ 282 763 031

Museu Municipal
✉ Rua General Alberto da Silveira ☎ 282 762 301 🕐 Tue–Sun 9:30–12:30, 2–5 💰 Inexpensive

The Algarve for Kids

If your children have grown bored with the beaches, here are some suggestions:
• **Capela dos Ossos**, Faro (▶ 163), where the walls are covered in skulls and other body parts.
• **Museu Municipal**, Lagos (▶ above), with a collection of oddities from mosaics to pickled animals.
• **Zoomarine** (on N125 near Guia; closed Mon), an aquarium with dolphin and parrot shows.
• **Slide and Splash** (on N125 near Lagoa; open Easter–Oct), Algarve's biggest waterpark.
• **The Big One** (on N125 near Porches; open Easter–Oct), a waterpark that is good for younger children.
• **Lagos Zoo** (in the village of Barão de São João; May–Sep daily 10–7; Oct–Apr 10–5), birds, primates and a children's farm.

Where to... Stay

Prices

Expect to pay for a double room with bathroom in high season

€ = under €60 €€ = €60–€120 €€€ = €121–€180 €€€€ = over €180

Convento de Santo António
€€–€€€€

This gem of a hotel was converted from a 17th-century Capuchin convent, and has been in the same family for the past 200 years. From the exterior you wouldn't know it was a hotel – the large white portal of the chapel hides the garden and the 17th-century cloisters. The atmosphere and peace of the former convent have been preserved, and most of the rooms are converted monks' cells. Breakfast is served in the arched courtyard and guests are free to linger here or by the pool. Booking in advance is essential and

minimum stays are two to four nights, depending on the season.

🚹 202 D1 ⊠ Rua de Santo António 56 ☎ 281 321 573, fax: 281 321 573 ⓒ Closed Jan

Hotel Quinta do Lago €€€€

Thirty minutes by car from Faro, the Quinta do Lago sits in verdant luxury, overlooking the lagoon and the sea. Arguably justified in calling itself "the finest hotel in the Algarve", it provides abundant facilities and luxurious accommodation. Sports enthusiasts are spoiled for choice, and it is particularly popular with golfers who can choose

from three different championship courses (▶ 170). You can dine on Portuguese gourmet fare watching the sun set in the Brisa do Mar, or feast on Venetian cuisine in the intimate Ca d'Oro. Stylish rooms come with spacious terraces, and little luxuries such as praline chocolates, a carafe of port and fresh flowers.

🚹 202 C1 ⊠ Quinta do Lago, Almancil ☎ 289 350 350, fax: 289 396 393; info@quintadolagohotel.com; reservations@quintadolagohotel.com; www.quintadolagohotel.com

Quinta dos Rochas €–€€

A guesthouse between Almancil and Quarteira, the Quinta dos Rochas offers six rooms in a peaceful rural setting. The house is southern Portuguese in style: whitewashed walls, Moorish arches, tiled floors and flowery terraces. The rooms all come with private bathroom and satellite TV and guests can relax in the lounge bar, library or on the

terraces. There is no restaurant but Almancil, near by, is the Algarve's gastronomic centre. The beach is 2km (1.2 miles) away, and there are excellent golf, tennis and riding facilities close to the hotel.

🚹 202 C1 ⊠ Fonte Coberta, Caixa Postal 600A, Almancil ☎ 289 393 165, fax: 289 399 198; quintadosrochas@mail.telepac.pt www.geocities.com/quintadosrochas/ ⓒ Closed Nov and Dec

Estalagem Monte do Casal €€€–€€€€

This small and exclusive English-run hotel is tucked away in the gentle hills above Faro, with fine views down to the sea. Surrounded by gardens and terraces, it has its own pool, bar and a first-class restaurant. The rooms have a private terrace where breakfast is served. The restaurant is a converted coach house that specialises in sophisticated French cuisine. In summer

Where to...
Eat and Drink

Prices
Expect to pay per person for a three-course à la carte meal, excluding drinks and tips
€ = under €12 €€ = €12–24 €€€ = €25–36 €€€€ = over €36

SILVES

Quinta do Rio €
Northeast of Silves, this rural guest house enjoys a peaceful setting in rolling hills and orange groves. The house has been enlarged to accommodate six bedrooms, all with their own shower room and four with a terrace. The rooms are simple and clean. Evening meals (first-class Italian) can be arranged in advance.

🔢 **202 C1** 🏠 **Sitio São Estevão, Apt 217** ☎ **282 445 528, fax: 282 445 528** 🕐 **Closed two weeks Dec**

LAGOS

Casa Grande €–€€
The Casa Grande is a rambling guest house furnished with antiques and curiosities. The house is a short walk from the beach. The rooms are large and upstairs they have their own balconies. There's a restaurant.

🔢 **202 B1** 🏠 **Burgau, Lagos** ☎ **282 697 416, fax: 282 697 825;** www.nexus-pt.com/casagrande

TAVIRA

Bica €
This is a no-frills café-style place, tucked down a side street north of the river. It's great value, but don't be surprised if the service is brusque and the waiter doesn't speak English. It's usually full of locals, watching TV and tucking into big helpings of sea bream or tuna fillet with onion sauce, fillet of turkey with shrimps or sole with orange sauce.

🔢 **202 D1** 🏠 **Rua Almirante Cândido dos Reis 22** ☎ **281 323 843** 🕐 **Daily noon–2, 7:30–10:30**

Portas do Mar €€
On the waterfront where the River Gilão meets the Rio Formosa estuary, the Portas do Mar is one of a cluster of fish restaurants downstream from Tavira. It's a modern building with a pretty blue-and-white interior and a terrace for fine views of the estuary. The choice of fish, the freshest of which is hauled ashore at the nearby port, ranges from lobster and crayfish to monkfish or shellfish *cataplana*.

🔢 **202 D1** 🏠 **Sítio das Quatro Águas** ☎ **281 321 255** 🕐 **Jul–Sep Wed–Mon 12:30–3, 7–midnight; Oct–Jun 12:30–3, 6:30–10:30**

---

guests can dine on the terrace under the palms; in cooler months, open log fires and candlelit tables provide guests with a warm welcome.

🔢 **202 D1** 🏠 **Cerro do Lobo** ☎ **289 990 140, fax: 289 991 341;** montedocasal@mail.telepac.pt; www.montedocasal.pt 🕐 **Closed late Nov–early Feb; open for Christmas**

ALBUFEIRA

Casa Bela Moura €€–€€€
A modern house in Moorish style, the Casa Bela Moura is a family-run guesthouse with rooms divided between the main house and a nearby annexe. The bar, breakfast room and reception are welcoming, and the 13 rooms are very clean. It has its own pool and is only 1.5km (1 mile) from the pretty cove of Nossa Senhora da Rocha.

🔢 **202 C1** 🏠 **Estrada de Porches 530, Alporchinhos** ☎ **282 313 422, fax: 282 313 025;** www.casabelamoura.com 🕐 **Closed Nov and Dec**

MONCHIQUE

Albergaria Bica-Boa €€

On a mountainside surrounded by flower-filled gardens, the Bica-Boa is a delightful guesthouse and restaurant, run by an Irish and Finnish couple. It provides a warm welcome and some of the best-value food in the region. The menu features Monchique dishes such as chicken *piri-piri* (with a chilli pepper sauce) and *cabrito estufado* (goat stew) as well as fish and a good choice of vegetarian dishes.

✚ 202 B1 ☒ Estrada de Lisboa 266 (1km/0.6 miles north of Monchique on the Lisbon road) ☎ 282 912 271 ⓖ Daily noon–2, 7:30–10:30

SAGRES

Pousada do Infante €€€

The Infante here was Henry the Navigator, and the *pousada* is set on the cliffs close to his famous navigation school at Sagres (▶ 156). Authentic Portuguese cuisine is served in an elegant dining room decorated with *azulejos*, or in the summer on a terrace with fine views of the fortress. The emphasis is on fresh fish and seafood, and the catch of the day will probably have been landed that morning at Sagres. Typical dishes are tuna steak in onion marinade, baked swordfish and shellfish *cataplana*. An extensive wine list ranges from house wine from Lagoa to the more pricey Bairradas or Dãos.

✚ 202 A1 ☒ Sagres ☎ 282 620 240 ⓖ Daily noon–2, 8–10:30

FARO

A Taska €€

Not far from Largo do Carmo this charming, no-frills eatery is particularly popular with the locals. The dining rooms are split between two floors and their walls are decorated with the work of local artists and verses by Antonio Aleixo, a well-known 20th-century Algarvian people's poet. An open fire burns in the winter months. A Taska serves authentic regional food in generous helpings, dishes here include rice with beans and razor fish, prawn curry, great fried squid and much more.

✚ 202 B1 ☒ Rua Alportel 38 ☎ 289 824 739 ⓖ Mon–Sat 12:30–3, 7:30–11:30

LOULÉ

Avenida Velha €€

This first-floor restaurant has been here for many years. It's a cheerful, friendly place, with wooden tables and walls crammed with ceramics. No sooner have you sat down than the appetisers arrive: fried squid, sardines, olives and home-made bread. To follow you could go for sole, tiger prawns, *cataplanas* or Portuguese meat dishes, accompanied by Algarve wine.

✚ 202 C1 ☒ Avenida José da Costa Mealha 40 ☎ 289 416 474 ⓖ Mon–Sat noon–3, 6–11, Sun 6–11

ALBUFEIRA

O Cabaz da Praia €€€

For many years "The Beach Basket" has been the best restaurant in Albufeira. Built on the cliffs, it overlooks the beach and has great views from the rooftop terrace. The service is excellent, the atmosphere friendly and the dishes well presented. The menu features French and international cuisine, and might include monkfish flambeed with spicy mango sauce, duck breast with quinces and honey or home-made tagliatelle with prawns.

✚ 202 C1 ☒ Praça Miguel Bombarda 7 ☎ 289 512 137 ⓖ Fri–Wed noon–2:30, 6:30–11

LAGOS

Dom Sebastião €€

The central location on the main pedestrian street and warm welcome here ensures a steady stream of visitors. It's not the cheapest place in town, but there are fine appetisers,

the fish and seafood excellent and there are home-made desserts. Choose from prawns, crayfish or lobster or the delicious fish risotto. Extensive wine list.

🕂 202 B1 ⊠ Rua 25 de Abril 20
☎ 282 762 795; domsebastiao@ip.pt
🕘 Daily noon–11 pm

SILVES

Rui Marisqueira €€–€€€

This is one of the Algarve's best-known fish restaurants, with a great choice of shellfish. The décor is nothing special, it's fairly noisy and the service can be offhand, but all is forgiven when the seafood platter arrives overflowing with lobsters and crabs, prawns and oysters. Main courses range from grilled fresh fish to clams *cataplana* and fish risotto. Fish dishes are priced by the kilo, so ask the price before you order that fat bass or bream.

🕂 202 C1 ⊠ Rua Commendador Vilarinho 27 ☎ 282 442 682
🕘 Wed–Mon noon–3:30, 6:30–10:30

Where to...
Shop

MARKETS

Olhão has the best fish market in the Algarve, held daily, except on Sunday, alongside the fruit and vegetable market.

Loulé is at its liveliest on Saturday mornings when the market is in full swing and all the surrounding streets are packed with stalls selling olives and sausages, poultry and pottery.

The covered food market in **Lagos** (Rua das Portas de Portugal, Mon–Sat 8–1) has a splendid display of fresh fish, fruit and vegetables, and there's a very colourful "gipsy market" in town on the first Saturday of every month.

The market in **Monchique** is held on the second Friday of each month.

CLOTHING AND CRAFTS

Many of Tavira's shops specialise in crafts. Visit the **Casa do Artesanato** (Calçada da Galeria II) or the **Artesanato Regional Bazar** (Rua José Pires Padinha) for baskets and woven goods, and **Alart** (Rua do Galria) for pottery. The **Casa Verde** (Rua Dr. Francisco Gomes, tel: 289 825 153) in Faro has excellen- lace, pottery and leather, while **Martinez** (Rua Tenente Valdim) is a stylish clothes shop with fashion for all ages. Loulé is one of the best towns to see Algarvio craft workers in action: old liquor stills and copper *cataplana* pots are sold at several shops along Rue de Barbacá. The **Centro de Artesanato** (Rua de Barbacá) offers a wide range of goods including ceramics and homemade rugs.

Chunky woollen cardigans and jumpers are sold at **Cabo de São Vicente** stalls.

In Silves, **Peter Liesegon** (Largo Jerónimo Osório) has an elegant antiques and art shop specialising in ceramics. There are several small craft shops on Rua Policarpo Dias.

FOOD AND DRINK

The markets on this page are the best places to stock up for picnics.

For a great choice of port try the **Supermercado Garrafeira** (Praça de Almeida 28, Faro), where you will be helped to choose a vintage.

The **Adega Cooperativa** on the road between Portimão and Lagoa (Lagoa wines are robust reds plus decent whites and rosés, the best in the Algarve) holds daily guided tours including tastings (tel: 282 342 181 to book). For delicious almond cakes try **Pastelaria Taquelim Concalvesa** (Rua Portas de Portugal, Lagos).

Caldas de Monchique, 7km (4.3 miles) south of Monchique, is famous for *medronho*, a firewater made from local arbutus berries – taste it at the craft centre in the former casino.

Where to...
Be Entertained

SPORT AND OUTDOOR PURSUITS

Watersports

Blessed with a mild climate all year round and Portugal's safest beaches, the Algarve is one of Europe's main centres for watersports. On the coast seek out opportunities for surfing, windsurfing, parasailing and boat trips, for example at the **Water-sports Centre** near Albufeira (tel: 289 394 929).

Waterparks

In Lagoa, **Slide & Splash** (along the N125, Vale de Deus, Estômbar, tel: 282 340 800) is a huge complex of water chutes, slides and swimming pools to keep water-babies amused. Water slides and parks have sprouted up all along the Algarve – they're not hard to find.

Golf

Golf (www.portugalgolf.pt) leads the way for land sports – there are 24 excellent courses in the region. The luxury resorts of **Quinta do Lago** and **Vale do Lobo** have six scenic courses between them, the most famous being the Quinta do Lago (tel: 289 351 900). The latest, in Vilamoura, is the **Millennium** (tel: 289 310 188), opened in 2000. **Penina** (5km/3 miles west of Portimão on the N125, tel: 282 420 223) is an 18-hole course designed by Henry Cotton, who also came up with **Alto Golf** between Alvor and Portimão (tel: 282 460 870), which has Europe's longest par five.

Tennis

The country's two leading tennis academies are **Vale do Lobo**

(tel: 289 357 850), with 14 courts plus a pool, sauna and gym, and **Barrington's** (tel: 289 351 940).

MUSIC AND NIGHTLIFE

Albufeira is the social hotspot. The best discos are out of town, such as top-rate **Locomia** (Praia de Santa Eulália), which has fantastic views and music from techno to dance.

For something more intimate there's the **St James's Club** in Almancil, an exclusive bar-disco enforcing a dress code and offering a drive-you-home service.

In Vilamoura **The Terrace** on Ermitage holds live jazz sessions every Sunday from 5 to 8pm (tel: 289 355 271) while folk dancing takes place at local hotels. Other popular venues for live music are **Harry's Bar** and **Central Station** on Largo Duarte Pacheco, Albufeira.

Faro's nightlife is concentrated on **Rua do Prior**, where you'll find **Emporium** (No 23). July is the best month for classical and jazz.

In **Lagos** there is the Centro Cultural (tel: 282 770 450) and is Almancil is the **Centro Cultural de São Lourenço** (tel: 289 395 475). Both host music festivals, concerts and recitals featuring international musicians. *Fado* nights are Saturday (and Tuesdays in summer) at **Adega do Papagaio** (Espiche, tel: 282 789 423), a converted wine cellar.

BOAT TRIPS AND FISHING

To see some of the least spoiled scenery in the Algarve, take a boat trip along the River Guadiana. These depart three times a week from Vila Real de Santo António; contact **Riosul** (Rua Tristão Vaz Teixeira, Monte Gordo, tel: 281 510 200). For trips to Alcoutim try **Turismar** (tel: 281 513 504).

Several companies offer half-day cruises from Portimão (not in winter), visiting caves, grottoes and beaches. These include **Portitours** (tel: 282 470 063) – they will arrange transport from hotels.

Walks & Tours

1 Lisbon 172 – 175
2 Port Country 176 – 179
3 Lower Alentejo 180 – 183
4 Lagos to Praia da Luz 184 – 186

1 LISBON
Walk

This walk introduces you to three very different districts – Alfama, Baixa and Bairro Alto – which together make up the historic core of Lisbon. The journey includes a tram ride and a climb on a funicular, which are not only enjoyable in themselves, but also a convenient way of getting up the hills. Although the walk can be done in as little as two hours, it is best to allow at least half a day, allowing some time for window shopping, cafés and visits to churches and museums along the way.

Top tip
A **one-day bus pass**, valid on buses, trams and funiculars and the Elevador de Santa Justa, is available at the ticket booth in Praça da Figueira (near Rossío).

DISTANCE 4km (2.5 miles) walking plus tram and funicular rides
TIME 2–2.5 hours
START/END POINT Praça do Comércio ✛ 196 C1

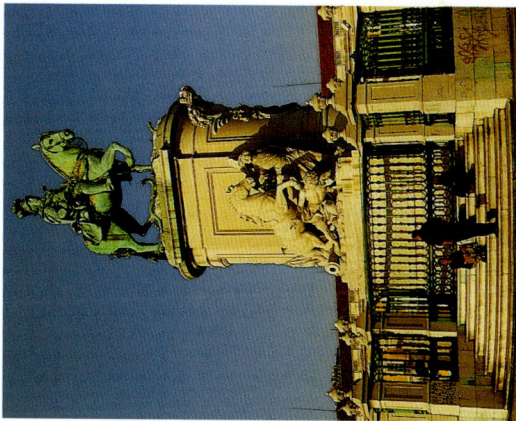

1–2
Start in **Praça do Comércio**, the large open square on the waterfront, with your back to the river. The square is still known as Terreiro do Paço, after the royal palace which once stood on this site. At the centre is a statue of Dom José I, king of Portugal at the time of the 1755 earthquake and the subsequent rebuilding of Lisbon. Walk straight ahead through the triumphal arch, the symbolic gateway to the city from the river. This brings you into Rua Augusta, the principal shopping street of the Baixa (lower town). On sunny days the promenade comes alive with buskers, street traders, busy news stands and café terraces. The shops along here are an eclectic mix of high street fashion chains and quirky

Previous page: Lamego is an attractive town of Renaissance and baroque mansions

Right: The walk begins on Praça do Comércio by the statue of Dom José I

local stores such as **Casa Macário** (No 272–274), an old-fashioned coffee shop where bottles of vintage port gather dust on the shelves. Approaching the top of the street, glance to your left to see the **Elevador de Santa Justa**, a much-loved iron lift designed

by a pupil of Gustave Eiffel, which opened in 1902 to connect Baixa with Chiado. Although the escalators inside the Baixa-Chiado metro station now do a more efficient job, the ride on the *elevador* is still an exhilarating experience and the views from the top are superb.

Rua Augusta ends in the **Rossio**, the nearest thing in Lisbon to a central square, with its fountains, flower stalls and a wavy mosaic pavement. The square is officially named Praça Dom

MOURARIA

ALFAMA

2–3

7 Largo do C de Dentro

■ **Museu e Casa do Fado**

Tejo

Rua Regueira

★ Largo de São Miguel

6

Museu das Artes Decorativas ■

✝ **Igreja da Santa Luzia**

✝ **Sé (Catedral)**

200 metres
200 yards
0
0

✝

Rua Augusta

★ **Arco da Rua Augusta**

■ **Praça do Comércio**

1

BAIXA

✝

Rossio ■
Praça da Figueira

2

Rua Augusta

Rossio ■
(Praça Dom Pedro IV)

Baixa-Chiado ●

Largo São Domingos

Elevador de Santa Justa ■

Largo do Carmo ■

4

CHIADO

5

Rua Garrett

Serpa Pinto

Rua A. Maria Cardoso

✝ ✝

Elevador da Glória ■

Praça dos Restauradores ■

Estação Central do Rossio ■

Restauradores

● ℹ

Palácio Foz

3

Miradouro de São Pedro de Alcântara
✝

RUA SÃO PEDRO ALCÂNTARA

BAIRRO ALTO

Rua do Diario d Noticias

Travessa da Queimada

Rua d Diario d Noticias

Igreja de São Roque ■

Largo Trinidade Coelho

Pedro IV after the statue of the king at its centre – though the statue was initially designed as a likeness of Emperor Maximilian of Mexico, who was executed before it could be completed. Café Nicola and Pastelaria Suiça, facing each other across the Rossio, offer a choice of terraces for people watching, and there are good views of the ruined **Igreja do Carmo** (▶ 175), high on the hill above the western side of the square. Leave the square by the far left corner and you find yourself in front of Rossio station, with its imposing neo-Manueline façade. Built as Lisbon's central station in 1892, it was the departure point for trains to Sintra (now Sete Rios Station).

Continue into **Praça dos Restauradores**, a large square with an obelisk at the centre commemorating Portugal's independence from Spain. On your left is **Palácio Foz**, a former nightclub and Ministry of Propaganda building now housing the city tourist office.

3–4

Just beyond the palace, the **Elevador da Glória** funicular trundles up to the Bairro Alto on what must be one of the world's steepest public transport rides, emerging opposite the **Solar do Vinho do Porto** (▶ 71–72). Turn right at the upper terminus to reach the garden

and *miradouro* of São Pedro de Alcântara, with magnificent views of the cathedral, castle and Tagus estuary. Now you can head into the warren of medieval streets that make up the **Bairro Alto** (▶ 63–64).

This area rewards random exploration, but one possible route is to take Travessa de São Pedro from opposite the fountain, take the second left along Rua dos Mouros (Street of the Moors), then turn left and immediately right along Rua do Diário de Notícias. As you reach Travessa da Queimada, turn left, passing Café Luso, one of Lisbon's famous *fado* houses, which has *fado* and folk dancing on most nights.

Lisbon stretches before you from the Miradouro de Santa Luzia

following the 1755 earthquake, is now an archaeological museum.

4–5

Leave the square by Rua da Trinidade. When you see a house with a fine *azulejo*-tiled façade on your right, turn left along Rua Serpa Pinto. This brings you out onto Rua Garrett, Chiado's most fashionable shopping street, heavily restored after a disastrous fire in 1988. Treat yourself to a coffee and pastry at one of two venerable institutions, Pastelaria Bernard and A Brasileira (➤ 70). The poet Fernando Pessoa used to meet his friends at A Brasileira and his statue on the pavement acts as a magnet for tourists.

5–6

Cross Rua Garrett to reach Rua António Maria Cardoso where you can hop on to tram 28, dropping back down to Baixa and passing the cathedral on the way up to Largo das Portas do Sol. Get off the tram opposite the **Museu de Artes Decorativas** (➤ 55).

From the *miradouro* (viewpoint) there are views over the Alfama rooftops to the churches of São Vicente de Fora and Santa Engrácia. From here you can plunge down to explore **Alfama** (➤ 54–57).

This brings you out opposite Largo Trinidade Coelho, known as Largo da Misericórdia and dominated by the Jesuit **Igreja de São Roque.** This is the headquarters of the Misericórdia charity, beneficiaries of Portugal's national lottery – hence the bronze statue of a ticket seller on the square in front of the church.

Leave this square by the Calçada do Duque steps and take the second right along Rua da Condessa to reach **Largo do Carmo,** a pretty square at the heart of the Chiado district. The ruined convent here, an empty shell

6–7

Take the staircase beside **Santa Luzia church** to enter a secret world of cobbled lanes, washing hanging from balconies, fountains, patios and hidden courtyards of orange trees. Turn left down more steps to reach Largo de São Miguel, where a tall palm tree stands guard in front of the church. Turn left here along Rua de São Miguel. At the end of this street, turn right and right again to reach Largo do Chafariz de Dentro, an open square facing the **Museu do Fado** (➤ 56–57).

7–8

Leave this square by the far corner along Rua de São Pedro, where women sell sardines from their doorways on weekday mornings. Look out in particular for **Beco de Azinhal,** a pretty courtyard with restaurant tables, immediately on your right at the start of the street. Continue along Rua de São Pedro, passing a rare surviving section of Moorish wall. The road widens and becomes Rua de São João da Praça, where several of the apartment blocks and shopfronts are decorated with *azulejo* tiles. Continue on this street, passing the *sé* (cathedral), then follow the tramlines down to Rua da Conceição and turn left along Rua Augusta to return to Praça do Comércio.

Taking a Break
Café Nicola
🚩 196 C4 ⊠ Praca Dom Pedro IV (Rossio) ◎ Mon–Fri 8am–10pm, Sat 9am–10pm, Sun 10–7 🍴€

Pastelaria Suíça
🚩 196 C4 ⊠ Praca Dom Pedro IV (Rossio) 96–104 ◎ Daily 7am–10pm (9 in winter) 🍴€

Pastelaria Bernard
🚩 196 B3 ⊠ Rua Garrett 104 ◎ Mon–Sat 8am–11pm 🍴€

Lautasco
🚩 197 F3 ⊠ Beco de Azinhal 7 ☎ 218 860 173 ◎ Mon–Sat lunch and dinner 🍴€€

2 PORT COUNTRY

Drive

This spectacular drive takes you through the steeply terraced vineyards of the Douro Valley, where the grapes in port wine are grown. The scenery is magnificent at any time of year but at its best in summer when the grapes are ripening on the vines, or in September and October when the harvest is taking place. Some of the roads are twisting and narrow, so allow plenty of time.

DISTANCE 130km (80.5 miles)
TIME 4 hours
START/END POINT Vila Real ✚ 198 C3

1–2

Start in **Vila Real** and follow signs for the IP4 in the direction of Porto and Amarante. Take care as this motorway climbs steeply and it is a notorious spot for accidents. After 24km (15 miles), turn off at the sign for "pousada" and cross the bridge to reach the **Pousada de São Gonçalo**. Turn right, follow the minor N15 for around 12km (7.4 miles) as it snakes down through the pine forests of the Ovelha Valley in the foothills of the Serra de Marão.

Lamego

A short detour south from Peso da Régua on the fast new IP3 motorway leads to Lamego, an attractive town of Renaissance and baroque mansions overlooked by two hills. On one of the hills stands a ruined 12th-century castle; on the other is the sanctuary of Nossa Senhora dos Remédios, reached by a magnificent baroque stairway similar to that at Bom Jesus near Braga (▶ 90). The chapel is the focus for a major pilgrimage, which takes place on 8 September each year. Lamego was the setting for the first Cortes (National Assembly), a meeting of the nobility, clergy and townspeople which proclaimed Afonso Henriques as first king of Portugal in 1143. These days it is better known as the centre of production for Raposeira, Portuguese sparkling wine. The wine cellars, which are 1km (0.6 miles) out of town on the road to Castro Daire, are closed for refurbishment. For details of reopening (tel: 254 655 003 or 254 612 005).

The fountain at Nossa Senhora dos Remédios, Lamego

mountains and their strange granite boulders, then reaches a plateau and drops down through the vineyards to **Mesão Frio**. Cross the stone bridge across the River Teixeira to enter the town and soon you have your first view of the great sweep of the River Douro down below.

3–4

Now you are in the heart of port wine country, surrounded by the steep slopes of the vineyards, painstakingly carved into fertile terraces by generations of farmers. As a local saying has it: "God created Earth, but man created the Douro." The road narrows, twisting and turning as it drops down to the river, passing the Pousada Solar da Rede, one of the finest of the *pousadas*, set on an 18th-century wine estate with great river views. Follow the river along its north bank (N108) through the spa town of Caldas de Moledo as far as **Peso da Régua**. This busy town, usually known as Régua, was built to serve the port trade and acts as a centre for transporting wine to Porto. *Barcos rabelos* boats, which these days serve a decorative purpose only, are moored on the riverbank

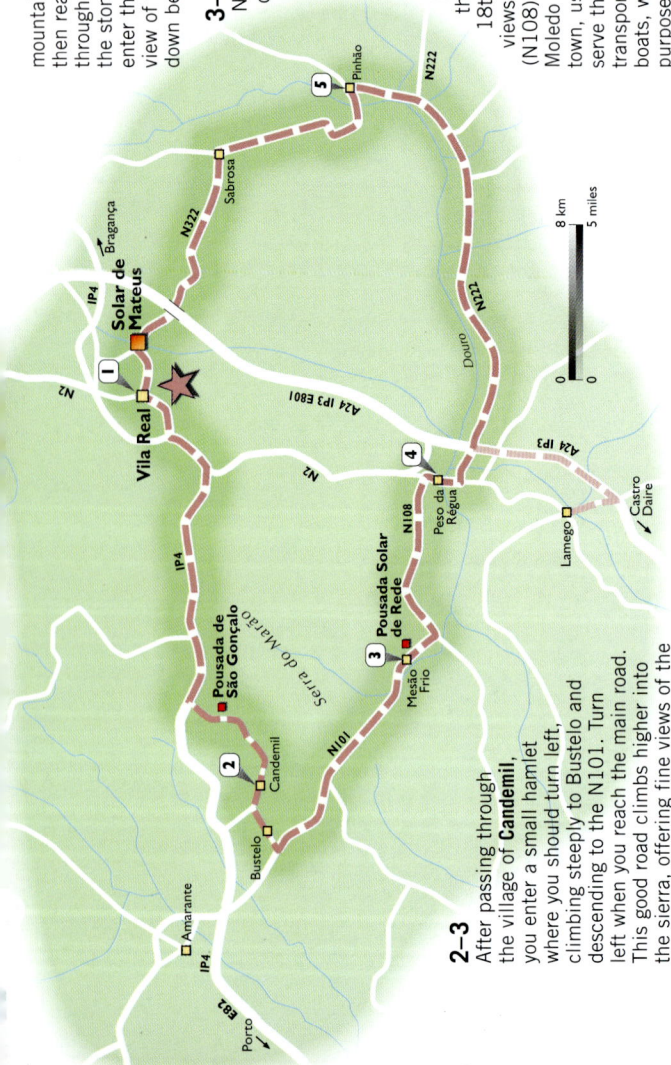

2–3

After passing through the village of **Candemil**, you enter a small hamlet where you should turn left, climbing steeply to Bustelo and descending to the N101. Turn left when you reach the main road. This good road climbs higher into the sierra, offering fine views of the

The dramatic landscapes of the Douro Valley can also be explored on scenic train and boat journeys from Porto. River trips run from Porto and Vila Nova de Gaia between March and October, typically travelling upstream as far as Peso da Régua and returning to Porto by train. Several trains a day leave Porto's São Bento station on the Douro Valley train line, which joins the river about 60km (37 miles) from Porto and follows its banks as far as Peso da Régua (2.5 hours), Pinhão (3 hours), Tua and Pocinho. Tickets are inexpensive and can be bought in advance or at the time of travel from São Bento station in Porto, or from the stations at Peso da Régua or Pinhão. There are also two scenic narrow-gauge branch lines along tributaries of the River Douro – the Corgo line running from Régua to Vila Real, and the Tua Valley line from Tua to Mirandela.

Leaving the Car Behind

Vila Real. You pass the Roman site of **Panóias** (▶ 86–87), on your way to **Solar de Mateus**, the impressive Portuguese manor house which you can see from a bend in the road as you approach. Turn right immediately after Mateus to return to Vila Real.

clinging close to the river with views of vineyards, olive groves, dry-stone walls and white-painted *quintas* with the names of the famous port houses emblazoned on the hillsides. Several of the *quintas* are open to visitors – **Quinta do Panascal** (on the slopes above the River Távora, tel: 254 732 321; Mon–Fri 10–5:30, also weekends Apr–Oct) has audio tours, vineyard walks and a stone *lagar* where the grapes are crushed by foot.

About 23km (14 miles) from Régua, turn left to enter **Pinhão**, crossing an iron bridge over the Douro to return to the north bank. Drive along the main street; don't miss the station building with its *azulejo* tiles depicting vineyards and rural scenes. This small town is one of the main centres of quality port production, and several of the leading houses have quintas here. For a glass of port, drop into Taylor's **Vintage House Hotel** (Lugar da Ponte, Pinhão, tel: 254 730 230), in a beautiful setting on the riverbank.

5–6

Leaving Pinhão, fork left where the road divides, following signs for Sabrosa and Vila Real. The road climbs through terraced vineyards. At **Sabrosa**, birthplace of the navigator Ferdinand Magellan (▶ 7), turn left towards

Taking a Break
O Malheiro
🚩 198 C4 ⊠ Rua dos Camilos, Regua ☎ 254 313 684 ⏰ Daily lunch and dinner 💰 €

and in summer you can take a cruise along the river to the nearby *quintas* (wine estates). **Quinta de São Domingos** (Peso da Régua, tel: 254 320 260; Mon–Fri 9–12:30, 2–5; Sat–Sun 9–6; tours take about 20 minutes, free), in the town centre, offers tours and tastings throughout the year. There are plenty of restaurants and cafés along the waterfront at Peso da Régua or try O Malheiro, set just back from the river on the main street. (For a detour to **Lamego** ▶ 176.)

4–5

Take the lower of the two bridges across the River Douro and keep right to swing back under the bridge and emerge beside the river. Now follow the N222 along the south bank of the Douro to Pinhão. This is a lovely drive,

Page 179: There are several *quintas* (wine estates) in and around Pinhão

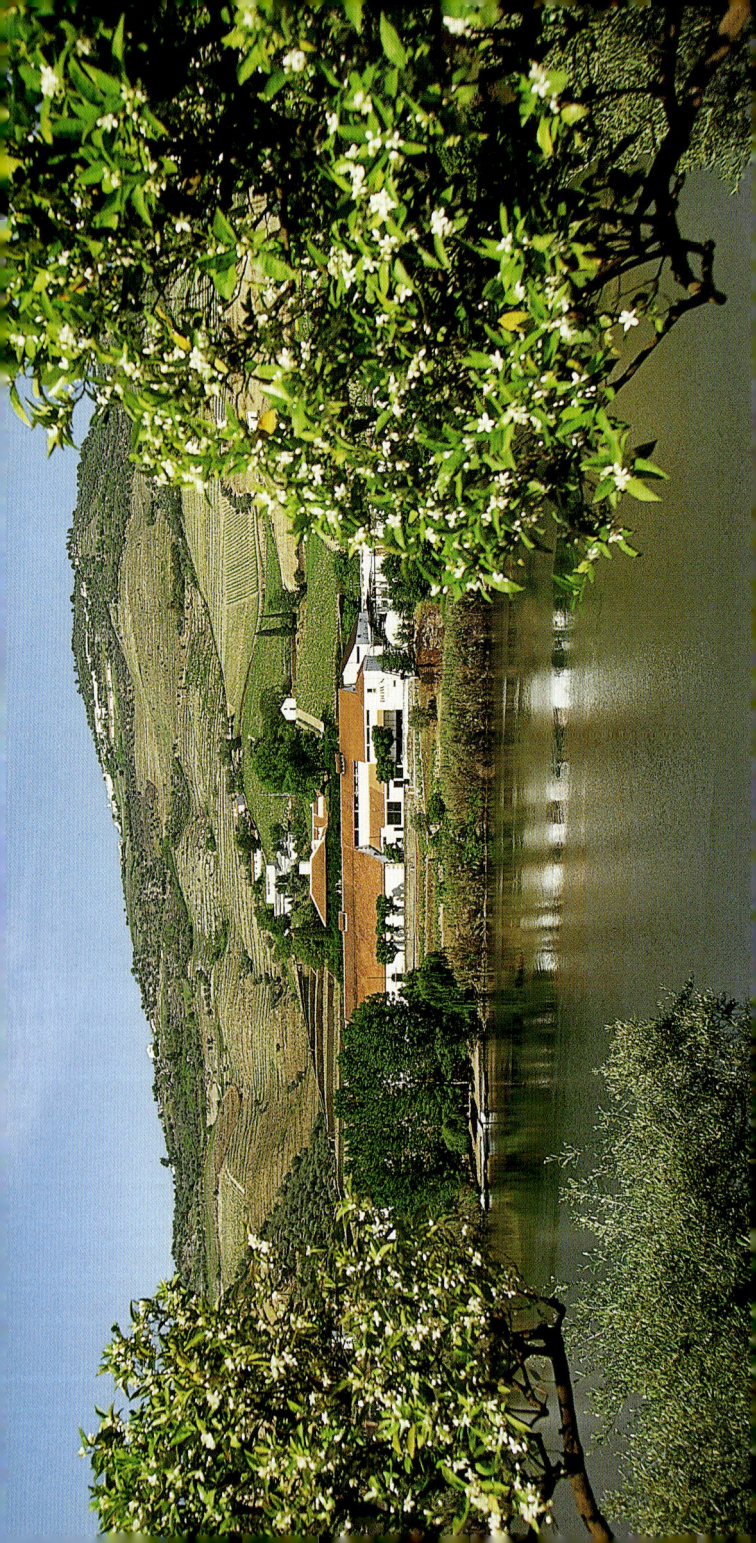

3 LOWER ALENTEJO
Drive

This enjoyable drive takes you into Lower Alentejo, a region ignored by most visitors in the dash from Lisbon to the Algarve. Few people live here and there are few must-see sights – the pleasures of this region are to be found driving along empty roads and pottering around small towns. Despite, or perhaps because of, the absence of other visitors, it is in places like Serpa and Moura that you can really feel the soul of southern Portugal and the influence of its Moorish past.

DISTANCE 222km (138 miles)
TIME 4 hours
START/END POINT Beja ✚ 201 D1

1–2
Start in **Beja** (➤ 142) and leave the city by following the IP2 in the direction of Faro. The road crosses a wide open landscape of wheat fields and cork oak trees, many with numbers painted on the stripped bark to indicate the

The convent at Beja, where the love letters of a Portuguese nun are said to have been written

date of the harvest. After 15km (9.3 miles), turn left on the N122 towards Mértola, on a quiet road with more cork oaks and the occasional isolated farmhouse or roadside hamlet. Turn right at the roundabout to enter **Mértola** (➤ 142) and park beneath the castle in the centre of town.

2–3
Once you have explored Mértola, leave by the same way you entered and take the bridge across the River Guadiana, following signs to Serpa – be sure to glance back as you cross the bridge for a lovely view of the town. The road climbs steeply at first, then levels out, with avenues of eucalyptus trees to either side. After 17km (10.5 miles) you reach **Mina de São Domingos**, an old copper-mining town first discovered by the Romans and still mined until the 1960s. The mines are now being turned into a tourist attraction with people visiting to see the effects of 2,000 years of mining on the landscape (free access at any

time). There is also a large reservoir here, with a picnic area and a small beach.

3–4

Continue driving across typical Alentejo countryside, with its cork oaks, wheat fields and sheep. The road is long and straight and the absence of traffic is remarkable – this is one of the most sparsely populated regions in Portugal. Shortly after passing through the olive and orange-growing village of **Santa Iria**, you reach a main road where you turn left and immediately left again to **Serpa**. Before entering the town, follow the signs to your left to climb the hill to the *pousada*, where there is a small whitewashed

Nossa Senhora de Guadalupe, Serpa

Moorish-looking chapel, **Nossa Senhora da Guadalupe**, and sweeping views over the plain.

4–5

Serpa is known as *vila branca* (white town) because of the typically Portuguese whitewashed houses lining its narrow cobbled streets. Like the other towns on this route, it makes a pleasant place to while away a

couple of hours. It has a watch museum, a folk museum, a botanical garden and a small archaeological museum housed within the castle walls. From the town's square, Praça da Republica, you can climb the steps past the tourist office to reach the parish church, with its separate bell-tower standing opposite. Cafés on the main square sell the strong local sheep's cheese, *queijão de Serpa*. For a fuller

The Story of Salúquia

Look at the coat of arms on the town hall in Moura and you will see a young girl lying dead at the foot of a tower. This is Salúquia, a Moorish princess, who lived in Moura at the time of the Christian conquest of the town in 1233. The story goes that on her wedding day her fiancé and his entourage were murdered by Christian knights on their way to the wedding ceremony. The Christians put on their victims' clothes and masqueraded as the wedding party in order to gain access to Moura. In this way they were able to capture the castle, and Salúquia threw herself from the tower in despair. There are many similar folk legends in Portugal, but this one is unusual as it casts Christians in the role of villains and Moors as their unfortunate victims.

Return to the N265 main road (signposted "Espanha" – Spain) and turn left, then take the next right towards Moura. Soon you reach the village of **Pias**, known for its strong red wines and the frescoes in the Santa Luzia church. Turn left to pass through the centre of the village then continue on this road through the vineyards and olive groves to the spa town of **Moura**.

5–6

Moura means "Moorish Maiden" and the town takes its name from the legend of the Princess Salúquia (▶ 181). This is another town with a ruined castle, cobbled streets and a long history. The Moorish quarter of Mouraria, which has

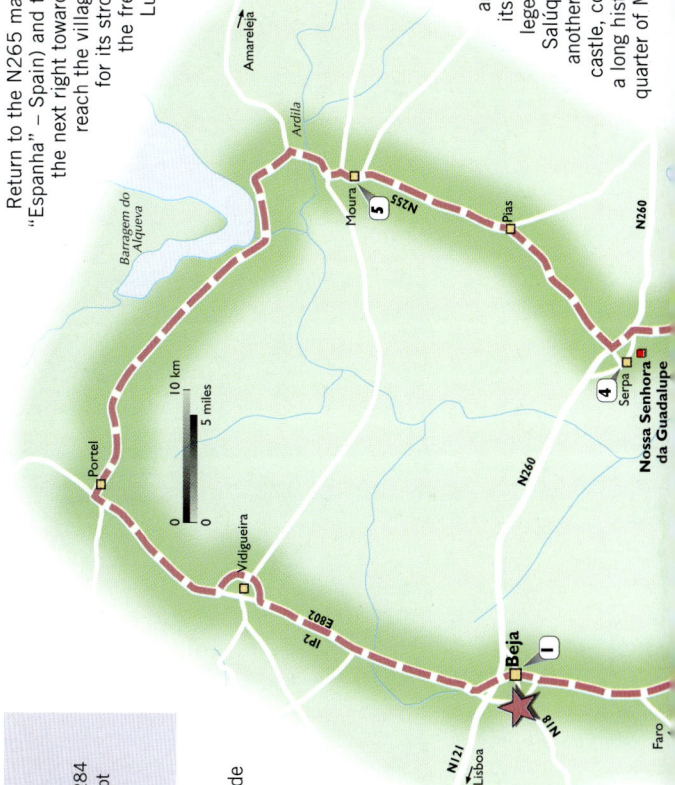

Taking a Break

Molhó Bico

✚ 202 D3 ⊠ Rua Quente 1, Serpa ☎ 284 549 264 ⓦ Daily lunch and dinner except Wed ⓦ €€

meal of hearty Alentejano specialities, walk up the street to Molhó Bico, beside the old town walls.

From here it is a short stroll to the castle, where you can walk around the ramparts for views over the town and its surroundings. The castle walls, which incorporate an earlier aqueduct, were built by Dom Dinis following the expulsion of the Moors in the 13th century, but were heavily damaged 500 years later during a raid by Spanish troops. Notice the boulder which forms a porch above the castle entrance, precariously balancing in the very spot where it was left hanging after the attack.

whitewashed houses and ornamental chimneys, is particularly atmospheric.

Follow signs to the castle and park your car near the parish church of São João Baptista, with its rich Manueline portal. There are also some fine Sevillian *azulejos* adorning the high altar, the side chapels and the niche in the façade of the bell-tower. Across the street, storks can sometimes be seen nesting

to Amareleja as the road swings round to the right beneath the gardens.

After crossing the River Ardila, the road forks – keep left for Portel. Soon you come to **Barragem de Alqueva**, where a dam crosses the River Guadiana (creating the largest artificial lake in the EU).

Continue on this road, crossing rolling countryside on the way to **Portel**, whose castle is visible from afar.

Follow signs to Beja and return on the IP2.

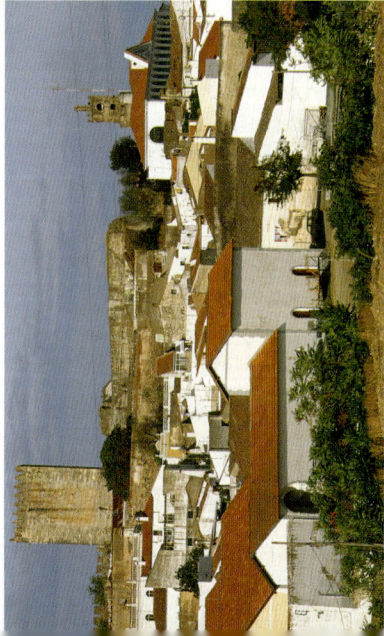

Map labels: Pulo do Lobo, Parque Natural do Vale do Guadiana, Guadiana, Mértola, Mina de São Domingos, Embalse del Chanza, N122, 265, E

in the castle tower. Near here are the peaceful public gardens of the old spa, where people come to enjoy sunset views over the hills.

Drive out of Moura with the castle on your right and stay close to the town walls, following signs

The thermal spa town of Moura has its own castle, grand mansions and pretty houses

Pulo do Lobo

The Pulo do Lobo (Wolf's Leap) waterfall is a place of rapids and weird rock formations in a deep gorge carved out by the River Guadiana between Mértola and Serpa. Although it is signposted from the Mértola to Serpa road, the easier approach is from a minor road 3km (2 miles) out of Mértola on the way to Beja.

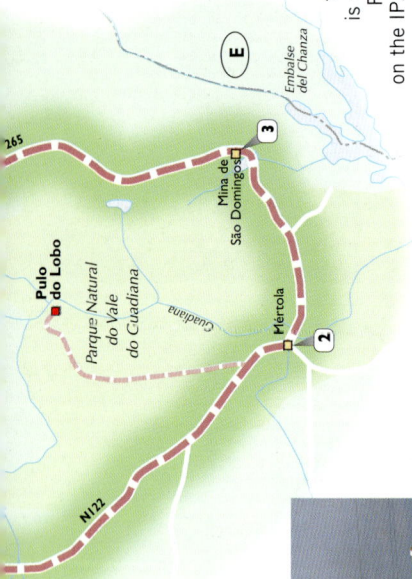

4 LAGOS TO PRAIA DA LUZ

Walk

The cliffs of western Algarve offer some superb walking, with sweeping views over the Atlantic and the bizarre rock formations that characterise this stretch of coast. Although you are hardly likely to find yourself alone, walking on the cliffs can be a good way of escaping the crowded beaches in summer. This walk is best done in the late afternoon or early evening, when the heat of the day has relented and the sunlight casts a softer glow of ever-changing colours on the ocean. If you are lucky you might catch one of the famous Atlantic sunsets from the cliffs above Praia da Luz.

DISTANCE 6km (3.7 miles)
TIME 2.5–3 hours
START POINT Lagos ✚ 202 B1 **END POINT** Praia da Luz ✚ 202 B1

1–2

Begin on the riverfront at **Lagos** (▶ 165), opposite the fishing harbour, and follow Avenida dos Descobrimentos towards the sea. Across the road is the municipal market, which opened in 1924. Fresh fish is sold downstairs, and there is a produce market upstairs selling fruit, flowers and jars of honey and piri-piri (hot pepper sauce).

Beside the market, **Praça Gil Eanes** contains an extraordinary statue of the boy-king Sebastião, a national hero who died in 1578 during a disastrous naval expedition from Lagos to Morocco. Take the opportunity for a coffee and snack at one of the pavement cafés here, as there will be few other opportunities for refreshment on this walk.

Continue walking along the riverside promenade, lined with palm trees. This place has a powerful feel of the great Age of Discovery, when Henry the Navigator's caravels sailed from here. There is a statue of Prince Henry across the road in Praça da República and a statue of the explorer Gil Eanes outside the nearby castle. To your left, beyond the harbour walls, ocean waves wash the shore of Meia Praia, Lagos' long and windswept town beach.

The beach at Praia de Dona Ana is typically Algarvian, with its curious rock formations on the sand

Walk past the Ponte da Bandeira fortress, which contains a small museum devoted to the discoveries. Alongside the fort is the pretty cove beach of Praia da Batata. Now climb the main road out of town, passing a *miradouro* with a monument to São Gonçalo, a local fisherman's son who became a monk and is now the patron saint of Lagos.

2–3
Reaching the top of the hill, leave the road by taking the path to the left, signposted to Praia do Pinhão. Continue on this path as it leads along the cliffs to **Praia de Dona Ana**, one of the most attractive of the Algarve's beaches, with its typical rock formations and sandstacks. Cross the car park above the

beach and climb back on to the cliffs, taking care on the partly eroded track. There is a choice of routes from here, but you really can't go wrong – just keep the sea to your left as you continue across the cliffs towards **Ponte da Piedade** (Bridge of Piety), a well-known beauty spot where the red rock has been sculpted by the wind and sea into a series of dramatic boulders, arches and caves.

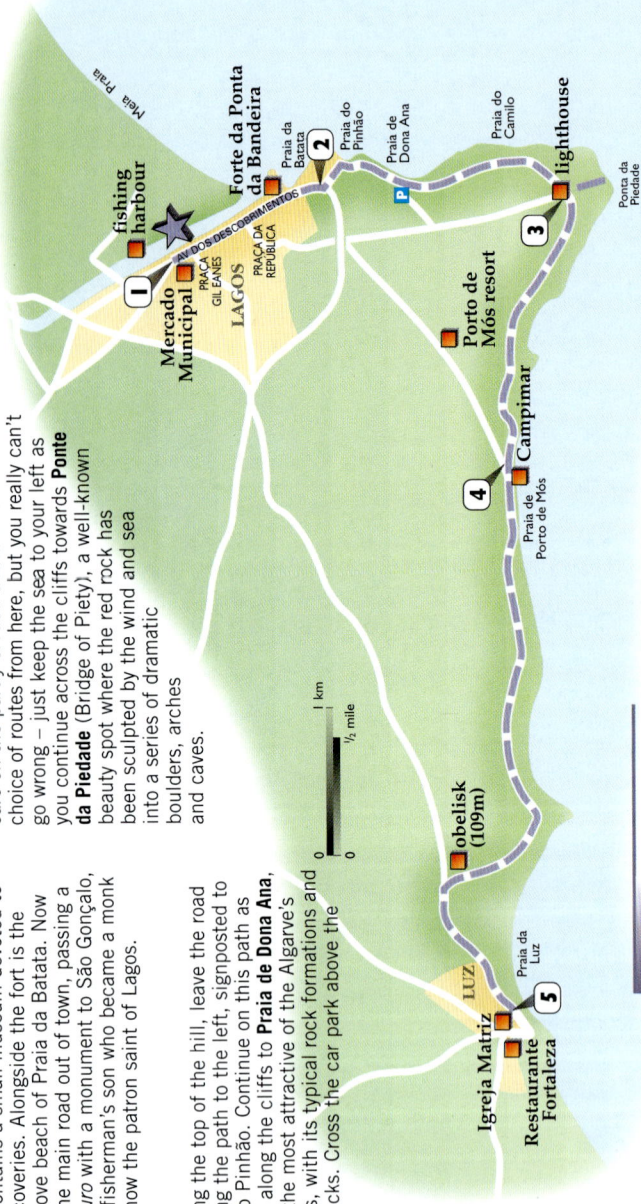

Map labels

fishing harbour

Forte da Ponta da Bandeira

Praia da Batata

Praia do Pinhão

Praia de Dona Ana

Praia do Camillo

lighthouse

Ponta da Piedade

AV. DOS DESCOBRIMENTOS

PRAÇA GIL EANES

PRAÇA DA REPÚBLICA

LAGOS

Mercado Municipal

Meia Praia

Porto de Mós resort

Campimar

Praia de Porto de Mós

obelisk (109m)

Praia da Luz

LUZ

Igreja Matriz

Restaurante Fortaleza

1 km

½ mile

0

and offers spectacular views over the Atlantic, as far as **Cabo de São Vicente** (➤ 157–158) on a clear day.

After about 45 minutes you reach an obelisk marking the summit (109m/358 feet). Just beyond the obelisk, look for a gap in the bushes to your left and scramble down towards **Praia da Luz**, emerging on a cobbled path that leads to the beach. Praia da Luz is a low-key but growing resort of whitewashed apartments and villas climbing above a splendid beach. Stroll along the beachfront promenade, with its mosaic pavement, to reach the balcony at the end. Near here is **Restaurante Fortaleza da Luz**, inside an old fortress, facing the parish church (➤ below). Regular buses to Lagos stop beside the church.

Walk out past the lighthouse on to a spit for the best views along the coast. In summer, fishermen offer boat trips into the grottoes from a small landing stage at the foot of the cliffs.

3–4
Leaving the lighthouse, head west along the clifftop path. You need to stay close to the sea to avoid being forced into the resort development at Porto de Mós. Instead, drop straight down to the **beach** where there are a couple of decent restaurants. If you feel you've done enough walking by now, there are occasional buses from here back to Lagos.

4–5
The next stretch of the walk is the hardest as it involves a long (but steady) climb to the highest point of the cliffs. The path is clear

Escape Route
The coastal footpath between Praia de Dona Ana and Ponte da Piedade also gives access to Praia do Camilo, a classic Algarve cove beach that may be less crowded than the others on this walk.

Taking a Break

Campimar

☎ 202 B1 ⊠ Praia do Porto de Mós ☎ 282 762 957 ⏰ Daily lunch and dinner 🚗 €€

Fortaleza da Luz

☎ 202 B1 ⊠ Rua da Igreja 3, Praia da Luz ☎ 282 789 926 ⏰ Daily lunch and dinner (closed mid-Nov to mid-Dec) 🚗 €€

Stop to admire the views over the coves and grottoes of Ponte da Piedade

Practicalities

GETTING ADVANCE INFORMATION

Websites
- Welcome to Portugal:
www.portugal.org
- Portugal National Tourist
Office:
www.visitportugal.com

- Algarve Net:
www.visitalgarve.pt
- Pousadas de Portugal:
www.pousadas.pt
- Solares de Portugal:
www.solaresdeportugal.pt

In the UK
Portuguese National Tourist
Office
11 Belgrave Square
London SW1X 8PP
☎ 0845 355 1212

BEFORE YOU GO

WHAT YOU NEED

● Required ○ Suggested ▲ Not required △ Not applicable	Some countries require a passport to remain valid for a minimum period (usually at least six months) beyond the date of entry – check beforehand.	UK	Germany	USA	Canada	Australia	Ireland	Netherlands	Spain
Passport/National Identity Card		●	●	●	●	●	●	●	●
Visa (regulations can change – check before booking)		▲	▲	▲	▲	▲	▲	▲	▲
Onward or Return Ticket		○	○	○	○	○	○	○	○
Health Inoculations (tetanus and polio)		▲	▲	▲	▲	▲	▲	▲	▲
Health Documentation		▲	▲	▲	▲	▲	▲	▲	▲
Travel Insurance (▶ 192, Health)		○	○	○	○	○	○	○	○
Driver's Licence (national)		●	●	●	●	●	●	●	●
Car Insurance Certificate		●	●	●	●	●	●	●	●
Car Registration Document		●	●	●	●	●	●	●	●

WHEN TO GO

Faro

High season   Low season

JAN	FEB	MAR	APR	MAY	JUN	JUL	AUG	SEP	OCT	NOV	DEC
15°C	16°C	18°C	21°C	24°C	30°C	35°C	37°C	33°C	28°C	19°C	17°C
59°F	61°F	64°F	70°F	75°F	86°F	95°F	99°F	91°F	82°F	66°F	63°F

☀ Sun   🌦 Sunshine and showers

Temperatures are the **average daily maximum** for each month. Spring (April to June) and autumn (September to October) are the best times to visit Portugal as the summer months can be unbearably hot and crowded. Added attractions are wild flowers in spring and the Douro Valley grape harvest in autumn. Summer is hot and dry inland, and mild on the coast where sea temperatures vary from 16°C (61°F) on the west coast to 23°C (73°F) in the Algarve. Winters are cool and wet in the north, but pleasantly mild in the Algarve, where walking and golf are year-round activities and swimming is possible from March to November. Hotel rates tend to be much lower in January and February, making this a good time to visit Lisbon and the Algarve.

In Ireland
Portuguese National Tourist
Office
54 Dawson Street
Dublin 2
☎ 01 670 9133

In the USA
Portuguese National Tourist
Office
590 Fifth Avenue
4th Floor
New York NY 10036-9702
☎ 646/723 0200

In Canada
Portuguese National Tourist
Office
60 Bloor Street West
Suite 1005
Toronto, Ontario M4W 3B8
☎ (416) 921 7376

GETTING THERE

By Air There are international airports at Lisbon, Porto and Faro. **British Airways** and the Portuguese national airline **TAP-Air Portugal** operate scheduled flights from London to all three cities, with a flight time of around two and a half hours. There is also a wide selection of charter flights, especially to Faro in summer, from British, Irish and European airports. Most seats on charter flights are sold by tour operators as part of a package holiday, but it is usually possible to buy a flight-only deal through travel agents or on the internet. The disadvantage of charter flights is that you are sometimes restricted to periods of 7 or 14 days. **From the USA** TAP has scheduled flights to Lisbon from New York (6.5 hours), with connections to other North American cities.

By Car There are numerous entry points along the border with Spain, with little or nothing in the way of border controls. The main roads into Portugal are from Vigo to Porto, Zamora to Bragança, Salamanca to Guarda, Badajoz to Elvas and the motorway from Seville to the Algarve. From Britain, take a car ferry to Bilbao or Santander in northern Spain, from where it is a drive of about 800km (500 miles) to Porto and 1,000km (620 miles) to Lisbon.

By Rail There are regular trains to Lisbon from Madrid (10 hours) and Paris (24 hours). A train line from Vigo in Spain crosses the border at Valença do Minho to Porto and Lisbon.

TIME

Portugal is on Greenwich Mean Time (GMT), and one hour behind most of continental Europe. During the summer, from the last Sunday in March to the last Sunday in October, the time in Portugal is GMT plus one hour (GMT+1).

CURRENCY AND FOREIGN EXCHANGE

Currency The euro (€) is the official currency of Portugal. Euro coins are issued in denominations of 1, 2, 5, 10, 20 and 50 euro cents and €1 and €2. Notes are issued in denominations of €5, €10, €20, €50, €100, €200 and €500. Note: €200 and €500 notes are not issued in Portugal, but those issued elsewhere are valid.

Foreign currency and traveller's cheques can be changed at banks and exchange bureaux, as well as in many hotels. Exchange bureaux generally offer the best deal, but it pays to shop around and compare commission charges. You will need to show your passport when cashing traveller's cheques.
  You can also withdraw cash from ATM (cashpoint) machines using your credit or debit card and a PIN (personal identification number). Your own bank will usually make a charge for this service.

Major credit cards are accepted in most resorts. When in the countryside it is advisable to have small denomination notes to hand. It is easier and no more expensive (depending on your credit card charges) to rely solely on plastic, rather than taking travellers' cheques or buying cash in advance.

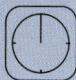

GMT 12 noon	Portugal 12 noon	USA (New York) 7am	USA (Los Angeles) 4am	Spain 1pm	Sydney 10pm
		←	←	→	→

WHEN YOU ARE THERE

CLOTHING SIZES

UK	Portugal	USA	
36	46	36	Suits
38	48	38	
40	50	40	
42	52	42	
44	54	44	
46	56	46	
7	41	8	Shoes
7.5	42	8.5	
8.5	43	9.5	
9.5	44	10.5	
10.5	45	11.5	
11	46	12	
14.5	37	14.5	Shirts
15	38	15	
15.5	39/40	15.5	
16	41	16	
16.5	42	16.5	
17	43	17	
8	34	6	Dresses
10	36	8	
12	38	10	
14	40	12	
16	42	14	
18	44	16	
4.5	38	6	Shoes
5	38	6.5	
5.5	39	7	
6	39	7.5	
6.5	40	8	
7	41	8.5	

NATIONAL HOLIDAYS

1 Jan	New Year's Day
Feb/Mar	Shrove Tuesday
Mar/Apr	Good Friday/Easter Monday
25 Apr	Day of the Revolution
1 May	Labour Day
May/Jun	Corpus Christi
10 Jun	National Day
15 Aug	Feast of the Assumption
5 Oct	Republic Day
1 Nov	All Saints' Day
1 Dec	Independence Day
8 Dec	Feast of the Immaculate Conception
25 Dec	Christmas Day

OPENING HOURS

○ Shops ● Post Offices
● Offices ● Museums/Monuments
● Banks ● Pharmacies

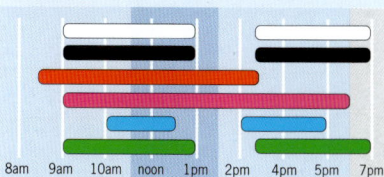

☐ Day   ☐ Midday   ☐ Evening

Shops In general 9–1, 3–7. Large stores and supermarkets open continuously from 9 to 7. Some supermarkets open until 10 (5 on Sundays).
Offices Generally offices are open 9–12:30, 2:30–6:30.
Banks Generally banks are open 8:30–3.
Post offices Mon–Fri 9–6, Sat 9–noon at main branches in cities, shorter hours in provincial areas.
Museums and churches Generally 10–12:30, 2–5, but this can vary so check before visiting.
Pharmacies They are usually open 9–12:30, 2–7, but duty chemists will be open longer (► 192).

PERSONAL SAFETY

Violence against tourists is unusual in Portugal. Theft from cars is the most common form of crime.

- Do not leave valuables on the beach or poolside.
- Always lock valuables in hotel safety deposit boxes
- Never leave anything inside your car. If you have to, lock it out of sight in the boot.
- Beware of pickpockets in crowded markets, and on crowded buses in Lisbon and Porto.
- Do not leave bags unattended while standing at a car hire desk or loading suitcases onto a bus.

Police assistance:
☎ 112 from any phone

TELEPHONES

There are public telephones on almost every street corner. They take coins, credit cards or phonecards, available from post offices, kiosks and shops displaying the PT (Portugal Telecom) logo.

International calls are cheaper between 9pm and 9am and at weekends.

Calls from hotel rooms will invariably attract a heavy premium.

International Dialling Codes

Dial 00 followed by

UK:	44
USA/Canada:	1
Irish Republic:	353
Australia:	61
Spain:	34

POST

Stamps (selos) can be bought at post offices, kiosks and tobacconists.

Letters to European Union countries will arrive within five to seven days, and to the USA within 10 days.

Send urgent mail by correio azul and ensure that you post it in a blue postbox.

Other postboxes are red.

ELECTRICITY

The power supply is 220 volts AC. Sockets take two-pronged round continental plugs.

Visitors from the UK will need an adaptor, and visitors from the USA will need a transformer for 100–120 volt devices.

TIPS/GRATUITIES

Tipping is not expected for all services and rates are lower than elsewhere in Europe. As a general guide:

Restaurant bill	(service not included) 10%
Taxis	10%
Tour Guides	half day €3
	full day €5
Porters	€1 per bag
Chambermaids	€2 per night
Toilet attendants	small change

UK	USA	Ireland	Australia	Canada
☎ 213 924 000	☎ 217 273 300	☎ 213 929 440	☎ 213 101 500	☎ 213 164 600

HEALTH

Insurance Citizens of EU countries receive reduced-cost emergency health care with relevant documentation (European Health Insurance Card), but private medical insurance is still advised and essential for all other visitors.

Dental Services The standard of dental care is generally excellent. Dental practices advertise in the free English-language magazines and newspapers at hotels. You have to pay for treatment, but your insurance should cover the costs.

Weather The sun is intense at all times of year, and it is possible to burn very quickly, even on cloudy days. Cover up with high-factor sunscreen, wear a hat and drink plenty of water, especially if walking in the hills or along the coast.

Drugs Chemists (*farmâcia*) are open Mon–Fri 9–1 and 2:30–7, and Sat 9–12.30. Some open through lunch and the late-night duty chemist is posted in pharmacy windows. Pharmacists are highly trained and can sell some drugs that require prescriptions in other countries. However, take adequate supplies of any drugs you take regularly as they may not be available.

Safe Water Tap water is safe but its mineral content may make it taste unpleasant. Ask for sparkling (*água com gás*) or still (*água sem gás*) bottled water.

CONCESSIONS

Young People Most museums have lower admission rates for students (and entry is generally free for children) on production of a passport or valid student identity card.

Senior Citizens Senior citizens from many European countries come to the Algarve for its year-round warmth and long-stay low-season rates. Travellers over 65 are usually entitled to discounted admission at museums and reduced fares on public transport (proof of age needed). If mobility is a problem getting around can be a bit of a trial (▶ Travelling with a Disability, opposite).

TRAVELLING WITH A DISABILITY

Facilities for disabled travellers in Portugal are slowly improving, but many older hotels and public buildings are still inaccessible, especially in cities where hotels tend to be situated on the upper floors of apartment blocks. Cobbled streets are a particular problem for wheelchair users. There are "blue badge" car parking spaces in most town centres, and adapted toilets at airports and railway stations.

It is best to discuss your particular needs with your tour operator or hotel before booking a holiday.

CHILDREN

Hotels and restaurants tend to be child-friendly, and many coastal hotels have playgrounds and children's pools. Facilities like baby-changing rooms are improving.

TOILETS

There are public toilets in shopping centres and some of the larger beaches.

CUSTOMS

The import of wildlife souvenirs sourced from rare or endangered species may be illegal or require a special permit. Check your home country's customs regulations.

There are two distinctive Portuguese sounds: firstly, the nasalised vowels written with a til (~, like the tilde on Spanish ñ): (so "bread", *pão*, is pronounced "pow!" with a strong nasal twang; secondly, "s" and "z" are often pronounced as a slushy "sh" (so "banknotes", *notas*, is pronounced "not-ash").

GREETINGS AND COMMON WORDS

Yes/No **Sim/Não**
Please **Se faz favor**
Thank you **Obrigado** *(male speaker)*/
  Obrigada *(female speaker)*
You're welcome **De nada/Foi**
  um prazer
Hello/Goodbye **Olá/Adeus**
Welcome **Bem vindo/a**
Good morning **Bom dia**
Good evening/night **Boa noite**
How are you? **Como está?**
Fine, thank you **Bem, obrigado/a**
Sorry **Perdão**
Excuse me, could you help me?
  Desculpe, podia-me ajudar?
My name is… **Chamo-me…**
Do you speak English? **Fala inglês?**
I don't understand **Não percebo**
I don't speak any Portuguese **Não**
  falo português

EMERGENCY! Urgência!

Help! **Socorro!**
Stop! **Pare!**
Stop that thief! **Apanhe o ladrão!**
Police! **Polícia!**
Fire! **Fogo!**
Go away, or I'll scream! **Se não se**
  for embora, começo a gritar!
Leave me alone! **Deixe-me em paz!**

I've lost my purse/wallet **Perdi o meu**
  porta-moedas/a minha carteira
My passport has been stolen
  Roubaram-me o passaporte
Could you call a doctor? **Podia**
  chamar um médico depressa?

DIRECTIONS AND TRAVELLING

Airport **Aeroporto**
Boat **Barco**
Bus station **Estação de camionetas**
Bus/coach **Autocarro**
Car **Automóvel**
Church **Igreja**
Hospital **Hospital**
Market **Mercado**
Museum **Museu**
Square **Praça**
Street **Rua**
Taxi rank **Praça de táxis**
Train **Comboio**
Ticket **Bilhete**
  Return **Ida e volta**
  Single **Bilhete de ida**
Station **Estação**
I'm lost **Estou perdida**
How many kilometres to…? **Quantos**
  quilómetros faltam ainda para
    chegar a…?
Here/There **Aqui/Ali**
Left/right **À esquerda/À direita**
Straight on **Em frente**

NUMBERS

0	zero	16	dezasseis
1	um	17	dezassete
2	dois	18	dezoito
3	três	19	dezanove
4	quatro	20	vinte
5	cinco	21	vinte e um
6	seis	30	trinta
7	sete	40	quarenta
8	oito	50	cinquenta
9	nove	60	sessenta
10	dez	70	setenta
11	onze	80	oitenta
12	doze	90	noventa
13	treze	100	cem
14	catorze	101	cento e um
15	quinze	500	quinhentos

DAYS

Today	Hoje
Tomorrow	Amanhã
Yesterday	Ontem
Tonight	Esta noite
Last night	Ontem à noite
In the morning	De manhã
In the afternoon	De tarde
Later	Logo/Mais tarde
This week	Esta semana
Monday	Segunda-feira
Tuesday	Terça-feira
Wednesday	Quarta-feira
Thursday	Quinta-feira
Friday	Sexta-feira
Saturday	Sábado
Sunday	Domingo

MONEY: Dinheiro

Bank **Banco**
Banknote **Notas**
Cash desk **Caixa**
Change **Troco**
Cheque **Cheque**
Coin **Moeda**
Credit card **Cartão de crédito**
Exchange office **Casa de Câmbio**
Exchange rate **Câmbio**
Foreign **Estrangeiro**
Mail **Correio**
Post office **Agência do correios**
Traveller's cheque **Cheque de viagem**
Could you give me some small
  change, please? **Podia-me dar
  tambén dinheiro trocado, se faz
  favor?**

ACCOMMODATION

Are there any...? **Há...?**
I'd like a room with a view of the sea
  **Queria um quarto com vista para
  o mar**
Where's the emergency exit/fire
  escape? **Onde fica a saída de
  emergência/escada de salvação?**
Does that include breakfast? **Está
  incluido o pequeno almoço?**
Do you have room service? **O hotel
  tem serviço de quarto?**
I've made a reservation **Reservei
  um lugar**
Air-conditioning **Ar condicionado**
Balcony **Varanda**
Bathroom **Casa de banho**
Chambermaid **Camareira**
Hot water **Água quente**
Hotel **Hotel**
Key **Chave**
Lift **Elevador**
Night **Noite**
Room **Quarto**
Room service **Serviço de quarto**
Shower **Duche**
Telephone **Telefone**
Towel **Toalha**
Water **Água**

RESTAURANT: Restaurante

I'd like to book a table **Posso reser-
  var uma mesa?**
A table for two, please **Uma mesa
  para duas pessoas, se faz favor**
Could we see a menu, please?
  Poderia dar nos a ementa, se faz favor

What's this? **O que é isto?**
A bottle of... **Uma garrafa de ...**
Alcohol **Alcool**
Beer **Cerveja**
Bill **Conta**
Bread **Pão**
Breakfast **Pequeno almoço**
Café **Café**
Coffee **Café**
Dinner **Jantar**
Lunch **Almoço**
Menu **Menú/ementa**
Milk **Leite**
Mineral water **Água mineral**
Pepper **Pimenta**
Salt **Sal**
Table **Mesa**
Tea **Chá**
Waiter **Empregado/a**

SHOPPING

Shop **Loja**
Where can I get....? **Em que loja
  posso arranjar...?**
Could you help me please? **Pode-me
  atender, se faz favor?**
I'm looking for... **Estou a procura de...**
I would like... **Queria...**
I'm just looking **Só estou a ver**
How much? **Quanto custa?**
It's too expensive **Acho demasiado
  caro**
I'll take this one/these **Levo este(s)/
  esta(s)**
Good/Bad **Bom/Mau**
Bigger **Maior**
Smaller **Mais pequeno**
Open/Closed **Aberto/Fechado**
I'm a size... in the UK **Na Grã
  Bretanha o meu número é...**
Have you got a bag please? **Tem um
  saco, se faz favor?**

TOWN PRONUNCIATION GUIDE

Braga **brag-uh**
Bragança **bra-gan-suh**
Coimbra **queem-bruh**
Évora **e-vor-uh**
Faro **far-ooh**
Fátima **fa-tee-muh**
Lagos **lah-goosh**
Lisboa **leezh-boh-ah**
Marvão **mar-vow**
Porto **port-ooh**
Sagres **sar-gresh**
Tavira **ta-veer-ah**
Vila Viçosa **vee-lah-vee-soh-sah**

Atlas

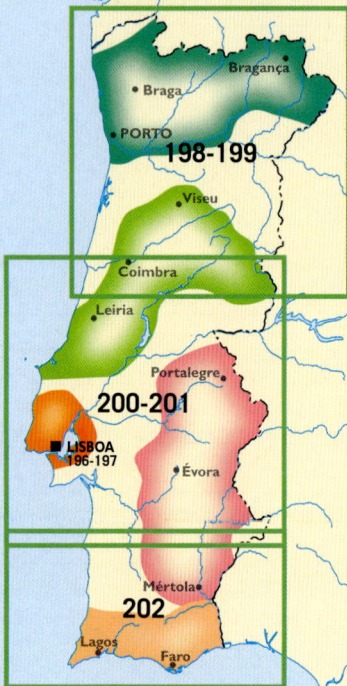

Bragança

• Braga

• PORTO

198-199

• Viseu

• Coimbra

• Leiria

Portalegre •

200-201

■ LISBOA
196-197

• Évora

Mértola •

202

Lagos •

Faro •

To identify the regions, see the map on the inside of the front cover

Regional Maps

| 198-202 | 0 5 10 15 20 25 km |
| | 0 5 10 15 miles |

– · – · – · – International boundary
━━━━━ Major route
▭▭▭▭▭ Motorway/toll motorway
▪ ▪ ▪ ▪ ▪ Road under construction
━━━━━ National road
━━━━━ Regional road
━━━━━ Other road
━━━━━ Railway
▢ City
▫ Town/village
✈ Airport
    Built-up area
    National/Natural park
▣ Featured place of interest
◼ Place of interest

▲ Height in metres

City Plan

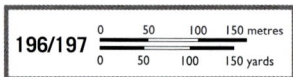

| 196/197 | 0 50 100 150 metres |
| | 0 50 100 150 yards |

════════ Main road
──────── Other road
──────── Minor road
━━━━━━ Railway
◖──◗ Funicular railway
    Important building
    Park/garden
▣ Featured place of interest
● Metro station
[i] Tourist information
✝ Church
✉ Post Office
☼ Miradouro/viewpoint

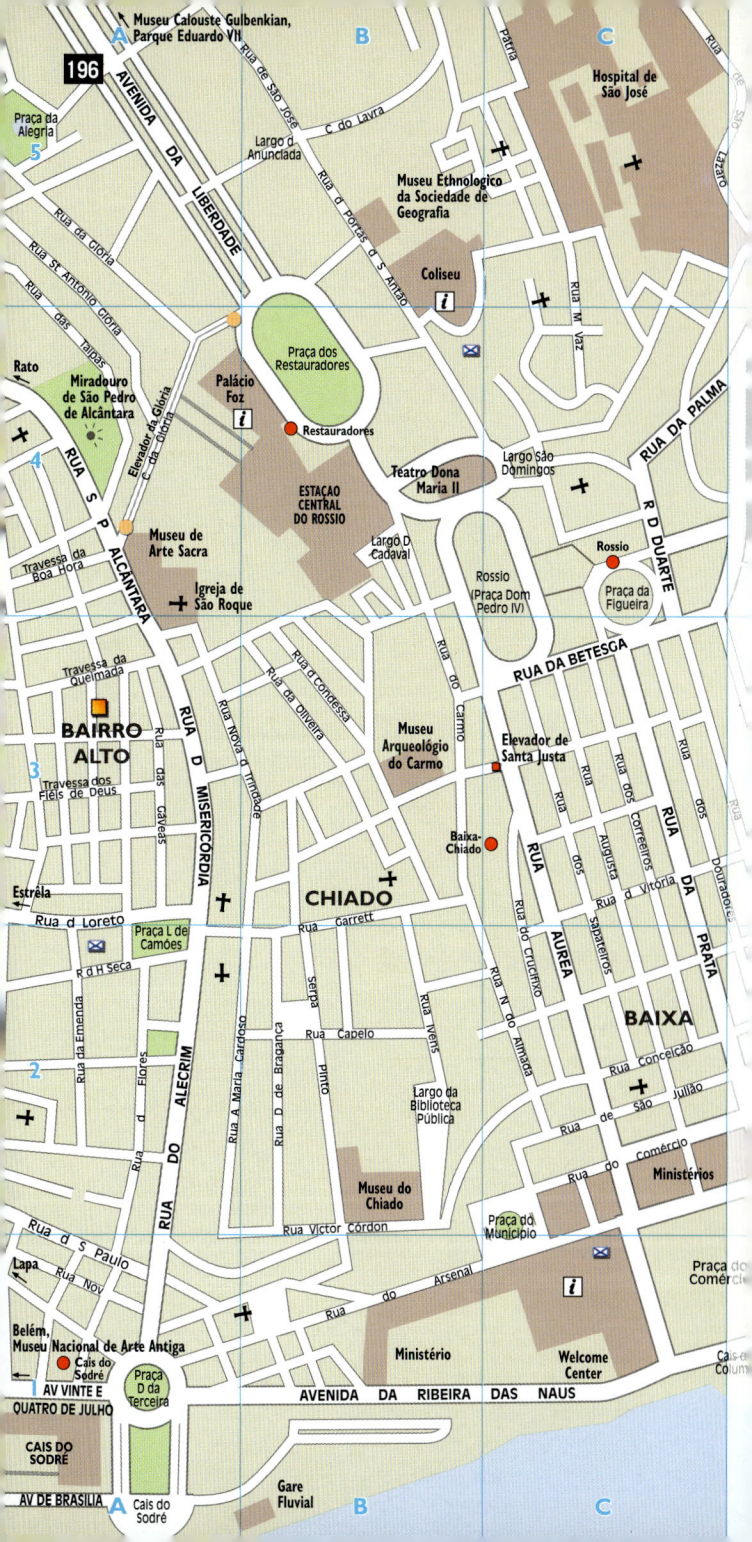

196

Museu Calouste Gulbenkian,
Parque Eduardo VII

B

C

Praça da
Alegria

5

Hospital de
São José

Rua de São José

C do Lavra

Largo d.
Anunciada

Rua d Portes d s Antão

Museu Ethnologico
da Sociedade de
Geografia

AVENIDA DA LIBERDADE

Rua da Gloria

Rua St Antonio Gloria

Rua das Taipas

Coliseu

Praça dos
Restauradores

Rato

Miradouro
de São Pedro
de Alcântara

Palácio
Foz

Restauradores

4

Rua S P ALCÂNTARA

Elevador da Gloria C. da Gloria

Rua M Vaz

RUA DA PALMA

R D DUARTE

Travessa da
Boa Hora

Museu de
Arte Sacra

ESTAÇÃO
CENTRAL
DO ROSSIO

Teatro Dona
Maria II

Largo São
Domingos

Igreja de
São Roque

Largo D.
Cadaval

Rossio
(Praça Dom
Pedro IV)

Rossio

Praça da
Figueira

Travessa da
Queimada

BAIRRO
ALTO

Travessa dos
Fiéis de Deus

3

Rua das Gáveas

RUA D MISERICÓRDIA

Rua Nova d Trindade

Rua da Oliveira

Rua d'Condessa

Museu
Arqueológio
do Carmo

Rua do Carmo

RUA DA BETESGA

Elevador de
Santa Justa

Baixa-
Chiado

RUA AUREA

Rua dos Correeiros

Rua Augusta

Rua da Prata

Rua dos Douradores

Estrela

Rua d Loreto

CHIADO

Rua Garrett

Praça L de
Camões

R d H Seca

Rua do Crucifixo

BAIXA

2

Rua da Emenda

RUA DO ALECRIM

Rua das Flores

Rua A Maria Cardoso

Rua D de Bragança

Serpa

Pinto

Rua Capelo

Rua Ivens

Rua N do Almada

Rua Conceição

Rua de São Julião

Lapa

Rua d S Paulo

Rua Nov

Largo da
Biblioteca
Pública

Museu do
Chiado

Rua Victor Córdon

Rua do Comércio

Ministérios

Praça do
Município

Praça do
Comércio

Belém,
Museu Nacional de Arte Antiga

Cais do
Sodré

Praça
D da
Terceira

Rua do Arsenal

Ministério

Welcome
Center

Cais
Colu

AV VINTE E
QUATRO DE JULHO

CAIS DO
SODRÉ

AV DE BRASILIA

A

Cais do
Sodré

AVENIDA DA RIBEIRA DAS NAUS

Gare
Fluvial

B

C

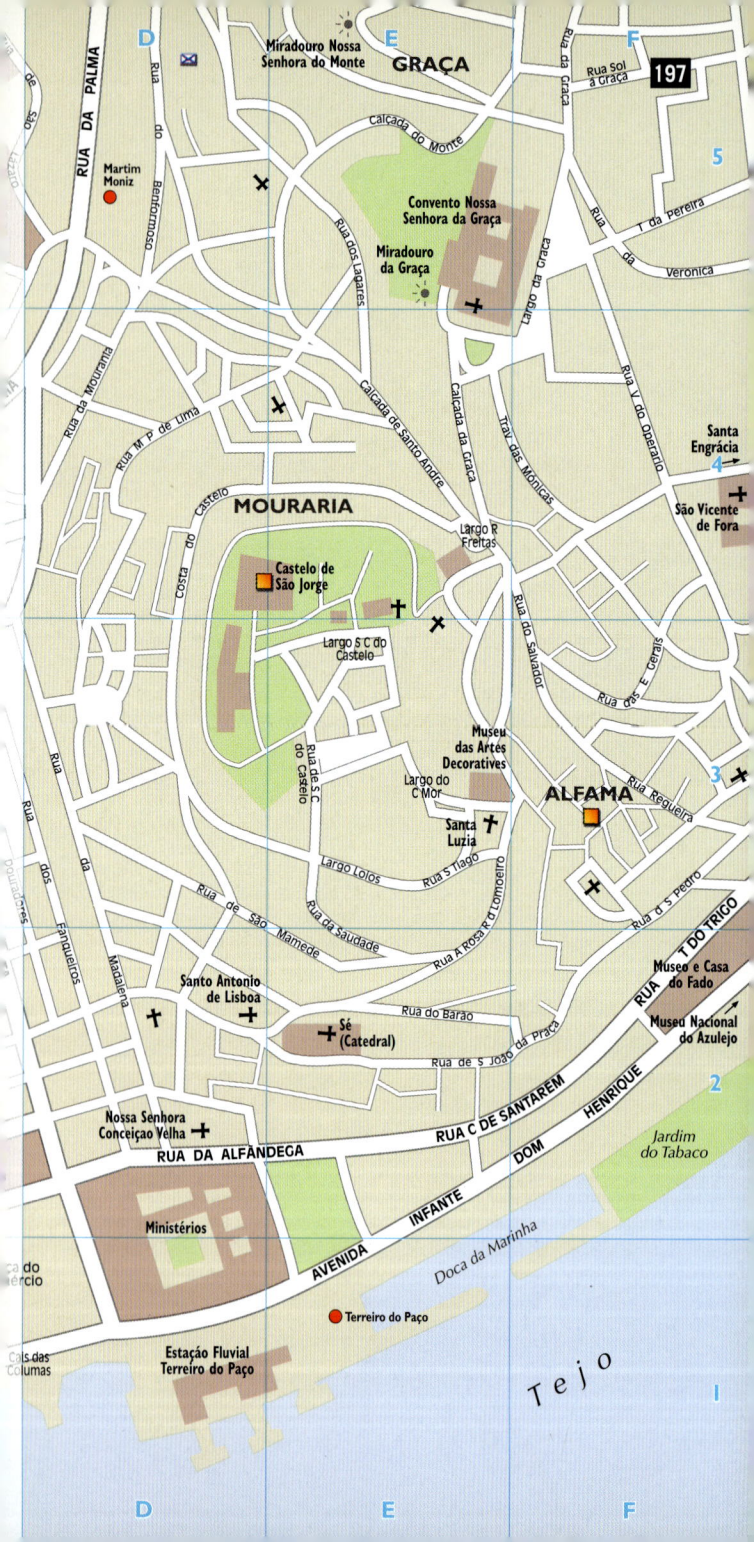

GRAÇA

Miradouro Nossa
Senhora do Monte

Calçada do Monte

Rua da Graça

Rua sol
à Graça

5

Rua da Palma

Rua do Benformoso

Martim
Moniz

Rua dos Lagares

Convento Nossa
Senhora da Graça

Miradouro
da Graça

Rua da Graça

T da Pereira

Rua da Veronica

Calçada de Santo André

Calçada da Graça

Trav das Mónicas

Rua da Mouraria

Rua M P de Lima

MOURARIA

Largo R
Freitas

Rua do Operario

Santa
Engrácia

São Vicente
de Fora

4

Costa do Castelo

Castelo de
São Jorge

Largo S C do
Castelo

Rua de S C do Castelo

Rua das E Gerais

Rua do Salvador

Rua da Regueira

Museu
das Artes
Decoratives

Largo do
C Mor

ALFAMA

3

Rua das Escolas Gerais

Rua A Rosa R d Lomoeiro

Rua S Tiago

Santa
Luzia

Largo Lolos

Rua d S Pedro

Rua de São Mamede

Rua da Saudade

Rua T do Trigo

Museu e Casa
do Fado

Santo Antonio
de Lisboa

Rua do Barão

Sé
(Catedral)

Museu Nacional
do Azulejo

2

Rua de S João da Praça

Nossa Senhora
Conceiçao Velha

RUA DA ALFÂNDEGA

RUA C DE SANTAREM

DOM HENRIQUE

INFANTE

Jardim
do Tabaco

Ministérios

AVENIDA

Doca da Marinha

Terreiro do Paço

Estaçáo Fluvial
Terreiro do Paço

T e j o

I

D   E   F

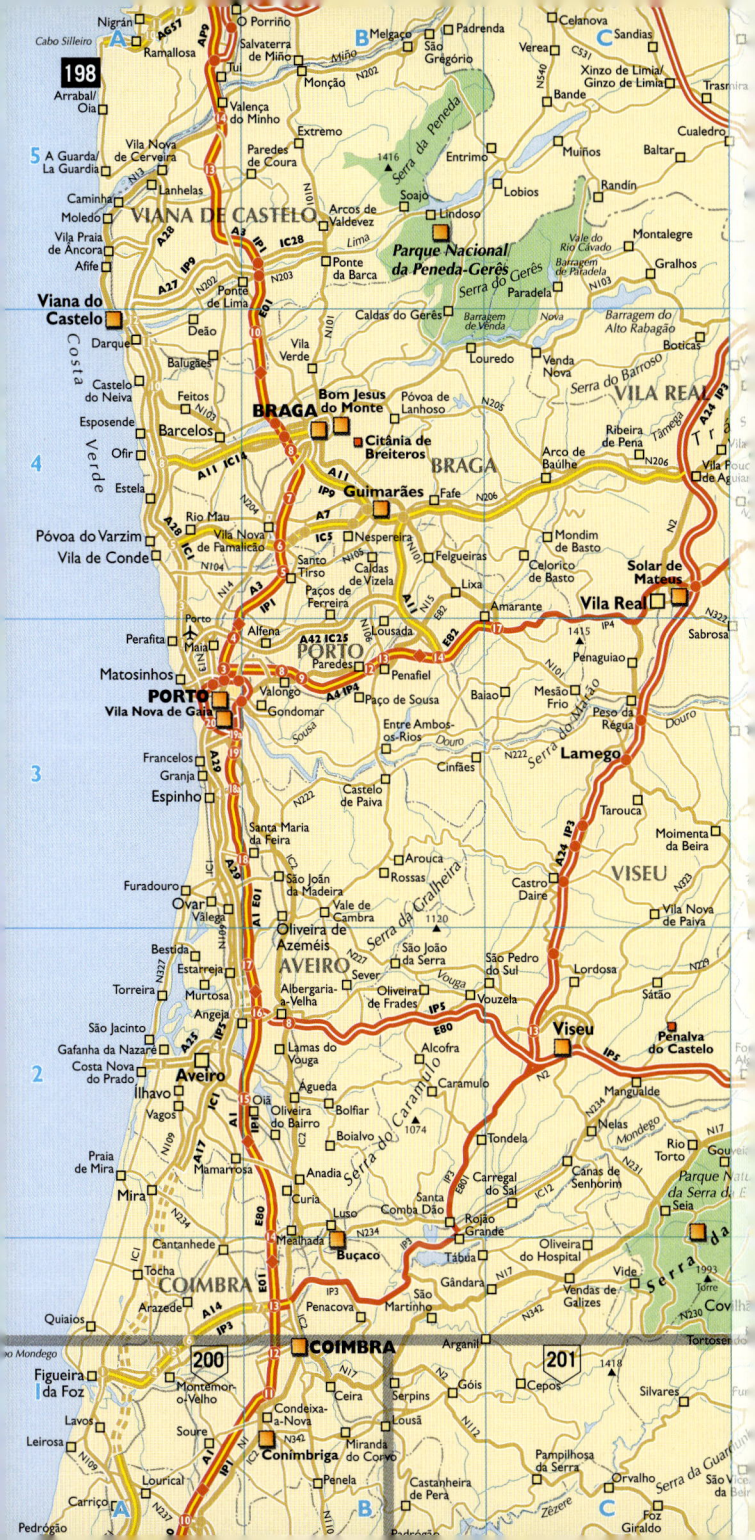

Nigrán
Cabo Silleiro
Ramallosa
AP9
O Porriño
B
Melgaço
Padrenda
Celanova
Sandias
Salvaterra de Miño
Miño
São Grégorio
Verea
C531
Xinzo de Limia
Arrabal/
Oia
AP9
Monção
N202
Bande
Ginzo de Limia
Trasmiras
A
A657
Valença do Minho
Extremo
Muíños
Baltar
Cualedro
5
A Guarda/
La Guardia
Vila Nova de Cerveira
Paredes de Coura
N13
Lanhelas
Arcos de Valdevez
Soajo
Serra da Peneda
1416
Entrimo
Lindoso
Lobios
Randín
Montalegre
Gralhos
Caminha
Moledo
VIANA DE CASTELO
A28
IP9
Ponte de Lima
N101
A3
IP1
IC28
N203
Lima
Ponte da Barca
Parque Nacional da Peneda-Gerês
Serra do Gerês
Paradela
Vale do Rio Cávado
Barragem de Paradela
N103
Vila Praia de Âncora
Afife
A27
Caldas do Gerês
Barragem de Venda
Nova
Barragem do Alto Rabagão
Viana do Castelo
Darque
Deão
Balugães
Vila Verde
Loureiro
Venda Nova
VILA REAL
Boticas
Serra do Barroso
Castelo do Neiva
Feitos
N101
Esposende
Barcelos
Ofir
Estela
A11
IC14
BRAGA
Bom Jesus do Monte
Citânia de Breiteros
Póvoa de Lanhoso
N205
BRAGA
Arco de Baúlhe
Ribeira de Pena
N206
Vila Pouca de Aguiar
A24
N2
4
Póvoa do Varzim
Vila do Conde
A28
IC1
Rio Mau
Vila Nova de Famalicão
N104
A11
A7
IP9
Guimarães
IC5
Fafe
N206
Nespereira
Felgueiras
Mondim de Basto
Celorico de Basto
Solar de Mateus
Vila Real
N322
Perafita
Maia
A3
IP1
Santo Tirso
Paços de Ferreira
N101
Caldas de Vizela
Lixa
A11
N15
Amarante
1415
IP4
Penaguião
Sabrosa
PORTO
A42
IC25
Alfena
Lousada
E82
17
N101
Vila Nova de Gaia
Paredes
Penafiel
A4
IP4
Baião
Mesão Frio
Serra do Marão
Peso da Régua
Douro
Matosinhos
PORTO
Valongo
Gondomar
Paço de Sousa
Entre Ambos-os-Rios
Douro
Lamego
3
Francelos
Granja
Espinho
A29
A1
IC2
A20
N222
Cinfães
Serra de Montemuro
Tarouca
A24
IP3
Moimenta da Beira
N323
Santa Maria da Feira
Castelo de Paiva
Arouca
Rossas
Serra da Gralheira
1120
Castro Daire
VISEU
Vila Nova de Paiva
Furadouro
Ovar
Válega
Oliveira de Azeméis
São João da Madeira
Vale de Cambra
Sever
São João da Serra
São Pedro do Sul
Lordosa
N228
Bestida
Estarreja
Murtosa
Angeja
A1
E01
A25
IP5
Albergaria-a-Velha
Oliveira de Frades
Vouga
Vouzela
E80
Viseu
IP5
Sátão
N234
Mangualde
2
São Jacinto
Gafanha da Nazaré
Costa Nova do Prado
Ilhavo
AVEIRO
IC1
A17
A1
A25
Lamas do Vouga
Águeda
Alcofra
Caramulo
Serra do Caramulo
N2
Nelas
Mondego
N234
Rio Torto
N17
Gouveia
Parque Nat. da Serra da E
Seia
Vagos
Oiã
Oliveira do Bairro
Bolfiar
Boialvo
1074
Tondela
Cañas de Senhorim
N231
Praia de Mira
Mira
Mamarrosa
E80
Anadia
Curia
Luso
Santa Comba Dão
Carregal do Sal
IC12
Oliveira do Hospital
Vide
1993
Torre
Serra da E
Cantanhede
N234
Buçaco
Mealhada
Rojão Grande
Tábua
Gândara
N17
Vendas de Galizes
Covilh
N230
1
Tôcha
Arazede
A14
IP3
COIMBRA
Penacova
São Martinho
N342
Tortosei
Quiaios
IP3
A1
12
COIMBRA
Arganil
201
1418
Cepos
Silvares
Serra da Guar
São J
200
Montemor-o-Velho
N17
Ceira
Góis
Figueira da Foz
Lavos
Soure
Condeixa-a-Nova
Lousã
Serpins
Pampilhosa da Serra
Orvalho
Serra da
Leirosa
A14
IP1
IC2
Conímbriga
Miranda do Corvo
Penela
Castanheira de Pera
Foz Giraldo
Carriço
A
N350
B
Penacova
Pedrógão
Zêzere
C

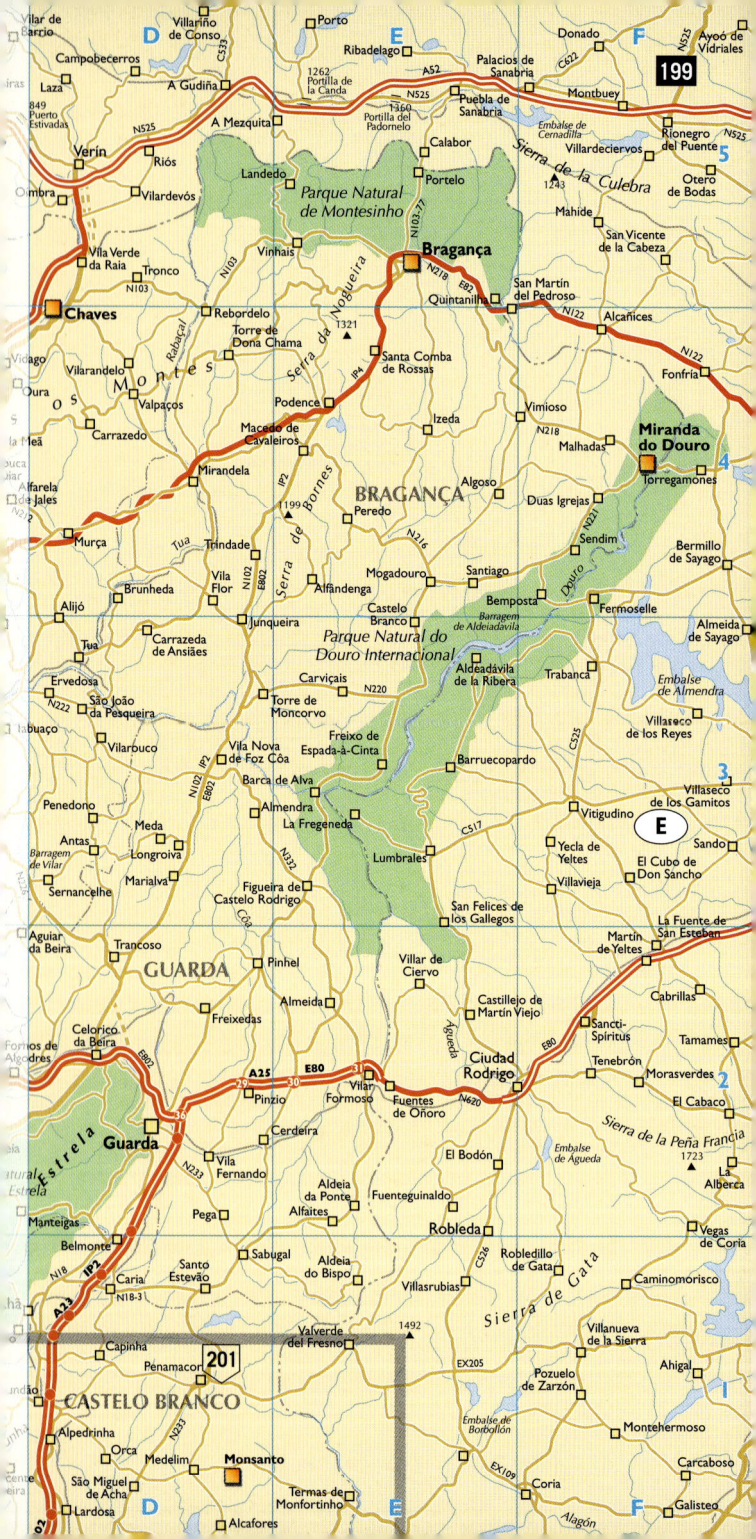

199

D · E · F

Vilar de Barrio
Campobecerros
Laza
849 Puerto Estivadas
Villariño de Conso
Porto
Ribadelago
Donado
Ayóo de Vidriales
A Gudiña
Portilla de la Canda
1262
A52
Palacios de Sanabria
Montbuey
N525
Verín
Riós
Vilardevós
A Mezquita
Portilla del Padornelo
N160
N525
Puebla de Sanabria
Calabor
Villardeciervos
Rionegro del Puente
N525
Ombra
Vila Verde da Raia
N525
Landedo
Vinhais
Portelo
Sierra de la Culebra
1243
Otero de Bodas
N103
Tronco
Parque Natural de Montesinho
Mahide
San Vicente de la Cabeza
Chaves
N103
Rebordelo
Torre de Dona Chama
Bragança
N218
Quintanilha
San Martín del Pedroso
N122
Alcañices
Vilarandelo
Valpaços
Podence
1321
Santa Comba de Rossas
Izeda
Vimioso
Malhadas
Fonfría
N122
Montes
Rabaçal
Carrazedo
Macedo de Cavaleiros
N218
Miranda do Douro
Mirandela
IP2
BRAGANÇA
Peredo
Algoso
Duas Igrejas
Torregamones
N221
Murça
199
Trindade
Vila Flor
N102
Alfândenga
Mogadouro
N216
Santiago
Sendim
Bermillo de Sayago
Tua
Brunheda
Junqueira
Castelo Branco
Bemposta
Barragem de Aldeiadávila
Fermoselle
E
Alijó
Carrazeda de Ansiães
Parque Natural do Douro Internacional
Almeida de Sayago
Ervedosa
São João da Pesqueira
N222
Vilarbuco
Torre de Moncorvo
N220
Carviçais
Aldeadávila de la Ribera
Trabanca
Embalse de Almendra
Villaseco de los Reyes
Vila Nova de Foz Côa
Freixo de Espada-à-Cinta
C535
Villaseco de los Gamitos
Penedono
IP2
Barca de Alva
Barruecopardo
Sando
Antas
Meda
Almendra
La Fregeneda
C517
Vitigudino
Yecla de Yeltes
El Cubo de Don Sancho
Longroiva
Lumbrales
Villavieja
Sernancelhe
Marialva
Figueira de Castelo Rodrigo
San Felices de los Gallegos
Martín de Yeltes
La Fuente de San Esteban
Aguiar da Beira
Trancoso
Pinhel
Villar de Ciervo
Cabrillas
GUARDA
Freixedas
Almeida
Castillejo de Martín Viejo
Sancti-Spíritus
Tamames
Celorico da Beira
A25
E80
Pinzio
Vilar Formoso
Fuentes de Oñoro
Ciudad Rodrigo
Tenebrón
Morasverdes
El Cabaco
29
30
31
Cerdeira
N620
Sierra de la Peña Francia
1723
La Alberca
Guarda
N233
Vila Fernando
Pega
Aldeia da Ponte
Alfaites
Fuenteguinaldo
Robleda
Embalse de Águeda
Manteigas
Belmonte
IP2
Caria
N18
Santo Estevão
Sabugal
Aldeia do Bispo
Villasrubias
Robledillo de Gata
C526
Vegas de Coria
A23
Capinha
N18-3
Valverde del Fresno
1492
Sierra de Gata
Caminomorisco
Villanueva de la Sierra
Pénamacor
201
EX205
Ahigal
CASTELO BRANCO
Alpedrinha
Orca
Medelim
Monsanto
Termas de Monfortinho
Embalse de Borbollón
EX109
Pozuelo de Zarzón
Montehermoso
São Miguel de Acha
Coria
Carcaboso
Lardosa
Alcafores
Alagón
Galisteo

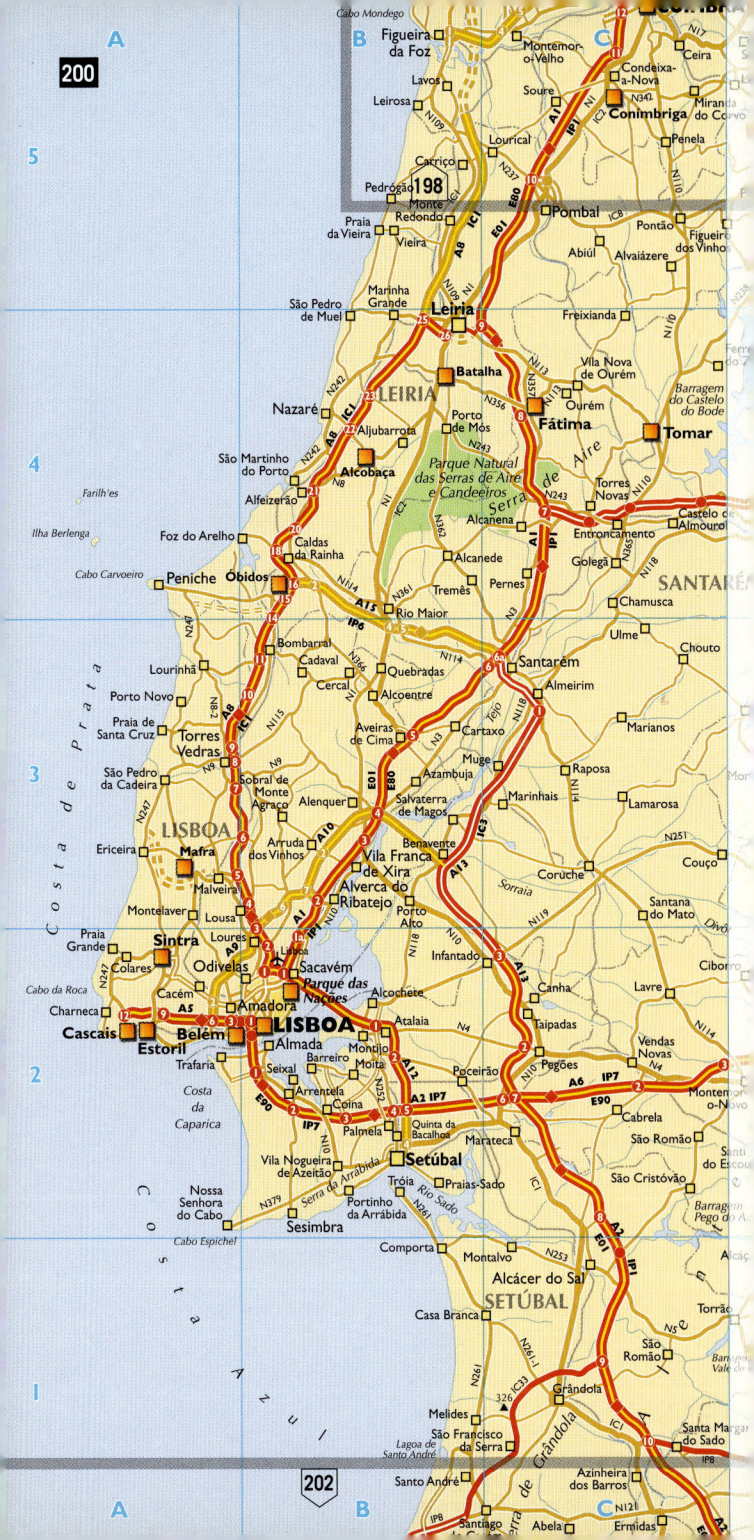

Cabo Mondego

Figueira
da Foz

Montemor-
o-Velho

Condeixa-
a-Nova

Ceira

Lavos

Soure

Conímbriga

Miranda
do Corvo

Leirosa

Louriçal

Penela

Catriço

Pombal

Figueiró
dos Vinhos

Monte
Redondo

Pedrógão

Abiúl

Alvaiázere

Praia
da Vieira

Vieira

Marinha
Grande

Freixianda

São Pedro
de Muel

Leiria

Vila Nova
de Ourém

Nazaré

LEIRIA

Batalha

Ourém

Fátima

Tomar

São Martinho
do Porto

Aljubarrota

Porto
de Mós

Alcobaça

Parque Natural
das Serras de Aire
e Candeeiros

Serra
de
Aire

Barragem
do Castelo
do Bode

Alfeizerão

Alcanena

Torres
Novas

Castelo de
Almourol

Caldas
da Rainha

Alcanede

Entroncamento

Foz do Arelho

Pernes

Golegã

SANTARÉM

Peniche

Óbidos

Cabo Carvoeiro

Tremês

Chamusca

Ulme

Rio Maior

Santarém

Chouto

Bombarral

Quebradas

Lourinhã

Cadaval

Almeirim

Marianos

Porto Novo

Cercal

Alcoentre

Cartaxo

Praia de
Santa Cruz

Aveiras
de Cima

Muge

Raposa

Lamarosa

São Pedro
da Cadeira

Torres
Vedras

Sobral de
Monte
Agraço

Azambuja

Marinhais

Couço

Alenquer

Salvaterra
de Magos

Ericeira

LISBOA

Mafra

Arruda
dos Vinhos

Benavente

Coruche

Santana
do Mato

Malveira

Vila Franca
de Xira

Montelavar

Lousa

Alverca do
Ribatejo

Praia
Grande

Sintra

Loures

Porto
Alto

Infantado

Ciborro

Colares

Odivelas

Cacém

Sacavém

Alcochete

Canha

Lavre

Cabo da Roca

Parque das
Nações

Charneca

Amadora

LISBOA

Atalaia

Taipadas

Vendas
Novas

Cascais

Belém

Almada

Montijo

Moita

Poceirão

Pegões

Estoril

Seixal

Barreiro

Cabrela

São Romão

Trafaria

Arrentela

Coina

Palmela

Quinta de
Bacalhôa

Montemor-
o-Novo

Costa
da
Caparica

Vila Nogueira
de Azeitão

Setúbal

Marateca

São Cristóvão

Nossa
Senhora
do Cabo

Serra da Arrábida

Tróia

Praias-Sado

Barragem do
Pego do Altar

Sesimbra

Portinho
da Arrábida

Cabo Espichel

Comporta

Montalvo

Alcácer do Sal

SETÚBAL

Casa Branca

Torrão

Melides

São
Romão

Barragem
Vale de...

São Francisco
da Serra

Grândola

Santa
Margarida
do Sado

Lagoa de
Santo André

Azinheira
dos Barros

Santo André

Santiago

Abela

Ermidas

Costa de prata

Costa Azul

Farilhões

Ilha Berlenga

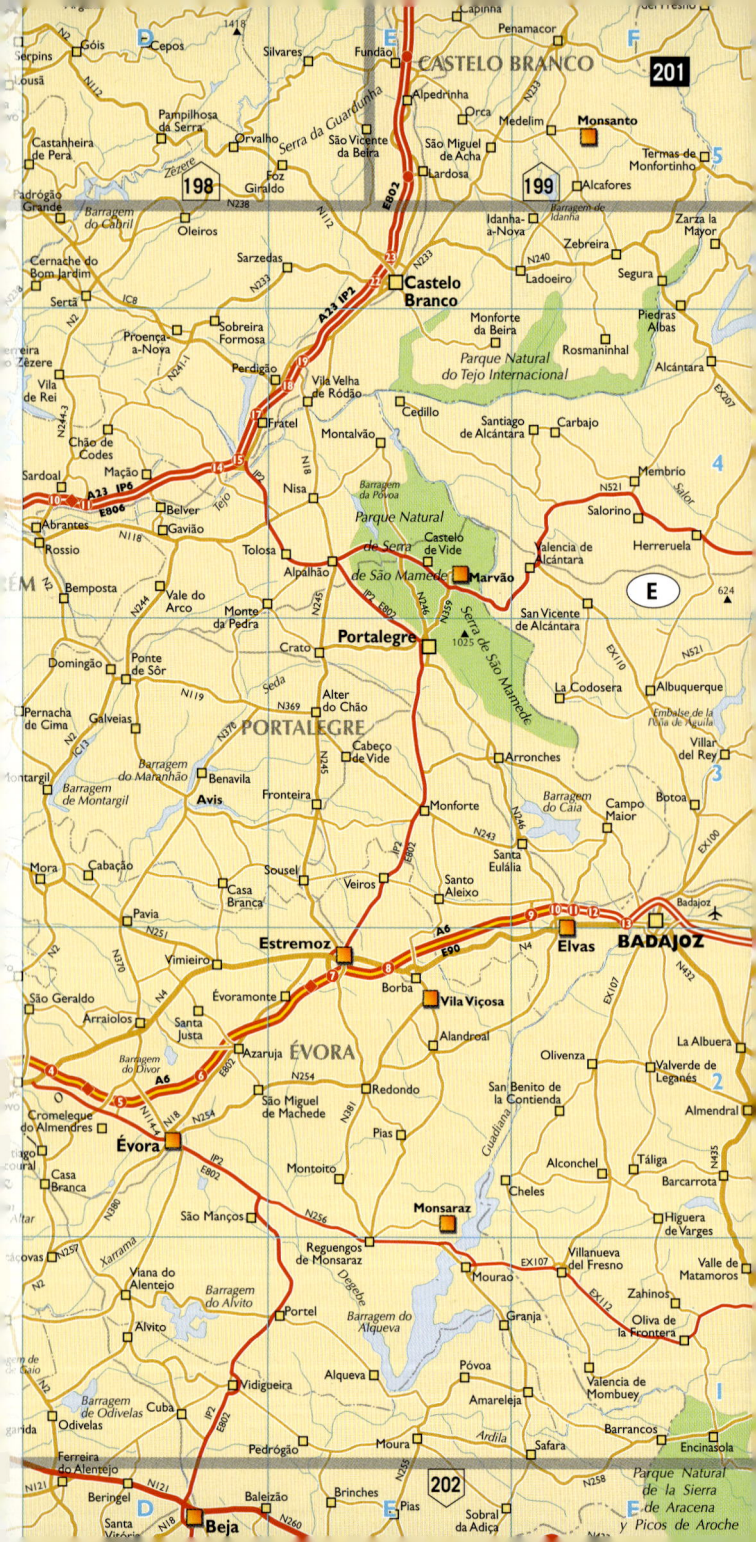

CASTELO BRANCO

Cepos
Silvares
Fundão
Alpedrinha
Orca
Penamacor
Capinha
Medelim
Monsanto
Termas de Monfortinho
Góis
Serpins
Lousã
Pampilhosa da Serra
Castanheira de Pêra
Orvalho
Serra da Gardunha
São Vicente da Beira
São Miguel de Acha
Lardosa
Alcafores
Zarza la Mayor
Foz Giraldo
198
Barragem do Cabril
Oleiros
N238
N112
N233
199
Idanha-a-Nova
Barragem de Idanha
Zebreira
Segura
Piedras Albas
Cernache do Bom Jardim
Sertã
IC8
Proença-a-Nova
Sobreira Formosa
Castelo Branco
A23 IP2
Monforte da Beira
Rosmaninhal
Alcántara
EX207
Ferreira do Zêzere
Vila de Rei
N141
N2
Perdigão
Vila Velha de Ródão
Parque Natural do Tejo Internacional
Santiago de Alcántara
Carbajo
Membrio
N4+3
Chão de Codes
Sardoal
Mação
A23 IP6
Belver
Gavião
Fratel
Nisa
Montalvão
Cedillo
N521
Salorino
Herreruela
Salor
10
Abrantes
E806
Rossio
N118
Tolosa
Alpalhão
Barragem da Póvoa
Parque Natural do Serra de São Mamede
Castelo de Vide
Marvão
Valencia de Alcántara
E
Bemposta
N244
Vale do Arco
Monte da Pedra
N245
de São Mamede
San Vicente de Alcántara
624
Domingão
Ponte de Sôr
Crato
Portalegre
1025
Serra de São Mamede
La Codosera
Albuquerque
Embalse de la Peña de Águila
Pernacha de Cima
Galveias
N119
N369
Seda
Alter do Chão
PORTALEGRE
Cabeço de Vide
Arronches
Botoa
Villar del Rey
Montargil
N2
IC13
Barragem do Maranhão
Benavila
N245
Fronteira
Monforte
N243
N246
Campo Maior
Badajoz
Barragem de Montargil
Avis
Mora
Cabação
Pavia
N251
Casa Branca
Veiros
Sousel
Santo Aleixo
Santa Eulália
Barragem do Caia
EX100
São Geraldo
Arraiolos
N370
Vimieiro
N4
Santa Justa
Estremoz
A6
E90
Borba
Elvas
BADAJOZ
Évoramonte
7
8
Vila Viçosa
9 10 11 12
N4
EX107
N432
Azaruja
ÉVORA
Alandroal
La Albuera
4
Barragem do Divor
A6
6
Olivenza
Valverde de Leganés
Almendral
Cromeleque do Almendres
N114-4
N118
5
IP2
Redondo
São Miguel de Machede
San Benito de la Contienda
Guadiana
Casa Branca
Évora
E802
Montoito
Pias
Alconchel
Táliga
Barcarrota
N380
N254
São Manços
N256
Monsaraz
Cheles
Higuera de Vargas
N257
Xarrama
Viana do Alentejo
Reguengos de Monsaraz
Mourão
EX107
Villanueva del Fresno
Valle de Matamoros
N2
Degebe
Barragem do Alvito
Portel
Barragem do Alqueva
Granja
EX112
Zahinos
Oliva de la Frontera
Alvito
Vidigueira
Alqueva
Póvoa
Valencia de Mombuey
Barragem de Odivelas
Cuba
IP2
E802
Pedrógão
Moura
Amareleja
Barrancos
Odivelas
Ferreira do Alentejo
N121
N259
N121
Beringel
Baleizão
202
Ardila
Safara
N258
Encinasola
Parque Natural de la Sierra de Aracena y Picos de Aroche
Santa Vitória
Beja
N18
N260
Brinches
Pias
Sobral da Adiça

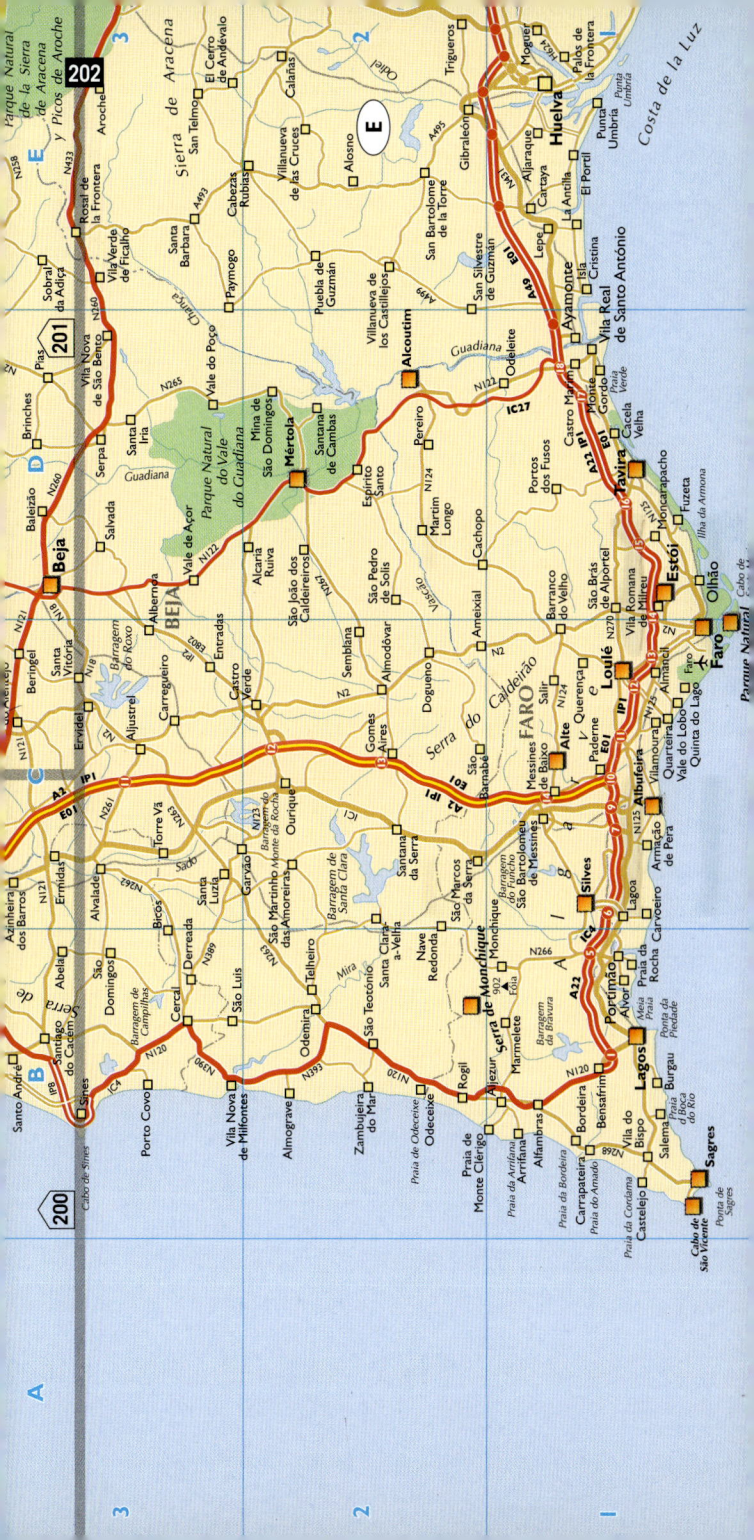

Index

Picture credits

The Automobile Association wishes to thank the following photographers and libraries
for their assistance in the preparation of this book.
Front and back covers: (t) AA Photo Library/Alex Kouprianoff; (ct) AA Photo Library/
Peter Wilson; (cb) AA Photo Library/Alex Kouprianoff; (b) AA Photo Library/Alex
Kouprianoff; Spine, AA Photo Library/Alex Kouprianoff.
EMPICS LTD 14c; MARY EVANS PICTURE LIBRARY 30; NATURE PHOTOGRAPHERS
24b (H Clark); PICTURES COLOUR LIBRARY 135, 139; JON LUSK/REDFERNS MUSIC
LIBRARY 18/19; REX FEATURES LTD 13; WORLD PICTURES 3ii, 15, 20, 89, 127,
132, 138.
The remaining photographs are held in the Association's own photo library (AA PHOTO
LIBRARY) and were taken by ALEX KOUPRIANOFF, with the exception of the following:
M BIRKITT 3iii, 147, 156/157; MICHELLE CHAPLOW 8t, 8c, 78t, 148b, 152/153, 154t,
155, 160/161, 162t, 163, 165, 184, 186, 191r; J EDMANSON 80t, 130b, 131c, 133b, 148t,
150b, 151b, 154b, 156t, 156b, 180, 183, 191t; TERRY HARRIS 2ii, 2iv, 6(background), 7t,
9, 10, 11, 12c, 18, 22/23, 24(background), 31, 43, 46/47, 47, 52, 53t, 53c, 56t, 57, 58c, 58b,
59c, 59b, 60/61, 61, 62, 75, 77, 78c, 78b, 79b, 80/81, 81, 83, 84, 85t, 85c, 86/87, 87, 91c,
91b, 103, 105b, 117, 118, 119(main), 119(inset), 172, 174, 179; CAROLINE JONES 6, 20/
21, 94, 150c, 151t, 152c, 153; JAMES A TIMS 21t, 114, 114/115, 115c; PETER WIL-
SON 14bl, 14br, 17c, 21b, 26c, 27t, 29cb, 65, 88, 93, 104b, 106, 107b, 116c, 133t, 134, 181.

SPIRAL GUIDES

Questionnaire

Dear Traveler

Your comments, opinions and recommendations are very important to us. So please help us to improve our travel guides by taking a few minutes to complete this simple questionnaire.

Send to: Spiral Guides, MailStop 66, 1000 AAA Drive, Heathrow, FL 32746–5063

Your recommendations...

We always encourage readers' recommendations for restaurants, nightlife or shopping – if your recommendation is added to the next edition of the guide, we will send you a FREE AAA Spiral Guide of your choice. Please state below the establishment name, location and your reasons for recommending it.

_____

_____

_____

_____

_____

Please send me AAA Spiral _____

(see list of titles inside the back cover)

About this guide...

Which title did you buy?

_____ **AAA Spiral**

Where did you buy it? _____

When? m m / y y

Why did you choose a AAA Spiral Guide? _____

_____

_____

_____

_____

Did this guide meet your expectations?

Exceeded ☐   Met all ☐   Met most ☐   Fell below ☐

Please give your reasons _____

_____

_____

_____

_____

continued on next page...

Were there any aspects of this guide that you particularly liked?

_____

_____

_____

_____

_____

Is there anything we could have done better?

_____

_____

_____

_____

_____

About you...

Name (Mr/Mrs/Ms) _____

Address _____

_____

_____ Zip _____

Daytime tel nos. _____

Which age group are you in?

Under 25 ☐ 25–34 ☐ 35–44 ☐ 45–54 ☐ 55–64 ☐ 65+ ☐

How many trips do you make a year?

Less than one ☐ One ☐ Two ☐ Three or more ☐

Are you a AAA member? Yes ☐ No ☐

Name of AAA club _____

About your trip...

When did you book? m m / y y   When did you travel? m m / y y

How long did you stay? _____

Was it for business or leisure? _____

Did you buy any other travel guides for your trip? ☐ Yes   ☐ No

If yes, which ones? _____

_____

Thank you for taking the time to complete this questionnaire.